JOHN BRIGHT
VICTORIAN REFORMER

JOHN BRIGHT

JOHN BRIGHT
VICTORIAN REFORMER

BY HERMAN AUSUBEL

JOHN WILEY & SONS, INC.

NEW YORK   LONDON   SYDNEY

BOOKS BY HERMAN AUSUBEL

John Bright, Victorian Reformer (1966)
In Hard Times: Reformers among the Late Victorians (1960)
The Late Victorians: A Short History (1955)
The Making of English History (with R. L. Schuyler) (1952)
Some Modern Historians of Britain (with J. Bartlet Brebner and Erling M.
    Hunt) (1951)
The Making of Modern Europe (1951)
Historians and Their Craft (1950)

Library of Congress Catalog Card Number: 66-14126
Printed in the United States of America

In Memory of HARRY AUSUBEL
and LOTTIE WEISINGER

PREFACE

A great deal of nonsense was written about John Bright during his lifetime. This is not surprising, for he was a highly controversial public figure. But the flow of nonsense has continued since his death in 1889. Just recently, for instance, one historian labeled him a republican "through and through." Another described him as an "uncompromising champion of laissez-faire" and another as a believer in "absolute freedom in all matters." Another placed him among those who consider government intervention in economic life "always wrong." Still another used him to typify those people who found trade unions "an outrage on the face of nature." And many historians have classified him as a rigid pacifist. All these statements —and dozens of others made about him—are demonstrably false. That they still flourish suggests that myths about him continue to be far more influential than the truth.

Bright was neither the saint his admirers found him to be nor the monster his enemies were certain he was. But although the saint in him far outweighed the monster, he became one of the most hated men in early Victorian England. At worst his enemies entertained death wishes for him that would have delighted and reassured some modern Freudians. At best they hoped that he would join the hordes of malcontents who were moving each year to the United States— the country he praised so much:

> Perish England's Constitution! he respects it not a jot,
> For this fine old English Radical, America's the spot!
> And there indeed were he to go and ever fix his lot
> On not too many cheeks would flow the tear so scalding hot. . . .

Bright did not have to work hard to achieve his unpopularity—he only had to be himself. Sincere, earnest, and self-righteous, he possessed, as he was aware, "a warm temperament" that rarely permitted him to keep his opinions to himself. Since his opinions were almost always critical of the Victorian Establishment, the results were predictable. Do away with the privileges of the great landowners, the Anglican Church, *The Times,* the armed forces, and the Foreign Office—this was the message that Bright preached during the course of almost a half-century of public service. It was a message guaranteed to win for him the hatred of the people who mattered in Victorian society.

Like other Englishmen who came of age during the agitation that resulted in the Reform Act of 1832, Bright started out as an angry young man. But his distinction was that he lived to become both an angry middle-aged man and an angry old man. What sustained his anger was his sense of the slowness of the change from the old social order to what he regarded as a wholesome modern society. Government of the people by the great landowners for the great landowners was the essence of the old order, as Bright saw it. He considered it his mission as a public instructor and Member of Parliament to end this aristocratic domination of British life and the military, religious, social, and political abuses that accompanied it.

Despite what some historians have said, however, Bright rarely derived a sense of success from his efforts as a reformer. Far more often he was overwhelmed by a sense of failure, and he was frequently tempted to give up public life because progress of the sort he favored did not seem to be taking place. He wanted very much to be what many historians have called him—a spokesman for the Victorian middle classes; and he would have relished exercising the "immense influence" that his eminent biographer, G. M. Trevelyan, was to ascribe to him. But he repeatedly made the devastating discovery that he spoke only for himself, some relatives and friends, and a tiny and insignificant section of the British public. Far from being a spokesman for the middle classes, he became one of their most formidable critics. At times he was as hard on them as Karl

Marx—so hard that his closest friend had to caution him against encouraging "a feeling of alienation from the capitalist class."

What disillusioned and embittered Bright more than anything else was middle-class subservience to the great landowners. For it was this deference that made the Victorian Era much less an age of reform and international peace than, according to Bright, it could and should have been. And he was right.

In order to avoid cluttering the text with a hopelessly large number of footnotes, I have followed the increasingly widespread practice of documenting by paragraphs. I hope that this will not be too much of an inconvenience for the small number of scholars who will have occasion to track down references.

For an excellent guide to the recent literature of nineteenth-century English history, see the footnotes and bibliography in S. G. Checkland, *The Rise of Industrial Society in England, 1815–1885* (New York, 1964); the best general accounts of Bright's England are still Sir Llewellyn Woodward, *The Age of Reform, 1815–1870* (rev. ed., Oxford, 1962) and Asa Briggs, *The Age of Improvement* (London, 1959).

Columbia University   *Herman Ausubel*
November, 1965

ACKNOWLEDGMENTS

My chief debt is to the owners, keepers, and assistant keepers of manuscripts who gave me permission to use the documents in their possession or care. I am particularly grateful to the following: the late Roger Clark, John Bright's grandson; Miss Patricia H. Allderidge; Miss W. D. Coates of the National Register of Archives; the Rev. R. G. Bliss of Dunford College, Richard Cobden's former home; Mr. Joseph W. Scott of the Library of University College, London; Mr. Ernest Taylor of the Rochdale Public Libraries; Dr. Frank Taylor and Miss Glenise Matheson of the John Rylands Library; Mr. Sidney Horrocks of the Manchester Central Library; Mr. D. S. Porter of the Bodleian Library; Mr. R. J. Hayes of the National Library of Ireland; Mr. Robert W. Hill of the New York Public Library; Mr. Herbert Cahoon and Miss Mary M. Kenway of the Pierpont Morgan Library; Dr. David C. Mearns of the Library of Congress; and Mr. Kenneth A. Lohf of the Columbia University Library.

I also wish to thank the Fulbright authorities who enabled me to spend a year as a visiting research professor at the University of Manchester. For a generous research grant I should like to express my gratitude to the William A. Dunning Fund of the History Department of Columbia University.

I owe much to some friends who criticized this book in manuscript: William Bridgwater, Stanley Burnshaw, Norman F. Cantor, James L. Clifford, Joseph Dorfman, A. S. Eisenstadt, Ainslie T. Embree, David H. Flaherty, Albert Hofstadter, Lawrence Ritt, and Chilton Williamson.

I wish to thank Donald F. Gerardi for his kind assistance during the various phases of production.

At every stage of research, writing, and proofreading, my wife, as usual, contributed heavily to the making of this book.

CONTENTS

SHORT TITLES

Addresses James E. Thorold Rogers, ed., *Public Addresses by John Bright, M. P.* (London, 1879)

Diaries R. A. J. Walling, ed., *The Diaries of John Bright* (New York, 1931)

Letters H. J. Leech, ed., *The Public Letters of the Right Hon. John Bright, M. P.* (London, 1885). A second edition (London, 1895) contains letters written until the end of 1888.

Magnus Sir Philip Magnus, *Gladstone: A Biography* (London, 1954)

Morley Lord Morley, *The Life of Richard Cobden* (13th edition, London, 1906)

Parl. Deb. *Parliamentary Debates*

Ramm Agatha Ramm, ed., *The Political Correspondence of Mr. Gladstone and Lord Granville, 1868–1876* (London, 1952), vol. I, 1868–1871, vol. II, 1871–1876.

Agatha Ramm, ed., *The Political Correspondence of Mr. Gladstone and Lord Granville, 1876–1886* (Oxford, 1962), vol. I, 1876–1882, vol. II, 1883–1886.

Speeches James E. Thorold Rogers, ed., *Speeches on Questions of Public Policy by John Bright, M. P.* (second edition, London, 1869, 2 vols.)

Trevelyan George Macaulay Trevelyan, *The Life of John Bright* (new edition, Boston, 1925)

ABBREVIATIONS

BI	Bishopsgate Institute
BL	Bodleian Library
BM	British Museum Additional Manuscripts
BPL	Birmingham Public Library
CUL	Columbia University Library
D	Dunford (Midhurst, Sussex)
FHL	Friends House Library (London)
HCL	Harvard College Library
HL	Henry E. Huntington Library and Art Gallery
HSP	Historical Society of Pennsylvania
JRL	John Rylands Library
LC	Library of Congress
LSEL	London School of Economics Library
MCL	Manchester Central Library
MHS	Massachusetts Historical Society
NLI	National Library of Ireland
NLS	National Library of Scotland
NLW	National Library of Wales
NYPL	New York Public Library
PML	Pierpont Morgan Library
PRO	Public Record Office
PUL	Princeton University Library
RGL	Rochdale Art Gallery and Museum and Public Library
S	Street, Somerset (home of the late Roger Clark)
UCLL	University College, London, Library
ULL	University of London Library
YUL	Yale University Library

JOHN BRIGHT
VICTORIAN REFORMER

CHAPTER ONE

A FIGHTER EMERGES
1811–1846

John Bright never forgot the year 1841. He was to celebrate his thirtieth birthday on November 16, but on that day there was little to celebrate. By then he had found out "how uncertain is life and how little durable our greatest earthly enjoyments." His model Quaker wife, to whom he had been married for not even two years, died of a lung hemorrhage in September. "Until I knew her," he told one of her childhood friends, "I had no knowledge that so much of purity and simplicity, so much of innocence and disinterested devotedness was to be found in our erring race." All the evidence makes it clear that Bright was not idealizing her; she *was* the admirable figure whose memory he was to cherish until his own death. (1)

Among those who called to express their condolences was Richard Cobden, the Manchester businessman, free trader, and recently elected Member of Parliament for Stockport, whom Bright had come to know in the last few years and whom he had kept informed about the condition of his "dear invalid." Cobden was aware that Bright's life had centered on his wife, and he knew how despondent he was. As the older man by seven years, he ventured the advice that Bright above all should try to keep himself busy. His father and brothers could run the family cotton business in Rochdale without him. One of his sisters could look after his infant daughter Helen. And he should bury his sorrow in a worthy cause—the struggle in behalf of the downtrodden in British society. There was no better way to honor the memory of his wife than by participating actively in the movement to repeal the corn laws, the despicable protective tariffs that made the cost of bread prohibitively high for the poor and kept them on the verge of starvation. (2)

At first Cobden's advice was hard for Bright to consider seriously, much less to take. He was a Quaker; most Quakers were wary of involvement in public affairs, regarding them as hopelessly noisy, corrupt, and corrupting; and he did not want to offend either his wife's family or his own. Before long, however, he did take Cobden's advice; for he discovered that to survive he had to lose himself in some meaningful activity. And so, what had previously been a lively interest in the political and social issues of his world rapidly became an obsession. The death of Elizabeth Priestman Bright was the birth of John Bright as a public figure. (3)

II

The young widower who emerged on the British political scene in the early 1840's had until then led an uneventful life. Although he was the second child born to Jacob and Martha Bright, the death of his brother in early childhood left him the eldest—and, as he was aware, the favorite—of what eventually became a family of eleven children. His parents were religious people who treasured their Quaker heritage and communicated to their children their admiration for their one notable ancestor—a seventeenth-century hero in the agitation for religious freedom. Martha Bright's wish for her son always remained what she had written on the back of his birth certificate: "May he indeed love his Creator in the days of his youth and continue stedfast unto the end." Her wish was certainly granted. John Bright, secure in his religion, was not to suffer any of those fierce crises of faith that shook so many Victorian luminaries in the Age of Darwinism and Higher Criticism. (4)

Jacob Bright was one of the band of energetic, ingenious, and self-made cotton millowners who helped to convert Lancashire into the most important region of steam and smoke in the early nineteenth-century world. He started out poor—a fact to which his son would often refer proudly—but in time his business successes enabled him to send his boys to the best schools then available for Quakers. Although for the rest of his life John Bright was to remember a few of his teachers with affection and respect, his school life was marred by a number of those harrowing experiences and sadistic masters described so well in nineteenth-century novels. The intellectual demands that his formal education made on him were unimpressive; but he did develop a love of reading in general and a passion for poetry in particular. Furthermore, he discovered the consolations of fishing, if not of music or philosophy—a discovery that would serve him well in later years. (5)

At fifteen—early in 1827—and with no sense of loss, he ended his school career and entered his father's business in Rochdale. Then he really began to learn, and for the next nine years he was immersed in the first-hand study of the technical, scientific, and economic changes that were reshaping the British scene. He learned about the disabilities and needs of the manufacturing and commercial classes of Lancashire, about the complicated relations of masters and men, and about the difficulties and sufferings of the working classes.

During the lively and prolonged agitation that had its anticlimax in the Reform Act of 1832, Bright knew where he stood. Traditionalists everywhere in Britain feared that their country was about to have its own ugly version of the French Revolution. As one of them aptly put it, "The great Majority have found out that the small Minority enjoy the good things, and as they have not the knowledge to inform them that this is the necessary condition of Society, they think it a shocking usurpation and they will endure it no longer." But there was no question about where Bright's sympathies lay. He rejoiced over the extension of the suffrage and the redistribution of seats in the House of Commons that occurred in 1832. He would have preferred a much more thoroughgoing transformation of Parliament than actually took place; but at least he was reassured that reformers like Joseph Hume, a particular hero of his father's, were in the House of Commons, where they could continue the fight for the interests of the people. Fortunately, Bright did not know how discouraged, even despairing, Hume often was because of the difficulty of getting much done in a Parliament dominated by Whigs and Tories who outdid one another in their devotion to the old aristocratic order. (6)

By the time he was in his mid-twenties Bright held a host of convictions that mirrored his religious, social, and family background. He revealed the intensity of these beliefs in a journal that he kept from 1835 to 1836 during a grand tour of the Mediterranean. Appalled by what he saw of laziness in Portugal, of begging and bribery in the Italies, and of torpor in the lands of the Ottoman Empire, he had no doubt that the poverty, ignorance, and degradation of the peoples of those countries were due to bad government, false religion, and lack of education. Yet what repelled him particularly was the fatalistic outlook of the Turks—their notion that whatever happened would have happened despite their efforts to prevent it from happening. "Thus," he noted with disgust, "the Turks are not solicitous about bettering the condition of their neighbours, nor do they trouble themselves for the sake of any prospective advantage which posterity might reap from their labours; but they come into the world, live as their fathers did, with as little trouble as possible, and sink into the grave without having performed any positive and visible service to their fellow men." The Turkish way of life was repugnant to everything that Bright stood for—his family, his religion, his class, his community. (7)

There was, in short, nothing vague or indecisive about the John Bright who came into prominence by the early 1840's. Proud of the Society of Friends, of Lancashire, and of the industrial—and industrious—classes, he had a powerful and rare sense of identity. He knew what was wrong with other countries. He also knew what was wrong with his own. And he knew what should be done about it: Since he believed that the source of most of the abuses that afflicted early Victorian society was the great landowning class, a large-scale crusade against the landowners was necessary. Once they were deprived of their unwarranted privileges, the United Kingdom would be a better place for politics, religion, culture, and social and economic life. Corn laws, the Established Church, and the landlord-dominated Parliament—all these survivals from an unsavory past had to be discarded. Bright looked forward to stirring and happier times for the British people: "A large and powerful party in the country will back a powerful party in the House, and

instead of 'faction fights' [among cliques of Whig and Tory aristo-
crats] we may hope for the assertion of great principles and for
deeds based upon them." (8)

III

The first of the great principles that Bright asserted as a public
figure—the one that made him famous and infamous—was free
trade. He was not one of the pioneers of the nineteenth-century
anti-corn law movement. Long before Bright became an eminent
free trader, T. Perronet Thompson had published his passionate
Catechism on the Corn Laws (1827); Ebenezer Elliott had brought
out his catchy and moving *Corn-Law Rhymes* (1831); Charles
Pelham Villiers had started his relentless parliamentary agitation
for the repeal of the corn laws; and the unjustly forgotten John
Benjamin Smith had worked assiduously to convert the Manchester
Chamber of Commerce to the cause. (9)

Even among the spokesmen of the Anti-Corn Law League itself
Bright emerged late. Richard Cobden, the man of ideas, and George
Wilson, the master of administrative details and delicate inter-
personal relations, sustained that small and unpromising organization in the difficult years after its founding in the late 1830's. It
was, in fact, a reflection of the competence and sound judgment of
Cobden and Wilson that they detected and encouraged Bright's
talents as an agitator. Cobden, in particular, proved himself a
genius at building up the self-esteem and confidence not only of
Bright but of other Leaguers as well. (10)

Although Bright did not pioneer in the movement, one gift
made him by the mid-forties the most important popularizer of
free trade doctrines. The Anti-Corn Law League had in its ranks
a number of first-rate speakers, but none of them could capture
and hold an audience as Bright could; none could so effectively
stimulate what he liked to call "the fierce democracy." Poised, com-
manding in appearance, brimming over with earnestness, enthusiasm, and passion, quick-witted, brief, clear, incredibly articulate,
and eminently hearable, he was an orator of orators. Sometimes, in
fact, he was so overwhelmed by his own performance at a public

meeting that he would unashamedly give Cobden a glowing account of how he had excited and won over his audience; but then his family training in Christian humility would reassert itself, and he would beg Cobden to forgive his inexcusable outburst of vanity. (11)

As early as 1842 Cobden urged Bright to consider entering Parliament—a speaker with his exceptional gifts would be invaluable there to the free-trade cause. A year later, in July, 1843, Bright took his seat in the House of Commons as Member for the City of Durham, but only after one of those episodes that demonstrated that eighteenth-century ways still operated in early Victorian politics. A select committee, headed by his future antagonist Lord Ashley, found the election of Bright's rival, Lord Dungannon, void because his agents had bribed "a large number of voters." A new election was held, and Bright was returned. The "Durham feat," as he liked to call it, marked the beginning of a parliamentary career that was to last almost without interruption until 1889. (12)

Between 1842 and 1846—the last stages of the campaign against the corn laws—Bright was totally committed to free trade. His activities were far-ranging, his energies unflagging. He urged his patient and cooperative father to make a generous contribution to the League. He pressed Cobden to found a free-trade newspaper in Manchester, for the *Guardian* was too unreliable and the *Anti-Corn Law Circular* was limited in its influence and controlled by an impossible editor. He suggested the closing of factories to dramatize the plight of both employers and workers under the corn law regime. (13)

So his efforts continued. He devised a scheme to unite the working and middle classes. He proposed to memorialize Queen Victoria not to prorogue Parliament until the corn laws were repealed. He wrote to the veteran reformer Lord Brougham to enlist his aid on the League's side. He prepared a paper for the Duke of Wellington setting forth the true remedy for economic distress—freer trade. He urged the planning of bigger and better bazaars, tea parties, and soirées to spread anti-corn law doctrines. He checked on the activity, or lack of it, of a free trade club. (14)

Both in Parliament and on countless "agitating tours" through-

out the country, Bright preached the virtue and sanity of free trade
and the baseness and stupidity of protective tariffs. Indefatigably he
addressed public meetings—in London, Nottingham, Derby, Devon-
port, Tavistock, Dorchester, Newcastle-on-Tyne, Worcester, Carlisle,
Gravesend, among many others. There was hardly a town in
Britain that he did not visit, and he learned more about British
geography than he could ever have learned at school. At times he
feared that his voice had "given up almost for good" and that his
power to serve the cause was gone. Exhaustion from over-work was
a feeling he knew both regularly and well. It was fitting, in short,
for *Punch,* when it published "Peel's Parliamentary Drinking Song,"
to include the line, "Here's unto Cobden, and here's to friend
Bright." (15)

Bright condemned the corn laws as inhumane, immoral, un-
Christian. "Give us this day our daily bread," so went the beautiful

words that the League quoted on its membership cards; but the selfish, callous, wicked landowners of Britain used their control of Parliament to shut out foreign grain, keep their rents high, and deprive the poor of cheap bread. In Bright's view, they were an oligarchy of the worst sort, attentive only to their class interests and scornful of the common good; and their legislation displayed their lack of sympathy for the needs of the great body of British consumers. At the same time that they prevented the people from eating the inexpensive food of other countries, they maintained lavish private parks that left thousands of acres of fertile land unproductive. And through the vicious device of game laws—a subject on which Bright became an authority—they prevented their tenant farmers from safeguarding crops against the ravages of rabbits, hares, pheasants, and partridges whose only purpose was to satisfy the landowners' insatiable passion for hunting. *Punch* could quip that as long as there were game laws country gentlemen would have something to do, but once those laws were abolished real problems would arise because country gentlemen would have nothing to do, and might even turn to writing to while their hours away. But game laws were never a laughing matter to Bright. (16)

Nor were corn laws. They were the worst crime ever committed against a people; they were "the most daring outrage upon human rights which has ever been perpetrated under the name of Law." And the Leaguers who were fighting to repeal the corn laws were emissaries of Christ, laboring to attain a noble and holy object. (17)

"You might as well try to persuade the leopard to change his spots as the English aristocracy to give up bread-taxing," Cobden wrote to Bright in a moment of discouragement. But Bright found the validity of free trade so overwhelming that he believed the subject needed only to be talked about "to make all doubt who now support the Law, and many come over entirely." Just as such seemingly impossible concessions as Catholic Emancipation and the Reform Act of 1832 had been wrested from reluctant aristocrats, so, too, the repeal of the corn laws would be wrung from them. The words of one of the many poetic outbursts that the free-trade crusade inspired summed up Bright's outlook:

> While the burden remains on our backs,
> Let the shout for repeal ne'er relax,
> Till, like Jericho's wall, Protection shall fall,
> And give us our loaf without tax. (18)

Victory was inevitable; therefore, as Bright repeatedly told his colleagues in the House of Commons, it made sense for them to repeal the corn laws while they could do so gracefully, instead of waiting for repeal to be extorted from them. Property, he reminded them, had duties as well as rights. Furthermore, Adam Smith had long since written his masterpiece, and so there was no excuse whatever for the persistence of the economic follies and fears of earlier times. Tariff protection acted as "a sort of opiate," and as long as it continued to be used the national interest would be sacrificed to selfish class interests. Constantly, Bright argued that the fears of the landowners—"the *Corn*servatives," as he called them—were unfounded. No calamities would result from the repeal of the corn laws. The British market would not be inundated by foreign wheat. Britain would not become excessively dependent on foreigners. Agriculture would not be ruined. (19)

IV

Making masterly speeches in behalf of cheap bread was Bright's chief contribution to the League's cause, but he served in other important ways, too. One of the most vital roles he played was that of morale-lifter, a role that has never been adequately appreciated by scholars. Time and again Bright cheered up both Cobden and Wilson when they became discouraged. They had, to be sure, good reason to be disheartened, for things went wrong far more often than right. The idyllic, upward-and-onward treatment of the League that has dominated history books—that it was founded, moved into action, won widespread support, was flooded with money, and in an incredibly short period swept away the corn laws—bears little relation to historical reality. The truth is that the League had almost chronic financial difficulties; agents of the League, when not drunk, were too often lazy, incompetent, or dishonest; converts were hard to win and keep; audiences were frequently hostile; the *Manchester*

Guardian caused no end of trouble; and the vilest kinds of accusations were constantly hurled at the Leaguers, especially the charge that they were trying to line their own pockets. (20)

Small wonder that Cobden and Wilson were often dispirited. "The work has been done by a very few—so few that we have been the laughing stock, *even of ourselves,* as we sat and chuckled over the splutter we were making in the name of 'the League,'" Cobden confessed in 1841. "We have made less real progress than we imagined," he acknowledged as late as 1844. (21)

In these circumstances, Bright took on particular importance. Filled with a sense of the justice and righteousness of repeal, he assumed that the cause had to triumph. The day of victory would soon come, he repeatedly told Cobden; the phenomenal growth of the British population, modern methods of communication, and the hard work of the League would see to that. Brimming over with faith and euphoria, he was able to cheer up his colleagues year after year, often at critical junctures. "I find many people saying that they have ceased to hope for or to expect improvement, unless our remedy be applied," he reported to Cobden in 1842. "The Whigs see their powerlessness and that you are carrying all the real liberals from them," he reassured Cobden in 1843, adding that it was only a question of time before even the opportunistic Whigs would be converts to the doctrines of the League. The noble struggle would go on, and justice would soon win out, he wrote to Wilson in 1844. "We are destined to survive the foe we are contending with," he predicted a year later, and the monopolists would get what they deserved. Constantly, Bright sent Cobden and Wilson accounts of public meetings that he described either as good, tremendous, or capital. He told them what they wanted—and needed—to hear. Indeed, if *Punch* was able to describe the League as an association "formed to do a certain thing, and wonderful to relate, actually doing it," it was because of the fierce dedication of a handful of people like Bright. (22)

V

As a free trader, he made a notable contribution in one other sphere: that of Chartist–League relations. These relations were for the most part hostile; but they would have been worse without Bright's strenuous efforts. (23)

In the England of the early forties the number of outright Chartists was small, but, as the experienced agitator Francis Place noted, almost every worker could be considered a Chartist sympathizer. Bright understood that if the Anti-Corn Law League was to lead a mass movement, Leaguers had to win over these latent Chartists, as well as the people Place called "out and outers," to the position that repeal should take priority over a democratic suffrage. This was hard to do, but it was also important to do, especially since Chartists often reveled in breaking up meetings of the League. Indeed, Cobden assigned to Bright in 1842 the task of securing information about the itinerant Chartists who went from one League meeting to another spreading disruption. (24)

Bright was the ideal man to work for better relations, except for one difficulty: his hostility to factory legislation and to reformers like Lord Ashley (later Lord Shaftesbury) and John Fielden who were urging such legislation. Bright saw the point in restricting child labor, but he denounced governmental limitation of the hours of work of adults as well as of young people between thirteen and eighteen. His opposition was based on two considerations above all: since British factories had to compete with foreign factories, factory legislation would put the British at a serious competitive disadvantage and inevitably would result in unemployment for British workers; besides, it was unjust to use state power to prevent people from working longer hours so that they could improve their position and that of their families. Bright never pretended that the manufacturing districts were a paradise, but he insisted that people like Lord Ashley and Fielden failed to understand that the great evils were unemployment, violent business fluctuations, and restrictive tariffs, all of which were connected. (25)

Although Bright's opposition to factory laws was often used by his opponents to embarrass him, the fact remained that he was still a nearly perfect man to work for better Chartist–League relations. First, some Chartists were against factories and machinery in any case. Second, and far more important, Bright had strong feelings about the working classes. As he dared to say in his first speech in Parliament, "These men have too few representatives in this House; the rich here are attended to—the poor are too neglected." (26)

Furthermore, Bright was not only much more radical in his political ideas than were other Leaguers, but he had none of his colleagues' fears of a widespread extension of the right to vote. As a private individual, he attended in 1842 the Birmingham meeting of suffrage reformers that was arranged by the Quaker leader Joseph Sturge. There he was particularly impressed with the moderate Chartist spokesman William Lovett—"a very fine man in every way," he told Cobden. He was relieved, in fact, to learn at firsthand that Lovett and his followers were as much concerned as the Leaguers about the irresponsibility, ruffianism, and passion for physical force of those Chartists who admired Feargus O'Connor. (27)

Bright would have wanted the League to advocate a broad suffrage, but he recognized that such a step would alienate the leading businessmen who supported and financed the anti-corn law crusade. He also knew that from a tactical point of view it was better to concentrate on one main object at a time. He concluded, therefore, that it was unwise for the League to become embroiled in the suffrage question. But he was constantly aware of the importance of cooperation between the middle classes and the working classes, and he liked to predict that the time was fast approaching when the middle classes would stop aligning themselves with the great landowners to deprive the working classes of their rights. (28)

In his debates with Chartists Bright argued that in the short run the repeal of the corn laws was a more realistic and important goal than manhood suffrage. The tyranny and selfishness of the great landowners had produced both starvation laws and a narrow electorate. The first thing to do was to get rid of the corn legislation; suffrage reform would come next. For the rest, Bright worked hard to expose some of the "false" economic ideas that Chartists defended. As he reported from Rochdale to Cobden in March, 1842:

Last night I lectured to a very large meeting of working men here on "the causes of the fall of wages." I spoke 2 hours, and then for 1½ hours discussed with a Chartist leader the questions and points raised. I am told I made many converts from their absurd views on machinery, corn laws, and on their foolish plan of obstructing our meetings. I think they will never join heartily in any merely Anti-Corn Law agitation or association, but much would be gained if they would not oppose us and this I hope will before long cease.

After another debate with a Chartist a few months later, Bright confessed to Cobden that while it was "very easy trouncing these fellows," the trouble was that they were not particularly sensitive and did not know when they had been beaten. (29)

Difficulties with the Chartists continued. At a large League meeting in Rochdale in 1843 a few troublemakers intruded, but, Bright was happy to report, they behaved more mildly than on earlier occasions. If this had been the future pattern of Chartist–League relations, he certainly would have been pleased. As late as 1844, however, he informed Wilson of the elaborate precautions being taken against Chartist disturbances at League meetings. It is no surprise, therefore, that even when the corn laws were about to be repealed, Cobden, who was ordinarily a generous and forgiving man, thought it necessary to remind the public of the hostility that the Feargus O'Connor brand of Chartist had shown the League. "It is due to the working class to draw a distinction between them and the O'Connor crew," he told Bright. (30)

VI

The Great Famine in Ireland was the decisive event in the history of the British free-trade movement. It was something the League's leaders had not anticipated and without which their agitation would have had to go on for years. Unlike many modern historians, Bright and Cobden did not exaggerate the importance of the League—or of themselves— in bringing about the repeal of the corn laws. Except for the horrors of the Irish Famine, they knew that repeal would not have taken place when it did. True, Sir Robert Peel had been moving for some time toward freer trade; but without the disaster of the Irish potato blight, which pointed up the absurdity of restrictive legislation on food, it is certain that he would not have dared to undo the corn laws in 1845–1846. Even with the Irish Famine in the forefront of the news, Peel had a harder time pushing repeal through Parliament than some historians have recognized. Bright and Cobden appreciated the difficulties of his position—he was denounced as a traitor and as a lackey doing the bidding of the League's agitators—and in the course of the highly charged legislative struggle over repeal, Bright and Cobden developed an admiration for him as a statesman and as a human being that they had not had before. They knew how much their cause owed to his willingness to become what Bright had publicly hoped he would become: "not the Minister of the Queen merely, but the Minister of the people also." (31)

The Irish troubles encouraged the League to intensify its pressures on Peel's Tory Government. In October 1845, for example, a memorial from the League-infiltrated Manchester Chamber of Commerce urged the Prime Minister to permit the free admission of food into British ports. The memorialists pointed out that years of experience had taught them that the prosperity of the cotton industry depended chiefly on food costs, that a cheap and plentiful supply of food would increase employment and wages, and that a sparse and costly food supply would reduce wages and the demand for labor. Furthermore, the sad news from Ireland spread, in the apt words of the memorialists, "a fearful gloom over the prosperity of that portion of the empire, in whose fate this country is indissolubly involved." Speedy action was necessary, and so the members of the Chamber shrewdly urged Peel to apply their remedy of free trade by means of an Order in Council. It would take Parliament too long to act in this emergency, they suggested, displaying their ingenuity in constitutional matters. Peel, however, chose to work through more conventional channels. (32)

On November 4, 1845, Bright and Cobden read in *The Times* the news for which they had looked long and impatiently. Peel's Government planned to take up with Parliament the question of the repeal of the corn laws. It was not until June 26, 1846, however, that the royal assent was given to Peel's measure. The intervening months were nerve-wracking for both Bright and Cobden. They knew the disasters that might befall the bill in the House of Commons, to say nothing of the House of Lords. They were familiar with the subterfuges and delays that Members of Parliament might employ in the complicated British legislative process. They remembered only too well the emasculation of what became the Reform Act of 1832, and they were determined to benefit from the experiences of earlier reformers and not let happen to them what had happened to their predecessors.

So under their leadership the League worked feverishly. Speeches, tracts, advertisements, and petitions favoring the repeal of the corn laws filled the land. The Manchester Chamber of Commerce memorialized Queen Victoria, humbly but earnestly praying that "all the influence with which the Constitution invests [Her] Majesty may be graciously exerted in order that all duties upon Corn and such articles of food as are necessary for the support of a daily increasing population may be forthwith abolished...." As with the Queen, so with the Houses of Parliament. "Get petitions everywhere," Bright told George Wilson. (33)

In these circumstances, the fury of many of the large landowners, both Whig and Tory, was unspeakable. As one outraged Tory explained his bitterness: "The sudden conversion of the two great parties—both Whig and Tory—to the Repeal of the Corn Laws which they have hitherto equally resisted—apparently with no motive for their change of sentiment—but the increased violence of Demagogic agitation—and the substitution of a naked question of class interests for one of party traditions (which were at least clothed under the garb of *Principles*)—is very like the *commencement de la fin*." (34)

Because of the passion of many of the large landowners, it is understandable that Bright and Cobden suffered acute anxiety in the last months of their crusade. Bright, to be sure, was less gloomy than Cobden, but even he was not so confident as usual, and he haunted the clubs of London searching for the right kinds of predictions. As late as March 5, 1846, Cobden wrote revealingly, "I don't think there are 100 men in the House, and certainly not 40 in the Lords, who *in their hearts* desire the total repeal of the Corn Laws." On

C——N.   SIR R. P——L.   B——T.

THE SEVEN-LEAGUE BOOTS;

OR, DEATH OF GIANT MONOPOLY

☞ The labours of Messrs. Cobden and Bright procured the recognition of Free Trade principles, and, with Sir Robert Peel, extorted from a reluctant Parliament the repeal of the Corn Laws.—1846.

April 1 Bright noted disappointedly that there was no chance of getting the corn bill out of the House of Commons before the Easter recess. At last, however—on June 26, 1846—the measure became law, and Bright could report to Wilson, "The assent is given—it was 5 o'clock before the words were said which completed our labors...." During the performance of this last act Bright stood close to the speaker. "The sensations were worth having. I wish you had been there," he told Wilson. (35)

Bright felt good about the victory. At last a parliamentary session had ended in action, not just talk. He was happy because the great landowners had been shaken dramatically and because the needs of consumers had been taken into account. For him, as for Cobden, however, the repeal of the corn laws was chiefly a moral victory, a triumph of the national good over selfish aristocratic class interests. And, Bright thought, as other countries followed the admirable British example, the peoples of the nineteenth-century world would discover that freer trade, by strengthening the economic ties among nations, would contribute in an impressive way to international harmony. As Cobden put it (in words that reflected Bright's influence): "The best effect of all will be that the whole civilized world will become *quakers* in the practice of peace and mutual forbearance." The point is an important one, for both Bright and Cobden did not consider free trade an end in itself but an instrument for the promotion of international peace. In the lines of one of the League's poets:

> Free Trade will be the link to bind
>   Each nation to the other;
> 'Twill harmonize the rights of man
>   With every fellow brother.

At the same time, however, Bright and Cobden were sufficiently rooted in reality to recognize that the motives of some of their colleagues were less exalted. (36)

In one respect the aftermath of the victory was unpleasant. Cobden properly received the greatest share of credit for the part he had played in the League, and Bright was rightly recognized for what he had done. But through no fault of either, some other leaders of the movement did not secure the public praise they deserved. Charles Pelham Villiers and T. Perronet Thompson were particularly hurt and resentful. So the repeal of the corn laws, which was designed to further international harmony, promoted embarrassing disharmony among the free-trade leaders. (37)

Both Cobden and Bright learned a great deal from the experience, however, and for the rest of their lives they went out of their way to emphasize the contributions of their free-trade colleagues and to minimize their own roles. To be sure, Cobden found the whole controversy childish and silly. He was no publicity seeker. It was simply that newspaper writers had needed an individual on whom to focus attention in order to humanize and dramatize the repeal movement. They had seized on him, and so he became famous; but he could not have cared less. Bright, on the other hand, learned how powerful his own need for recognition was and how gratifying it was to be recognized. (38)

NOTES

(1) Bright to Sophia G. Gaselee, Dec. 8, 1841, Bright MSS, Fitzwilliam Museum, Cambridge.

(2) The first Cobden letter to Bright in the Cobden MSS in BM 43,649 is dated Dec. 14, 1837; Bright to Cobden, Mar. 25, 1841; June 5, 1841; July 5, 1841; Sept. 7, 1841, Bright MSS, BM 43,383; Cobden to Bright, Sept. 5, 1841, Cobden MSS, BM 43,649; Cobden to Bright, Sept. 9, 1841, Cobden MSS, Iowa State Department of History and Archives; Helen Priestman Bright Clark to W. H. Northy, Apr. 20, 1884, Northy MSS, BM 44,877.

(3) Bright to Cobden, Oct. 9, 1841; Oct. 23, 1841, Bright MSS, BM 43,383; Bright to Mrs. Bright, Apr. 18, 1864, Bright MSS, UCLL; Bright to George Wilson, May 9, 1839, Anti-Corn Law League MSS, MCL; cf. Norman McCord, *The Anti-Corn Law League, 1838–1846* (London, 1958), p. 112.

(4) Bright's birth certificate is in RGL; *Diaries,* Jan. 18, 1880; Bright to Mrs. Bright, June 18, 1854, Bright MSS, UCLL; *Diaries,* June 18, 1868; Hugh Barbour, *The Quakers in Puritan England* (New Haven, 1964) is the ablest recent account of the early history of the Society of Friends; J. Travis Mills, *John Bright and the Quakers* (London, 2 vols., 1935) is packed with valuable information; Bright to Mrs. Bright, Nov. 27, 1847; Aug. 11, 1872, Bright MSS, UCLL; Bright to John Albert Bright, Jan. 10, 1866, Bright MSS, RGL; Bright to Moncure D. Conway, Dec. 4, 1877, Bright MSS, Dickinson College Library;

A Testimony of Marsden Monthly Meeting of the Society of Friends, 1889, Local History Department, MCL.

(5) Bright to Cobden, Feb. 13, 1843, Bright MSS, BM 43,383; Bright to Mrs. Bright, June 18, 1854, Bright MSS, UCLL; Bright to W. R. W. Thorn, Feb. 23, 1869, Bright MSS, Folger Shakespeare Library; Bright to Gladstone, Sept. 17, 1873, Gladstone MSS, BM 44,113; *Addresses,* p. 410; Bright to John Butterworth, June 2, 1884, Bright MSS, BPL.

(6) Bright to Mrs. Bright, Feb. 16, 1862; Feb. 16, 1878, Bright MSS, UCLL; Ralph Sneyd to Henry Vincent, Dec. 4, 1831, Sneyd MSS, University of Keele; Joseph Hume to William H. Seward, June 15, 1840, Gratz MSS, HSP; Joseph Hume to Edward Davies Davenport, Apr. 12, 1841, Davenport MSS, JRL; later Bright was to complain of Hume's vanity and jealousy: Bright to Cobden, Oct. 15, 1852, Bright MSS, BM 43,383; Cobden to Bright, Oct. 18, 1852, Cobden MSS, BM 43,649.

(7) *Diaries,* ch. II; Bright to F. Cousinery, Apr. 1, 1845, Bright MSS, HSP.

(8) Bright to Cobden, July 5, 1841, Bright MSS, BM 43,383; it is understandable that such modern defenders of the Victorian landowning classes as G. Kitson Clark and David Spring do not like Bright; cf. Bright to Mrs. Bright, Feb. 17, 1866, Bright MSS, UCLL.

(9) See McCord for the best history of the League; Ebenezer Elliott to S. Smith, Nov. 16, 1839, Anti-Corn Law MSS, MCL; the George Wilson and John Benjamin Smith MSS in the MCL are an invaluable source.

(10) Cobden to Bright, May 5, 1841, Cobden MSS, BM 43,649; Cobden to Joseph Parkes, Jan. 12, 1854, Parkes MSS, UCLL.

(11) Samuel Smiles to Bright, Sept. 23, 1879, Bright MSS, BM 43,389; Bright to George Wilson, Feb. 12, 1844, Wilson MSS, MCL; Bright to Cobden, Oct. 18, 1843; Dec. 7, 1849, Bright MSS, BM 43,383; Bright to Wilson, Oct. 24, 1849, Wilson MSS, MCL; Bright to William Hickes, Dec. 6, 1860, Bright MSS, YUL; Bright to Mrs. Bright, Feb. 17, 1866, Bright MSS, UCLL; *Letters,* Oct. 15, 1888; Bright to Cobden, Sept. 7, 1841, Bright MSS, BM 43,383.

(12) Morley, p. 264; Cobden to Bright, no day, 1842, Cobden MSS, BM 43,649; *Parliamentary Papers,* 1843, VI; Bright to Wilson, July 28, 1843, Wilson MSS, MCL; Bright to Cobden, July 15, 1860, Bright MSS, BM 43,384; *Speech of John Bright, Esq., M.P., at the Nomination at Durham on Monday, July 24, 1843;* Bright to John T. Brook, June 29, 1843, Bright MSS, Friends Historical Library, Swarthmore College.

(13) Bright to F. Cousinery, Jan. 1, 1845, Bright MSS, PML; Bright to Cobden, Feb. 25, 1842; March 3, 1842; Apr. 19, 1842, Bright MSS, BM 43,383; cf. Cobden to Bright, Oct. 18, 1850, Cobden MSS, BM 43,649; Bright to Cobden, Apr. 19, 1842, Bright MSS, BM 43,383; Cobden to Bright, Mar. 12, 1842; Mar. 15, 1842; June 21, 1842, Cobden MSS, BM 43,649; Bright to Cobden, Mar. 9, 1842, Bright MSS, BM 43,383.

(14) Bright to William Lovett, Apr. 18, 1842, Lovett MSS, BM 47,663; Bright to Wilson, June 13, 1842, Wilson MSS, MCL; Bright to Brougham, June 15, 1842; June 20, 1842, Brougham MSS, UCLL; Bright to Wilson, July 18, 1842, Wilson MSS, MCL; Bright to Cobden, Dec. 11, 1842, Bright MSS, BM 43,353; Bright to Edward Watkins, Aug. 8, 1844, Autograph MSS, BL; Bright to G. J. Evans, Sept. 13, 1844, Bright MSS, RGL; Bright to Wilson, Dec. 23, 1843, Wilson MSS, MCL.

(15) *Parl. Deb.,* 76 (July 11, 1844), 635; Bright to Wilson, July 13, 1842; Oct. 17, 1843; Dec. 13, 1842; Apr. 12, 1843, Wilson MSS, MCL; Bright to Cobden, May 15, 1843; July 11, 1843, Bright MSS, BM 43,383; Bright to Wilson, Oct. 7, 1843; Jan. 8, 1844; June 13, 1844, Wilson MSS, MCL; Bright to W. M. Christy, Feb. 13, 1845, Bright MSS, FHL; Bright to William Bright, Dec. 18, 1843, Bright MSS, MHS; Bright to Wilson, Dec. 23, 1843; May 2, 1844, Wilson MSS, MCL; Bright to Joseph Sturge, Feb. 15, 1844, Sturge MSS, BM 43,723; *Punch,* VIII (1845), 118.

(16) *Corrected Report of Mr. Bright's Speech at the Public Meeting Held in the Music Saloon of the Corn Exchange, Wakefield, April 21, 1843* (Manchester, 1843); Bright to Joseph Sturge, Sept. 1, 1843, Sturge MSS, BM 43,845; Bright to Joseph Kay, Jan. 11, 1846, Kay MSS, NLI; *Parl. Deb.,* 78 (Feb. 27, 1845), 53ff.; *Punch,* VIII (1845), 120; Bright to W. H. Roberts, May 21, 1853, Lee Kohns MSS, NYPL; cf. F. M. L. Thompson, *English Landed Society in the Nineteenth Century* (London, 1963), p. 141.

(17) Bright to Brougham, Feb. 16, 1843; Feb. 22, 1843, Brougham MSS, UCLL.

(18) Cobden to Bright, Nov. 5, 1841, Cobden MSS, BM 43,649; Bright to Cobden, Sept. 7, 1841, Bright MSS, BM 43,383; National Anti-Corn Law League, *Bazaar Gazette,* No. 11 (London, 1845), p. 8.

(19) *Parl. Deb.,* 71 (Aug. 14, 1843), 666ff.; 73 (Mar. 12, 1844), 944ff.; 75 (June 26, 1844), 1542ff.; 76 (July 19, 1844), 1106, 1110; 77 (Feb. 24, 1845), 1140ff.; 80 (May 8, 1845), 321; 81 (June 10, 1845), 341ff.; 83 (Feb. 17, 1846), 1123ff.; cf. the vigorous protests in the House of Lords, 87 (June 25, 1846), 961ff.

(20) Cobden to Bright, Mar. 15, 1842; Apr. 15, 1842, Cobden MSS, BM 43,649; Cobden to John Benjamin Smith, Feb. 15, 1845, Smith MSS, MCL; Cobden to Smiles, Dec. 1, 1842, Cobden MSS, Fitzwilliam Museum, Cambridge; Cobden to Bright, June 2, 1842, Cobden MSS, BM 43,649; Bright to Cobden, Sept. 4, 1841; Sept. 7, 1841, Bright MSS, BM 43,383.

(21) Cobden to Smiles, Oct. 21, 1841, Cobden MSS, Fitzwilliam Museum, Cambridge; Cobden to Wilson, April 2, 1844; July 17, 1844, Wilson MSS, MCL.

(22) Bright to Cobden, June 5, 1842; Mar. 1, 1843; March 30, 1843; July 20, 1843; Oct. 2, 1843, Bright MSS, BM 43,383; Bright to Wilson, June 13,

1842; June 16, 1842; Mar. 30, 1844; Feb. 14, 1845; Feb. 20, 1845, Wilson MSS, MCL; *Punch*, X (1846), 270.

(23) The best general discussion is Lucy Brown, "The Chartists and the Anti-Corn Law League," in Asa Briggs, ed., *Chartist Studies* (London, 1959), pp. 342–371.

(24) Francis Place to unnamed correspondent, Sept. 29, 1840, Anti-Corn Law League MSS, MCL; Cobden to Bright, no day, 1842, Cobden MSS, BM 43,649.

(25) *Parl. Deb.*, 73 (Mar. 15, 1844), 1132ff., 1148ff.; 74 (May 13, 1844), 1063ff., 1070; 75 (June 10, 1844), 451ff.; 86 (May 22, 1846), 1050ff., 1054, 1057; Bright to Joseph Sturge, Apr. 18, 1853, Sturge MSS, BM 43,723; J. T. Ward, *The Factory Movement, 1830–1855* (London, 1962) is invaluable.

(26) *Parl. Deb.*, 71 (Aug. 7, 1843), 338ff.; 73 (Mar. 7, 1844), 659ff.

(27) Bright to Wilson, Apr. 7, 1842, Wilson MSS, MCL; Bright to Cobden, Apr. 10, 1842, Bright MSS, BM 43,383; Cobden to Bright, Apr. 15, 1842, Cobden MSS, BM 43,649; for years Bright was to speak with compassion about Chartism: *Parl. Deb.*, 105 (June 5, 1849), 1206; *The Times*, Nov. 24, 1885.

(28) Bright to Cobden, Oct. 9, 1841; March 5, 1842, Bright MSS, BM 43,383; Bright to Wilson, Aug. 12, 1842; Aug. 14, 1842, Wilson MSS, MCL; *Parl. Deb.*, 83 (Jan. 29, 1846), 408ff.

(29) *Letters* contains his public address of Aug. 1842 "To the Working Men of Rochdale"; Bright to Cobden, Mar. 5, 1842; May 28, 1842, Bright MSS, BM 43,383.

(30) Bright to Cobden, Mar. 3, 1843, *ibid.;* Bright to Wilson, Feb. 15, 1844, Wilson MSS, MCL; Cobden to Bright, May 7, 1846, Cobden MSS, BM 43,649.

(31) Cobden to Bright, Mar. 30, 1864, Cobden MSS, BM 43,652; *Parl. Deb.*, 84 (Mar. 6, 1846), 762; Bright to Cobden, July 29, 1846, Bright MSS, BM 43,383; Cobden to Bright, May 7, 1846, Cobden MSS, BM 43,649; Ralph Sneyd to Henry Vincent, Jan. 20, 1846, Sneyd MSS, University of Keele; Cobden to Parkes, May 26, 1856; June 10, 1857, Cobden MSS, BM 43,664; Bright to Mrs. Bright, Apr. 23, 1858, Bright MSS, UCLL; *Parl. Deb.*, 71 (Aug. 7, 1843), 341; 83 (Feb. 17, 1846), 1129; 302 (Jan. 12, 1886), 8–10. Bright's last speech in Parliament was in praise of Peel.

(32) Manchester Chamber of Commerce MSS, Oct. 22, 1845, MCL.

(33) Cobden to Wilson, Nov. 4, 1845, Wilson MSS; Manchester Chamber of Commerce MSS, Jan. 14, 1846; Bright to Wilson, Jan. 28, 1846, Wilson MSS, MCL.

(34) Ralph Sneyd to Henry Vincent, Jan. 2, 1846, Sneyd MSS, University of Keele.

(35) Morley, pp. 379–85; Cobden to James Mellon, Mar. 5, 1846; Cobden to Walter Wilson, Mar. 24, 1846, Cobden MSS, BM 43,667; Bright to Mrs.

Drummond, Apr. 1, 1846, Bright MSS; Bright to Wilson, Jan. 30, 1846; June 26, 1846, Wilson MSS, MCL.

(36) Cf. Bright to Joseph Sturge, Feb. 15, 1844, Sturge MSS, BM 43,723; Morley, p. 506; Cobden to Sturge, Mar. 26, 1846, Cobden MSS, BM 43,656; Bright to W. C. Bennett, Dec. 26, 1846, Bright MSS, Wellesley College Library; National Anti-Corn Law League, *Bazaar Gazette,* No. 12 (London, 1845); Bright to Cobden, Oct. 19, 1852, Bright MSS, BM 43,383.

(37) Cobden to Parkes, July 18, 1846, Cobden MSS, BM 43,664; Bright to Wilson, July 31, 1846, Wilson MSS, MCL; Ebenezer Elliott to unnamed correspondent, Aug. 31, 1849, Authors Club MSS, NYPL; Thompson to H. B. Peacock, June 14, 1846; June 30, 1846, Thompson MSS, JRL; Thompson to G. J. Holyoake, Jan. 26, 1864, Holyoake MSS, Cooperative Union Ltd., Manchester; increasingly, Cobden and Bright found Villiers' indecisiveness maddening: Cobden to Bright, Nov. 17, 1852; Jan. 1, 1853, Cobden MSS, BM 43,649–50; Villiers to Bright, Jan. 3, 1884, Bright MSS, BM 43,386.

(38) Morley, p. 368; Cobden to F. Buloz, Dec. 19, 1845, Autograph MSS, University of London Library; Cobden to Wilson, July 11, 1846, Wilson MSS, MCL.

CHAPTER TWO

NO REST
1846–1848

Bright's efforts in the struggle for cheap bread established his reputation as a defender of the working classes. "Bright in the lion's den,/Champion of honest men," wrote Ebenezer Elliott, the popular working-class poet. "Labour, and Labour's Sons, lay in sad plight,/When Rochdale John came forth, and all was BRIGHT," wrote another of the band of versifiers who drew inspiration from the crusade against the corn laws. And in the acrostic outburst of still another admirer:

Join'd in a league with all thy noble band,
On freedom's prow we see thee steadfast stand;
Hail'd by the wishes of the suffering poor,
No longer hopeless, though they still endure.

But Bright's role as a free trader also won him enemies—and on a grand scale. Newspaper attacks on him were both frequent and vicious, and all kinds of abusive names were heaped on him, ranging from hypocrite and liar to demagogue and traitor. He came to symbolize what one country gentleman called "the headlong downward course by which we are daily approximating an American form of Government and (what is even worse) an American tone of politics." (1)

Nor was it only great landowners who viewed him as a scourge and warned him that making bullying speeches was not the way to deal with gentlemen. Even within the ranks of the Leaguers he was under attack. Some of his opponents were jealous of him and his oratorical gifts; some found him unduly strong-minded, argumentative, tactless, reckless, aggressive, and lacking in deference; and some were alarmed by his radicalism, especially his intense hostility to the great landowners and his denunciations of their "selfish oligarchy." Bright knew, as he confessed to Cobden, that there were "incapacities" about him, but he was unaware of the extent to which he had offended and frightened some of his middle-class colleagues. (2)

Even in the last years of the crusade, when Bright's talents were so urgently needed, his enemies within the League took advantage of every opportunity to undermine his position. Cobden, always alert to the importance of unity and harmony, repeatedly came to Bright's defense. He made a point of reporting back to Wilson at the League's Manchester headquarters every new triumph of Bright, and in the most generous and flattering terms. It was then up to Wilson to pass along word of Bright's indispensability. Who else but Bright could make such a telling speech? Who else could do his work so admirably? (3)

The crisis came in the months following the repeal of the corn laws. Bright, with his passion for Lancashire, wanted as his reward the privilege of sitting in the House of Commons as a Member for Manchester. The center of the cotton trade was, for him, the center of the new world of the nineteenth century, and he could think of no greater distinction than that of representing this new locus of power in Parliament. Cobden, furthermore, had encouraged him in this ambition. Bright assumed, therefore, that at the appropriate time he would be invited to stand for Manchester, and so he informed his Durham constituents that he would no longer represent them.

Bright's enemies shrewdly insisted, however, that Cobden was the more suitable man for the Manchester seat, and Bright had to agree with them. Cobden, after all, personified the free-trade movement more than anyone else, and although he fully and freely acknowledged the contributions of his colleagues, unquestionably he had been the mainspring of the League. For all that, Bright felt hurt because Cobden had assured him repeatedly that he was satisfied to continue as Member for Stockport and that he had no desire whatever to sit for Manchester. As the son of a Sussex farmer, Cobden had none of Bright's strong personal feelings about Lancashire and the exalted position of Manchester, "the centre and heart of the greatest and most remarkable industry that the world has ever seen." (4)

Cobden, with his usual magnanimity, ended the difficulties. Despite the pressures that were brought to bear on him, he refused to be a candidate. Wilson, in the meantime, went to work and rallied the right people; and Bright secured the nomination to the seat that meant so much to him. The struggle made him so distraught that even on his thirty-fifth birthday, November 16, 1846, he took time to give Wilson detailed suggestions about how to manage his campaign and win over his enemies. Bright, in fact, became so dependent on Wilson as a peacemaker and organizer of victory that when the possibility arose that Wilson, too, might seek a seat in Parliament, Bright shamelessly discouraged him. "You pull many strings now which would not answer to your pull if you sat for Huddersfield or elsewhere," he wrote. "Your motives would always be suspected, and you would be only an M.P., whereas now you can make members through your influence." This side of Bright his biographers have conveniently ignored. (5)

It was clear from the outset that Bright would have trouble with his constituents even though he tried to convince himself that his sentiments largely accorded with theirs. For, while he and his constituents referred to themselves as "liberals," his idea of what the word meant was shared by few of them. He was far more advanced in his social and political thought, and since he insisted on making his views plain, friction was inevitable. He regarded the repeal of the corn laws as only the first major assault on the privileges of the aristocracy; other reforms—of the game, tax, land, and voting laws— were equally necessary for the health and decency of British society, and Bright could hardly wait for them to take place. Since many of his constituents were reluctant to press for further changes, he was bound to clash with them. He was not the kind of Member of Parliament who would let escape an opportunity to state what he thought should be done. Nor was he the kind to abstain from voting on a measure because it was controversial; such behavior he found repugnant. (6)

II

Fortunately for Bright, 1847 was the year not only of his parliamentary tie with Manchester but of his second marriage. His wife, the former Margaret Elizabeth Leatham, had led a sheltered and comfortable life with her Quaker banking family in the outskirts of Wakefield, Yorkshire. She knew almost nothing about politics, but her marriage quickly changed that. Bright, for his part, after six years as a widower, now had a companion and correspondent to whom he could talk and write about his fantasies and frustrations as well as his victories: "Thou wilt think I am vain, but I only write *thus* to my *wife*, who will not be sorry if her husband says anything worth saying, and in an effective manner." His marriage served as a buffer against a hostile political environment; and, as he told Cobden, he relished the prospect of domestic peace after the seven years' war of the League. (7)

Bright did not hold his new wife in the kind of awe in which he had held his first Elizabeth. Nor was his second marriage so idyllic as the editor of his diaries has painted it. Not infrequently Bright snapped at his wife for a variety of reasons—the illegibility of her handwriting, her mismanagement of the household help, the extravagance of some of her tastes, and her tendency to let trifles upset her and bring on seizures of self-pity. Indeed, what made their marriage a good one, and it became better as they aged, was the relatively free expression of their resentments and disagreements. Their Quakerism and Mrs. Bright's kindness to her stepdaughter were strong bonds; so, too, were "more kisses than [could] be counted." Probably the best sign of the success of the marriage was Bright's frequent wish, as the number of his children increased, to give up public life so that he could spend more time at home and make better provision for his family. (8)

III

In the early years of his career as Member for Manchester, Bright devoted his energies to clarifying what he considered to be the two leading problems that faced the United Kingdom: the Irish troubles and the restricted parliamentary franchise. Since he had no doubt whatever of the prime importance of domestic issues, he deplored Britain's chronic meddling in the affairs of other countries. A vigorous foreign policy meant large military expenditures, which resulted in a huge tax burden on the poor who obviously could least afford it. Small wonder that Bright detested politicians who made fiery speeches that stimulated jealousy and mistrust of foreign countries and encouraged gullible citizens to fear imaginary enemies. Small wonder, too, that he admired and envied the United States for its tiny military expenditures and for the ability of its people to concentrate on domestic questions and not get involved in the affairs of other countries. He conveniently ignored the Mexican War and the outbursts of the champions of manifest destiny. (9)

The Irish Question obsessed Bright for several reasons. As a Quaker and as a human being, he was appalled by the heartrending reports from the Ireland of the Great Famine, and it made him shudder to think that far more people had died recently of starvation in Ireland than had ever died in a British war. As an English patriot (which he was, despite what his enemies said about him), he was humiliated by the disrepute into which his country had fallen because of the maltreatment of Ireland—a disrepute of which Cobden reminded him constantly in bitter letters from the Continent. Furthermore, as a Lancashire man, he was horrified by the sight of the wretched Irish immigrants who were crowding into Liverpool and Manchester under inhuman conditions. In fact, he argued that many of the evils and abuses ascribed to industrialization were really due to the vast influx of Irish into Lancashire—an important truth that historians since his time have often forgotten. (10)

As Bright saw it and had seen it for years, there was nothing complicated about the Irish land question. Although Ireland was an overwhelmingly agricultural country, the masses of Irish peasants were dispossessed in their own land. Small numbers of landlords, many of them absentee owners, were destroying what should have been a prosperous society. As long as these landlords continued to enjoy a privileged position in British law and as long as their land remained absurdly "sacred," the bulk of the Irish peasants would be doomed to pauperism. Fortunately, the remedy for Ireland's plight was simple. Social harmony and peace would result if Irish tenant farmers were given a real stake in the land. This, to be sure, required a fundamental revision of Irish land law, and such preposterous vestiges from the feudal past as primogeniture and entail had to make way for the free sale of land. Bright was aware that because of these proposals he would be charged with undermining aristocratic institutions, but as he plainly put it, "...perish your aristocratic institutions rather than that a whole nation should be in this terrible condition." Indeed, he thought it would be a very good thing for the children of aristocratic families to learn how to earn a living. (11)

At a time when almost all Members of Parliament believed the Great Famine should be dealt with by temporary relief measures, Bright called for far-reaching and long-range land reform. The Irish economy would come into its own when the masses of peasants were motivated to make improvements and cultivate the land efficiently, and these things would happen when they enjoyed property rights. Peace and prosperity were impossible in Ireland until Parliament took steps to "set in motion her industry, create and diffuse capital, and thus establish those gradations of rank and condition by which the whole social fabric can alone be held together." (12)

So Bright pressed for land reform acts decades before such measures were passed. He was certainly ahead of his time, but he believed that a politician dealt with emergencies as they arose, while a statesman anticipated the problems of the future and, by acting with courage and foresight, prevented them from becoming insoluble. Bright was to discover frequently in the course of his career that the Irish Question brought out the politician, not the statesman, in Members of Parliament. The Whig and Tory leaders, Lord John Russell, Sir Robert Peel, and Lord George Bentinck, were merely waiting for things to quiet down in Ireland, as they so often had in the past. (13)

Bright realized that land reform alone would not soothe Irish discontent; church reform was also indispensable. Since so few Irish were Anglicans, the existence of an established Anglican Church in Ireland was a guarantee of disaffection. Indeed, the Church of

Ireland had for years inspired Bright's genius for invective. He repeatedly proclaimed it as foul a blot, as monstrous an evil, and as shameful and disgraceful an institution as existed in Christendom. Since religion, for him, was by its nature a private matter, he was convinced that a state church was bound to endanger public liberty and threaten Christianity itself. Avoid all kinds of evils, therefore, by separating church and state, he argued; and in disendowing the Church, use some of the funds for some important national need such as education. In the light of his attitude toward the Anglican Establishment, it is understandable that he joked with his wife about the ceremony preceding his assumption of his parliamentary seat: "Thou mayst imagine me at the Table of the House of Commons affirming allegiance etc., and that I will not injure the Church as by law established etc.!" It is also understandable that when *Punch* tried to dream as wildly as it could about the future, Bright appeared as the Archbishop of Canterbury. (14)

The disestablishment of the Church of Ireland and land reform would win the confidence of the Irish, make them stop feeling conquered and oppressed, alter the pattern of their wretched history of idleness, poverty, starvation, and insurrection, and cement the union between England and Ireland. Alms and force, the traditional British methods of dealing with Ireland, had not worked in the past and would not work in the future. As Bright reminded his colleagues in the House of Commons in 1848: "You have toiled at this Irish difficulty Session after Session, and some of you have grown almost from boyhood to grey-headed old men since it first met you in your legislative career, and yet there is not in ancient or modern history a picture so humiliating as that which Ireland presents to the world at this moment." (15)

Nor did Bright ignore the implications of the vast Irish migration to the United States and elsewhere. Decrying the myth of the Irish as a naturally lazy people, he liked to point out that the transplanted Irish showed how hard they could work when they had a chance to do so and how much they could enrich the communities in which they settled. At the same time, he cautioned that the transplanted Irish would be fierce enemies of Britain and would do everything they could to secure revenge. Long before the founding of the Irish Republican group known as the Fenian Brotherhood, he saw the inevitability of such an organization. And he predicted that in the event of a crisis between the United States and Britain the Irish in America would do all they could to strike back at their old oppressors. (16)

Bright's view of the Irish Question reveals the absurdity of much that has been said about his attitude toward the proper role of government. He certainly believed that the state should not intervene in matters which "experience showed might wisely, safely, and beneficially be left to private individuals, stimulated by the love of gain and the desire to administer to the wants and comforts of their fellow men." But there was nothing rigid or doctrinaire about Bright's position. In certain spheres he considered state intervention wise, safe, and beneficial. In other spheres he considered it unwise, unsafe, or harmful. Thus at the same time that he favored Irish land and educational legislation, he opposed the Factory Act of 1847 which in certain factories established the ten-hour day for "young people" between thirteen and eighteen. As has been noted, he condemned short-time legislation because it would injure those workers who wished to increase their earnings by extra labor, and because it would threaten the manufacturing supremacy of Britain. He considered the advocates of factory laws misguided patriots as well as fools and knaves who had convinced themselves that the British were such a naturally superior people that they had nothing to fear from foreign competition. He supported state intervention to promote railroad construction and the cultivation of cotton in British India; but he opposed legislation to control smoke as both unwise and ineffectual. (17)

IV

Just as Bright denounced British aristocrats for preventing Irish reform, so, too, he attacked them for blocking parliamentary reform. The much vaunted British Constitution, as he saw it, was a mass of hypocrisy. It was bad enough that the House of Lords was an aristocratic institution, but the real tragedy was that the House of Com-

mons was hardly less aristocratic. Furthermore, both the Whig and
Tory parties were dominated by the aristocracy, and all the members
of the cabinet were either aristocrats or their hangers-on. To Bright,
it was both a scandal and a disgrace that the Reform Act of 1832 had
not been followed by measures distributing the seats in the House
of Commons more equitably and extending the right to vote to
much more than one-seventh of the male adult population. (18)

The Continental Revolutions of 1848 impressed Bright with the
urgency of parliamentary reform. If the Government of Louis-
Philippe had made concessions in advance, the February Revolution
would have been averted. Stupidity and shortsightedness had prevented wise and generous actions, and so Louis-Philippe was a
refugee in England. Bright lacked the light touch that would have
permitted him, after the fashion of *Punch*, to quip:

> Louis-Philippe
> Has lost his sheep,
> And never again will find 'em;
> The people of France
> Have made an advance,
> And left their King behind 'em.

But Bright found the lesson clear and indisputable. Revolutions
were in fashion again—"a fresh revolution or a dethronement by
every post," as Cobden put it—and if British aristocrats wished to
survive, they had better institute changes from above. (19)

Bright had no doubt whatever that British workers could be
trusted with the right to vote. After all, he of all Members of Parliament probably knew Lancashire workers the best, and he could
testify that "communist principles" had found no support among
them as they had among groups of French workers. In short, the
time had come, he told his colleagues in the House, to extend

the pale of the constitution of which they boasted so much. The 800,000
electors of the country formed a kind of garrison, but it was surrounded
by 5,000,000 persons, who required to be admitted within its bounds, and
who, if admitted, would tend considerably to strengthen and support that
constitution which was so highly prized not only in this but in other
countries. He admitted the excellence of the constitution; but it was only

a mere theory to the great body of the people in this country, for the benefits it admitted of were not enjoyed by them; and that constitution would be strengthened to an extraordinary degree by admitting a large number of people to participate in its privileges and partake of its advantages. (20)

Bright saw parliamentary reform as an end in itself, an act of justice that would give more adult males the stake in society that was rightfully theirs. He also saw it as a device by which to reduce the vast authority of the great landowners, and he saw it as an opportune measure that would rule out the possibilities of bloodshed. Like many of his contemporaries, including the Duke of Wellington, Bright overestimated the strength of the Chartists in 1848; and he feared that those among them who recklessly advocated the use of force would come into their own in the infectious atmosphere of the year of European revolutions. (21)

As early as March 1848, Bright suggested to George Wilson that Manchester should launch another crusade—this time for the reshaping of Parliament. He argued that if parliamentary changes were not made peacefully, they would be made violently. Since Manchester had had more experience in the organization of agitation than any other British town, it was easily the best qualified to act in this new cause. "If we move," he told Wilson, "we shall strike terror into the enemy, because they will give us credit for resolution and sincerity, for money and labor." (22)

The more Bright thought about the state of Parliament, the more he raged at the aristocrats. They were Philistines who made the English people grind at their mills; they were wretches who by their failure to learn anything from the disturbances on the Continent showed their wish for self-destruction; they were brutal in their tendencies and blind to the retribution that awaited them. Unless they were ousted as the dominant class, Bright told Wilson, "they will destroy us." (23)

Bright knew what a new League would mean—the memory of the old League was still fresh. He understood how much energy and time it would consume and how much tension it would produce. He also knew that many of his fellow Quakers would disapprove of his behavior. His new mother-in-law, in particular, could not see a Quaker in the role of a noisy agitator, and she was disturbed by the reputation of her son-in-law. As Bright bluntly told his wife, however, "It is all well enough for rich and comfortably off people to complain that their quiet is disturbed by the growling of millions whom they tax to an enormous amount—and yet shut out from all share in the power by which taxes are imposed." It was obvious to Bright that things could not continue as they were, and that somebody had to work to change them. The remedy was certainly not to be found in "shutting our eyes and sticking our fingers in our ears, and railing at Chartists and Radicals." (24)

Despite the hardships that a new crusade would involve, Bright was willing to make sacrifices. Cobden and Wilson, on the other hand, had strong misgivings. Although they favored parliamentary reform, they lacked Bright's zeal for it. Having hardly recovered from the exhaustion of the anti-corn law struggle, they would not enter lightly on a new venture. Besides, Cobden doubted that Manchester and the old League officers should assume leadership in the new agitation because the impression would inevitably be created that they were insatiable seekers after power. He preferred that some other town and other leaders take the initiative. (25)

The weeks and months went by, the Chartist scare subsided, and it was plain that Parliament would not consent to reform itself. Since the Chartists had brought discredit on the holding of big public meetings, Cobden was convinced that the time was wrong for a new agitation on the lines of the old League. Bright was disappointed. He had been willing to settle for almost any scheme of parliamentary reform on which the middle classes of Manchester would agree. Recognizing the desirability of harmony, he was prepared to put up with less than what he really wanted just so that the middle classes could travel united "all in one boat." His efforts were all to no avail, however. The sad truth, he recognized, was that the aristocrats had exploited the Chartist menace to alarm the middle classes and to keep them from joining any movement for the extension of the suffrage. As Bright expressed his disgust: "The Government seem to make a great uproar about the Chartists. They have spies among these wretched fools, to stimulate them to conspiracy and to out-rage—and then getting a lot of them together they pounce upon them, and imprison or transport them.... The aristocracy want to frighten the middle classes from the pursuit of reforms, and to do this they and their emissaries stimulate a portion of the least wise of the people to menaces and violence, to damage the cause of reform...." (26)

At the end of the year Bright learned of the formation of a new organization in Liverpool that was to agitate for both financial and political reform. He was enthusiastic about its possibilities. But it is revealing that when he wrote to Cobden about it, he exercised great restraint: "Now don't be alarmed at all this, for it will not involve our old sacrifices. I think it may be done without killing either of us, or driving us from home as before." It is no less revealing that Cobden was firmly against combining in a single organization the two objectives of parliamentary and financial reform. He certainly favored an agitation that would dispel some of the ignorance of the British people about taxation, colonies, and armaments. But he told Bright that he dreaded "abortive efforts on a conspicuous stage," and he included parliamentary reform among such efforts. He urged Bright to talk as much as he wished about the subject at meetings but to accept the fact that the public mind was not yet ready for action. (27)

No doubt about it, 1848 was a hard year for Bright. His disappointments were profound, and for the rest of his life he was to insist that, if Ireland and Parliament had been properly dealt with in 1848, many tragedies that later took place could have been averted. In the meantime, however, he was sustained through the frustrations of the year by his belief that God would punish the great landowners for their outrageous behavior. He was also sustained by his family. He loved his wife, she loved him, she was taking excellent care of his daughter, and she gave birth to his first son. (28)

NOTES

(1) "On a FRIEND Indeed," by W. S., circular in FHL; National Anti-Corn Law League, *Bazaar Gazette*, No. 15 (London, 1845); *The Times*, Aug. 11,

1845; Aug. 18, 1845; Bright to Cobden, Mar. 22, 1843, Bright MSS, BM 43,383; Bright to Wilson, Mar. 9, 1844, Wilson MSS, MCL; Ralph Sneyd to Henry Vincent, July 10, 1846, Sneyd MSS, University of Keele.

(2) *Parl. Deb.,* 77 (Feb. 6, 1845), 199; *The Times,* Jan. 7, 1846; Morley, p. 465; Bright to Cobden, Sept. 20, 1845, Bright MSS, BM 43,383.

(3) Cobden to Wilson, Feb. 11, 1845; Feb. 28, 1845; Mar. 4, 1846; Aug. 26, 1848, Wilson MSS, MCL; Morley, p. 485.

(4) Bright to Cobden, July 29, 1846, Bright MSS, BM 43,383; Cobden to Wilson, Aug. 3, 1846; Bright to Wilson, Aug. 2, 1846; Aug. 4, 1846, Wilson MSS, MCL; *The Times,* Aug. 21, 1846; *Parl. Deb.,* 112 (June 18, 1850), 10; cf. Bright to A. Bauer, Sept. 28, 1850, Anthony MSS, NYPL.

(5) Bright to Wilson, Nov. 16, 1846; June 12, 1847, Wilson MSS, MCL.

(6) *The Times,* Oct. 19, 1846; Jan. 18, 1847; Bright to Cobden, Nov. 29, 1846, Bright MSS, BM 43,383; Bright to Wilson, Nov. 26, 1846; Cobden to Wilson, Dec. 29, 1846, Wilson MSS, MCL; Bright to J. Aspinall, June 8, 1847, Bright MSS, Friends Historical Library, Swarthmore College; cf. Bright to Joseph Sturge, Oct. 16, 1858, Sturge MSS, BM 43,723.

(7) Bright to Mrs. Bright, Aug. 17, 1847; Nov. 24, 1847; Dec. 7, 1847; Dec. 10, 1847; Feb. 20, 1850; Nov. 22, 1850, Bright MSS, UCLL; Bright to Cobden, July 29, 1846, Bright MSS, BM 43,383.

(8) *Diaries* p. 93; Bright to Mrs. Bright, Feb. 20, 1850; June 13, 1851; July 22, 1851; Oct. 13, 1851; Apr. 7, 1852; Dec. 10, 1852; June 11, 1854; July 19, 1854; July 29, 1854; Apr. 28, 1860; Feb. 13, 1862; Feb. 14, 1862; Feb. 15, 1862; Sept. 13, 1867; Mar. 19, 1874; Dec. 2, 1852; Nov. 27, 1847; Nov. 13, 1852; Apr. 23, 1858; Feb. 22, 1861, Bright MSS, UCLL; Cobden to Bright, Oct. 12, 1860, Cobden MSS, BM 43,651.

(9) Bright to J. Grave, Jan. 25, 1846, Bright MSS, JRL; Bright to Cobden, Nov. 29, 1846, Bright MSS, BM 43,383; Bright to Wilson, Jan. 24, 1847, Wilson MSS, MCL; *Parl. Deb.,* 96 (Feb. 18, 1848), 975ff.; 96 (Feb. 22, 1848), 1076ff.; 97 (Mar. 20, 1848), 839.

(10) Cobden to Bright, Jan. 18, 1847, Cobden MSS, BM 43,649; *Speeches,* I, 306ff., 310–11.

(11) *Parl. Deb.,* 71 (Aug. 7, 1843), 341; 71 (Aug. 14, 1843), 661; 73 (Mar. 7, 1844), 663; *Speeches,* I, 310.

(12) See R. Dudley Edwards and T. Desmond Williams, eds., *The Great Famine* (New York, 1957); *Speeches,* I, 307.

(13) Bright to Mrs. Bright, Aug. 20, 1848, Bright MSS, UCLL.

(14) *Parl. Deb.,* 79 (Apr. 16, 1845), 818ff.; 91 (Apr. 26, 1847), 1411; 97 (Apr. 4, 1848), 1282ff.; 99 (May 29, 1848), 6; 100 (July 17, 1848), 517; *The Times,* Jan. 18, 1847; Dec. 9, 1848; Bright to J. M. Hare, Apr. 18, 1848, Bright MSS, PUL; Bright to Mrs. Bright, Nov. 24, 1847, Bright MSS, UCLL; *Punch,* XIV (1848), 107.

(15) *Parl. Deb.,* 97 (Mar. 31, 1848), 1183ff.; *Speeches,* I, 320.

(16) Bright to Wilson, Apr. 6, 1848, Wilson MSS, MCL; *Speeches,* I, 315.

(17) Cf. W. L. Burn, *The Age of Equipoise* (London, 1964), p. 162; *Parl. Deb.,* 109 (Mar. 18, 1850), 1068ff.; 76 (July 11, 1844), 629; Bright to Joseph Kay, Jan. 11, 1846, Kay MSS, NLI; *Parl. Deb.* 89 (Feb. 10, 1847), 1136ff., 1144; 91 (Mar. 17, 1847), 126; Bright to Wilson, Mar. 3, 1847, Wilson MSS, MCL; *Parl. Deb.,* 92 (May 6, 1847), 476ff.; 95 (Dec. 10, 1847), 927; 105 (June 6, 1849), 1261ff.; 107 (July 11, 1849), 196ff.

(18) Bright to Wilson, Mar. 7, 1848, Wilson MSS, MCL; *Parl. Deb.,* 98 (Apr. 10, 1848), 117.

(19) *Punch,* XIV (1848), 100; Morley, p. 484; Bright to Wilson, June 12, 1848, Wilson MSS, MCL.

(20) *Parl. Deb.,* 98 (Apr. 18, 1848), 471ff.

(21) Cf. *Annual Register, 1848,* p. 123; Asa Briggs, ed., *Chartist Studies* (London, 1959) is invaluable, but a systematic history of Chartism is desperately needed.

(22) Bright to Wilson, Mar. 25, 1848; Apr. 18, 1848, Wilson MSS, MCL.

(23) Bright to Wilson, May 23, 1848; May 25, 1848, *ibid*.

(24) Bright to Wilson, June 7, 1848, *ibid.;* Bright to Mrs. Bright, June 10, 1848, Bright MSS, UCLL.

(25) Cobden to Wilson, May 11, 1848; Bright to Wilson, May 31, 1848; June 23, 1848; Cobden to Wilson, June 24, 1848, Wilson MSS, MCL.

(26) Cobden to Bright, Sept. 8, 1848; Nov. 1, 1848; Dec. 22, 1848, Cobden MSS, BM 43,649; Bright to Mrs. Bright, Aug. 20, 1848, Bright MSS, UCLL.

(27) Bright to Cobden, Dec. 21, 1848, Bright MSS, BM 43,383; Cobden to Bright, Dec. 23, 1848; Dec. 27, 1848, Cobden MSS, BM 43,649.

(28) Bright to Wilson, Dec. 24, 1848, Wilson MSS, MCL; Bright to Mrs. Bright, Aug. 20, 1848; Aug. 29, 1848, Bright MSS, UCLL.

CHAPTER THREE

CONTINUING THE STRUGGLE
1849–1851

Bright did not give up. He was still in his thirties, his recuperative powers were strong, and he remained as certain as ever of the soundness of his position. The deplorable condition of Ireland and the hardly less deplorable condition of Parliament—these were the important issues that needed to be dealt with in 1849. Furthermore, these issues were related, for without parliamentary reform it was improbable that the maltreatment of Ireland would be corrected. If his old friends in the free trade campaign would join with him again, that would be fine. If not, he would go it alone because that was the right thing to do.

Cobden was equally sure that Bright's estimate of the political situation was incorrect. But since he liked Bright and valued his friendship, he tried to avoid offending him. So both subtly and bluntly he attempted to persuade Bright that his hopes were, in the short run, unrealistic. In January 1849, for example, Cobden called on Francis Place, the old and experienced reformer, and when he wrote to Bright about the visit, he took obvious delight in reporting Place's belief that for the present it was futile to put parliamentary reform ahead of financial reform. (1)

Cobden did not succeed in his aim: he was simply wrong, Bright thought, and he told him so. Not without some malice, Bright insisted that the case for parliamentary reform was as strong or stronger than the case for free trade had ever been. More and more, in fact, he saw parliamentary reform as the subject that would separate the liberals from the spineless opportunists (like Lord John Russell) who made up the Whig Party. Bright was so disillusioned with these

Whigs that he could detect no real difference between them and the Tories. He regarded all people who would not support parliamentary reform as fitting colleagues of the unprincipled Whigs and the hopelessly stupid Tories. (2)

Even when Cobden showed enthusiasm for the qualification movement, Bright had some misgivings. It was fine to urge middle-class and working-class people to purchase forty shilling freeholds so that they could qualify as county voters. But Bright feared that this qualification movement (or freehold plan) would become an end in itself and that in the process parliamentary reform would be forgotten. As far as Bright was concerned no object short of a thoroughgoing reform of Parliament deserved serious effort. Cobden's answer was that the freehold plan was a means to the end Bright sought; though not a substitute for parliamentary reform, it was a valuable device by which to lessen the authority of the great landowners in their traditional strongholds. At the same time Cobden could not conceal his annoyance that "some of us have not clearly weighed the difficulties of our task." Nor did he fail to point out to Bright that the middle classes of Lancashire, though admirably suited to conduct the free trade agitation, were not at all ready to lead a democratic reform movement. (3)

Fortunately for their future relations, Bright was willing to do what he could "to prevent liberal principles from suffering by the open display of a schism." And fortunately for his own peace of mind he was to console himself for many years with the thought that the repeal of the corn laws had been so successful that people could not give themselves to any other important reform—their mouths were too filled with cheap bread. (4)

II

In the meantime, Bright used every opportunity to clamor for justice for Ireland. Whenever he could, he embarrassed the Government of Lord John Russell for its failure to cope with the Irish land question. He voted against any further suspension of habeas corpus in Ireland. He tried to talk privately with Sir Robert Peel about what should be done. He pleaded with his colleagues in the House to let bygones be bygones, to stop blaming one another for the blunders of the past, and to plunge into the complexities of the Irish Question without further delay. Finally, when the parliamentary session ended in July 1849, he spent a little time in Rochdale and then went to Ireland to see for himself what was happening. The day he arrived Queen Victoria was concluding a brief trip there, and he rejoiced to hear what a favorable impression she had made. (5)

Bright's visit was just what he needed. It proved to him that his analysis of Ireland's plight was sound and that the great landowners were the unmistakable villains. "Here we have in perfection the fruits of aristocratic and territorial usurpation and privilege," he wrote to his wife. The trials that the Irish people had been through were enough to "horrify the stoutest, and move the hardest heart." The signs of the Irish calamity were so frightful that Bright could not bring himself to write details of them to his wife. (6)

The Irish visit moved Bright for another reason: he learned that he was appreciated. He found that his attempts to plead the Irish case in England were well known in Ireland—even among humble people whom he would never have expected to be informed about such matters. This recognition was important to Bright. The rebuffs he had suffered in recent years had made him feel "nauseated with politics." It was not pleasant to be denounced for goading one class to hate another and for stimulating envy, a "levelling spirit," and the destruction of property rights. So he was encouraged to see that some of his contemporaries understood—and favored—what he was trying to do. He would certainly have been profoundly hurt by the failure of Mrs. Cecil Woodham-Smith and other twentieth-century historians to dwell on his contributions to the debate on the Great Famine. (7)

Bright spent more than a month in Ireland. He would have remained there longer, but his wife was nearing the end of a pregnancy and he wanted to be with her when the child was born. His Irish stay, though brief, made a lasting impression. Now he could talk at first hand about post-Famine Ireland—something that shockingly few of his English colleagues in Parliament were able to do.

Now, on the basis of his incessant inquiries, he could say with authority that the Irish people wanted land and parliamentary reform, and that most of them wanted disestablishment. Now he could point out the dangers of the Ministry's lack of a rational Irish policy and of its reliance on the passage of time as a panacea. The Irish situation required a government that would press for salutary changes, not a government that wallowed in ignorance and cowardice. If the United Kingdom was to remain united, Parliament had to do justice to the Irish and stop blaming their starvation on the potato and Providence. (8)

At times Bright hesitated to keep saying the same things, and *The Times* repeatedly criticized him for being repetitious; but he reassured himself that these were the things that had to be said. Besides, there was always Cobden urging him to give "another great Irish speech" and congratulating him for making the Irish Question clearer than it had ever been before. Cobden, indeed, enjoyed being able to claim the Irish masses as partisans of "the Manchester School," as Disraeli called the free traders of the League. (9)

III

Obsessed as Bright was with the importance of unsolved domestic problems, he disliked the prominence that foreign affairs came to assume for the British people in 1850. The culprit was the Whig Foreign Minister Lord Palmerston, whom Bright suspected at every turn and who symbolized everything that Bright despised. He was an Irish aristocrat and absentee landlord; he disapproved heartily of parliamentary reform; and, totally lacking in Christian humility, he displayed in his dealings with foreign countries the kind of rashness, arrogance, and insolence that was certain to bring on either war or war scares. (10)

There was no doubt about the side that Bright would take in the Don Pacifico affair. Pacifico, a Portuguese Jew who by reason of his birth in Gibraltar was a British subject, had made claims against the Greek government for certain property damages he had suffered in Athens. To support these claims of a British subject, Palmerston ostentatiously sent British naval units to Piraeus. If *Punch*, there-

A *BRIGHT* IDEA
THE PEACE RECRUITING SERGEANT
TRYING TO ENLIST THE DUKE

☞ Mr. Bright's peace principles were embodied in the plan proposed this year to settle all international differences by arbitration. The scheme was not viewed with much favor.—1849.

fore, called Pacifico the greatest British subject, the reason was that none other had had a Foreign Secretary as his sheriff and a British admiral as his bailiff. (11)

Like Cobden, Peel, and such followers of Peel as the vigorous William E. Gladstone, Bright was distressed by Palmerston's abuse of British power, his exploitation of British patriotism, and his conversion of John Bull into "John Bully." What was hardly less distressing to Bright was the discovery that in Manchester, as well as throughout Britain, pro-Palmerston sentiment was strong. It was clear that Britons loved the haughty "*Civis romanus sum*" spirit that their Foreign Minister embodied. Even middle-class Mancunians, who should have known better, were displaying feelings of national grandeur and superiority that Bright found sinful as well as disgusting in a professedly Christian country. And many of them were furious with him for having voted against Palmerston in the debate on the Pacifico affair. (12)

All this was bad enough. Yet the uproar over Don Pacifico had hardly subsided when the Whigs raised what from Bright's point of view was another false issue in the No Popery crusade of 1850–1851. This time the culprit was Lord John Russell, who succeeded in carrying through Parliament the Ecclesiastical Titles Bill, which forbade Roman Catholic bishops to assume any title already taken by clergy of the Church of England. Bright could hardly believe what was happening. Whig appeals to religious bigotry were so appalling (and at the same time so appealing to a large section of the public) that Bright saw himself being transported back to the age of the religious wars. All the while he could not help noting that the Whigs who were raving about the Pope and his alleged designs on Britain were the very people who were supposed to pacify Catholic Ireland. The No Popery episode, as Bright rightly saw it, was not only disgraceful but dangerous; for years it would exacerbate Anglo-Irish relations, which were alarming enough anyhow. For his efforts *Punch* rewarded Bright with a cartoon showing him embracing the leading British Roman Catholic dignitary, Cardinal Wiseman. (13)

Privately Bright scorned Roman Catholicism as a religion. Nevertheless, he was outraged by the ignorance and prejudice that dominated the No Popery campaign: they provided proof once more of the painful fact that "so much as we have of Churches and of religions, the true spirit of Christianity has made very little way amongst the Churches of the world." It was absurd to claim that a foreign power—the Papacy—was attacking the supremacy of the Crown. Since the Queen lacked the power to make Roman Catholic bishops, there could not possibly be an invasion of the Crown's prerogative when the Pope created bishops. To regard the papal action as a threat to the Crown and to the nation's independence was both stupid and ludicrous. For the rest, Bright insisted that Parliament was not the place to discuss religious questions: "...reflecting on the deep mysteries of religion, on my own doubts and frailties, on the shortness of the present time, and on the awful and unknown future—I ask what am I that I should judge another in religious things, and condemn him to exclusion and persecution?" The irony did not escape Bright that the year of the passage of the wretched papal bill was also the year of the Great Exhibition which was designed to demonstrate to the world the advanced state of British society. (14)

The combination of the Don Pacifico affair and the No Popery episode completed Bright's alienation from the Whigs. He had never had much faith in them; now he had none at all. They were opportunists who engaged in dangerous adventures and appealed to the worst in human nature. Instead of leading the British people, they misled them. They were feeble and unmanly, and anyone who expected anything good from them was a fool. Bright's disgust was so profound that he seriously considered withdrawing from public life. What was the point of making all the sacrifices that his membership in Parliament involved? Why should he spend so much time away from his family? Why should he bear the financial burdens that public service necessitated? There were few Members of Parliament whom he respected; and they became fewer still with the accidental death in 1850 of Sir Robert Peel. Perhaps Cobden was right when he suggested that the members of the Manchester School should stop trying to cram their programs "down the throats of unwilling customers." (15)

Bright's doubts about continuing in public life took on additional meaning because in 1851 he was to turn forty—allegedly a dangerous age for a successful man but probably an even more dangerous age for an idealist who was failing to win support for his ideals. The years were rushing by, and what had Bright accomplished? How much time did he have left? Should he continue to spend that time advocating policies that both Whigs and Tories repudiated? Should he endure further parliamentary sessions that promised to be conspicuous only for their worthlessness? Other distressing events contributed to his confusion about his future. Esther, his younger sister, had died suddenly in 1850, an event that shook him severely, and gave him hints of his own mortality. The family business in Rochdale, run by his brothers, had been in difficulties for several years. And in 1851 his father died. It is not surprising that Bright had come to believe that it was best when there was no news—news was more often bad than good. (16)

IV

Bright's doubts once more subsided and his fighting spirit asserted itself. His scorn of the Whigs was so intense that he felt he could not honorably withdraw from politics. To do so would be just what the enemy wanted—an act of cowardice that would reduce the already small number of independent Members of Parliament who could denounce any future Don Pacifico affairs and No Popery episodes and expose the immorality of Lord Palmerston and the stupidity of Lord John Russell. These aristocrats were the people who should be banished from politics, not he; they were the ones who were bringing Parliament into well-deserved contempt. (17)

When the session ended in July 1851, Bright took another of the short trips that invariably lifted his spirits. This time he went to France to see what was happening to the Second Republic under President Louis Napoleon Bonaparte. His wife had wanted to accompany him, but she was expecting another child, and he refused to let her go along. Filled with guilt about leaving her, he wrote to her about how unpleasant the trip had been. She was lucky to have avoided a very painful crossing; she could not have tolerated the heat of an August in Paris. He, on the other hand, needed the trip desperately—"after so much that is worrying that I have had to contend with during the past year." (18)

Naturally he found too many Englishmen in France, but there was more to criticize than that. Versailles was particularly repugnant to him. He granted that it was magnificent, but at what a cost! He saw it as a direct link with the revolutions of 1789, 1830, and 1848 that the poor French people had had to endure. A symbol of aristocratic extravagance and decadence, it could serve as a lesson to those who would try to learn from history. So, too, a parade of some fifty thousand troops that he saw on the streets of Paris had a lesson to teach of how tax money was wasted. At least this kind of military display could not happen in England. (19)

But there were things that happened in London that did not occur in Paris. Bright was impressed by the good behavior of the Parisians. They lived practically out of doors in the summer, but despite their singing, dancing, eating, and drinking in the open air, he witnessed none of the drunkenness, grossness, or vice that he associated with London. The Paris of 1851 was far more Victorian, he found, than mid-Victorian London. (20)

Bright went back to Rochdale in good spirits, and the news that greeted him made him feel still better. His second son had been born; his wife felt fine; and the family business had improved considerably. The prize his firm had won for its carpets at the Exhibition had brought expanded sales and profits. His only concern at the time of his return was that Queen Victoria was about to visit Manchester, and he feared that this occasion would bring out all the flunkeyism and snobbism in his middle-class colleagues. With his old passion, he urged the local officials in Manchester to treasure their self-respect and "not present an address as full of slip slop and flattery as the Queen is often condemned to listen to." (21)

V

The surest sign of his recovery was his renewed eagerness to agitate for parliamentary reform. The last session of Parliament had been a waste of time; the next must be different. In this spirit of determination he resumed his dialogue with Cobden. The response was the same. Cobden assured him that he would do his share, but he considered the cause hopeless for the present. Bright was far ahead of the middle classes in his political opinions. Besides, people were enjoying their new prosperity too much to participate in a parliamentary reform movement. (22)

Bright was not deterred. He visited some of the reformers in Leeds to find out what they were thinking, and with his old cheerfulness he reported the results of his conversations to Cobden. The people would move; they were simply waiting for leaders to point the way. Furthermore, Bright predicted, unless Parliament was changed, it would be impossible to do anything about the condition of the Irish people. Indeed, every time he thought of Ireland—and this was often—his hatred of the great landowners welled up. "Why cannot the Irish get and save money in Ireland? and why must they cross the Atlantic before they can get hold of a piece of land?" Bright found it utter nonsense to ascribe the plight of Ireland to race and religion. The great landowners were responsible, and the sooner their powers were curtailed, the sooner the regeneration of Ireland would take place. (23)

Cobden countered that important changes could be carried through Parliament even as it was then constituted; and reformers would serve their country better if they aimed at realistic objectives. There was so much that the people had to be taught. It was dangerous for them to be so ignorant of the virtues of religious freedom, land reform, financial retrenchment, and disarmament. Concentrate, therefore, on these issues, instead of on a campaign for the organic reform of Parliament that would arouse vast hostility among aristocrats and a great deal of hostility among the middle classes. The English, Cobden insisted, were as slow-moving a people as the Chinese, and to get them to do anything was much harder than Bright suspected, especially now that they were filled with feelings of Palmerstonian arrogance and superiority. It was revealing, after all, that so few young people showed any interest in parliamentary reform. Where were the young Brights and Cobdens?, Cobden asked pointedly. (24)

Bright's answer was that a parliamentary reform movement would emerge regardless of what Cobden and he did. Since this was so, it would be better if they were to lead it. They worked well together; their connection with the Anti-Corn Law League would bring prestige to the new agitation; and they—unlike other reformers—recognized the importance of cooperation between the middle classes and the working classes for the success of any new campaign. Thus Bright begged Cobden to overcome his hesitations and throw himself with enthusiasm into a cause worthy of his talents. (25)

Cobden remained unconvinced. Despite what Bright said, he was certain that the people were not ready for a crusade for parliamentary reform. Embittered by the No Popery episode, he insisted that at the moment it was more important for the country to learn something about the desirability of religious freedom. Besides, when the news came in December 1851 that the masses of the French people had used their right to vote to wipe out the Second Republic and restore a Napoleonic Empire, Cobden wondered whether this action was not an argument against extending the franchise in Britain. At the same time, however, he was generous in praising Bright for his efforts to stir up interest in parliamentary reform; and he urged him repeatedly not to underestimate the freehold movement as a device to forward the cause. (26)

Bright, for his part, was by no means the doctrinaire advocate of parliamentary reform that his enemies made him out to be; he did not commit himself to any rigid scheme of political change. He wanted "a full, fair, and free representation of the people in the House of Commons." Full representation meant as broad a suffrage as possible. Fair representation meant an allocation of parliamentary seats in harmony with the distribution of the population. Free representation meant a secret ballot and therefore the end of the cruelty, immorality, oppression, humiliation, and degradation that often accompanied the system of open voting. As much as possible, however, Bright tried to avoid the use of such expressions as universal manhood suffrage, household suffrage, and democratic suffrage for fear that they would do more harm than good. Yet what these phrases implied was certainly what he favored. His aim was "a peaceful, wise, and enduring democracy," a government based on respect for the dignity and worth of the five million grown men currently excluded from a role in politics. Bright had no fear of the working classes, insisting that it was perfectly safe to enfranchise them. They were not vicious, and their ignorance, he found, was vastly exaggerated. In fact, as he contemplated the reactionary behavior in the House of the parliamentary representatives of the Universities of Oxford and Cambridge, he had no doubt whatever that workers would choose their Members more wisely than university people chose theirs. He had long since pointed out what Oxford had done "to prove that there may be the greatest possible acquaintance with books, united to the profoundest ignorance of men." (27)

Repeatedly Bright emphasized that decrepit landowners dominated Parliament, that the people had almost no voice in their government, that it was high time for aristocrats to be prevented from preying on the industrious classes, and that the friends of parliamentary reform "were truly the conservative party." The British constitution was an "imposture," and it was absurd to attribute the greatness of Britain to this constitution and its monstrous and ridiculous scheme of parliamentary representation. Natural advantages, mineral wealth, geography, the industry of the people—these had made Britain great, not the sham Parliament with its "antediluvian" politicians who had repeatedly revealed their unworthiness and incompetence. (28)

As he exposed the inadequacies of the British system of government, Bright rarely resisted the temptation to dwell on the excellences of the United States. American presidents from George Washington to Zachary Taylor compared more than favorably with British prime ministers from Lord North to Lord John Russell. American ministers from Benjamin Franklin to George Bancroft compared more than favorably with the aristocratic ambassadors the British employed. Furthermore, the American people had low taxes, no national debt, and almost no military and naval expenditures. They were better educated than the British, they had far fewer paupers and criminals, and had experienced none of the shocking insurrections that had repeatedly disgraced British history since the French Revolution. Except for their institution of slavery, which Bright was sure would soon be abolished peacefully, he thought that the Americans afforded "a spectacle to the world to which history has no parallel, and which it would be a happy thing for the population of this country if we were only at some rapid and sensible pace approaching." (29)

Often Bright predicted that before long the power ruling Britain would be changed and that the "have nothings" would come into their own. Fortunately, he could not know how many years it would take for his predictions to come true. If he had known, there is no doubt whatever that he would have given up politics. His kind of activism—"we live in an age of agitation"—needed victories to sustain it. (30)

NOTES

(1) Bright to Wilson, July 12, 1849, Wilson MSS, MCL; Cobden to Bright, Jan. 3, 1849, Cobden MSS, BM 43,649.

(2) Bright to Cobden, Sept. 17, 1849, Bright MSS, BM 43,383; Bright to Wilson, Feb. 22, 1849; Sept. 18, 1849, Wilson MSS, MCL.

(3) Cobden to Bright, Oct. 1, 1849; Dec. 8, 1849, Cobden MSS, BM 43,649; Bright to Cobden, Dec. 7, 1849, Bright MSS, BM 43,383.

(4) Bright to Wilson, Jan. 17, 1850, Wilson MSS, MCL; Bright to Cobden, Oct. 12, 1850, Bright MSS, BM 43,383.

(5) *Speeches,* I, 323–47; II, 295; *Parl. Deb.,* 102 (Feb. 5, 1849), 286ff.; 104 (Apr. 26, 1849), 890; 105 (June 5, 1849), 1206; 113 (Aug. 7, 1850), 922ff.; 113 (July 30, 1850), 551ff.; 113 (Aug. 12, 1850), 1040–41; Bright to Wilson, Feb. 6, 1849, Wilson MSS, MCL; Bright to Mrs. Bright, Feb. 10, 1849; July 18, 1849; Aug. 14, 1849; Nov. 15, 1849, Bright MSS, UCLL.

(6) Bright to Wilson, Sept. 18, 1849, Wilson MSS, MCL; Bright to Mrs. Bright, Aug. 23, 1849; Sept. 2, 1849, Bright MSS, UCLL; cf. Robert Travers to Edward Edwards, June 20, 1849; Sept. 8, 1849, Edwards MSS, MCL.

(7) Bright to Cobden, Sept. 17, 1849, Bright MSS, BM 43,383; Bright to Mrs. Bright, Aug. 23, 1849; Aug. 26, 1849, Bright MSS, UCLL; Bright to Wilson, July 18, 1849, Wilson MSS, MCL; *The Times,* Mar. 19, 1849; Mar. 27, 1849; Apr. 3, 1849; Apr. 6, 1849.

(8) Bright to Cobden, Sept. 17, 1849, Bright MSS, BM 43,383; Bright to Wilson, Sept. 18, 1849; Oct. 29, 1849, Wilson MSS, MCL; cf. *Parl. Deb.,* 103 (Mar. 1, 1849), 34–35; Cobden to Bright, Oct. 1, 1849, Cobden MSS, BM 43,649; Bright to E. K. Tenisson, Oct. 1, 1849; Bright to G. Poulett Scrope, Nov. 9, 1849, Bright MSS, PUL; *Diaries,* Sept. 4, 1849; *The Times,* Sept. 26, 1849; *Parl. Deb.,* 108 (Feb. 22, 1850), 1306; 109 (Mar. 7, 1850), 494.

(9) Bright to Wilson, Jan. 1, 1850; Cobden to Wilson, Jan. 1, 1850, Wilson MSS, MCL; Cobden to Bright, Jan. 7, 1850, Cobden MSS, BM 43,649; cf. Cobden to Bright, Feb. 16, 1864, Cobden MSS, BM 43,652.

(10) Bright to Joseph Kay, Sept. 14, 1850, Kay MSS, NLI; *Letters,* July 3, 1850; Bright to Cobden, Oct. 12, 1850, Bright MSS, BM 43,383; cf. Bright to J. A. Langford, Apr. 1, 1863, Anthony MSS, NYPL; Cobden to Bright, Dec. 27, 1851, Cobden MSS, BM 43,649.

(11) *Punch,* XVIII (1850), 220.

(12) Cf. *ibid.,* 173; Bright to Wilson, July 10, 1850; July 15, 1850, Wilson MSS, MCL; *Diaries,* July 5, 1850; *The Times,* Jan. 25, 1851.

(13) Bright to Cobden, Oct. 12, 1850, Bright MSS, BM 43,383; Bright to Mrs. Bright, Nov. 22, 1850; Feb. 21, 1851; Mar. 20, 1851; June 2, 1851, Bright MSS, UCLL; Bright to Wilson, Mar. 12, 1851, Wilson MSS, MCL; *Parl. Deb.,* 114 (Feb. 7, 1851), 242ff.

(14) Bright to Duncan McLaren, Dec. 17, 1851, Bright MSS, NLS; Bright to Mrs. Bright, Sept. 16, 1852, Bright MSS, UCLL; *Speeches,* II, 471ff.; *Parl. Deb.,* 116 (May 12, 1851), 917ff.

(15) Bright to Wilson, Apr. 4, 1850; July 15, 1850; Feb. 28, 1851, Wilson MSS, MCL; Bright to Mrs. Bright, Mar. 12, 1851; May 22, 1851, Bright MSS, UCLL; Bright to Joseph Sturge, July 7, 1850, Sturge MSS, BM 43,723; Cobden to Bright, Oct. 18, 1850, Cobden MSS, BM 43,649.

(16) Bright to Mrs. Bright, May 28, 1851; June 12, 1851, Bright MSS, UCLL; Cobden to Bright, Oct. 4, 1850, Cobden MSS, BM 43,649; Bright to Cobden, Oct. 12, 1850, Bright MSS, BM 43,383; the will of Jacob Bright is in the Lancashire Record Office, Preston; Bright to Mrs. Bright, July 7, 1861; July 7, 1868; June 25, 1851, Bright MSS, UCLL.

(17) Bright to Wilson, Mar. 12, 1851, Wilson MSS, MCL; Bright to Mrs. Bright, July 31, 1851, Bright MSS, UCLL; Bright to Cobden, Nov. 4, 1851, Bright MSS, BM 43,383.

(18) Bright to Mrs. Bright, July 26, 1851; July 29, 1851; Aug. 2, 1851, Bright MSS, UCLL.

(19) Bright to Cobden, Aug. 29, 1851, Bright MSS, BM 43,383; Bright to Mrs. Bright, Aug. 4, 1851, Bright MSS, UCLL.

(20) Bright to Mrs. Bright, Aug. 5, 1851, *ibid.*

(21) Bright to Cobden, Aug. 29, 1851, Bright MSS, BM 43,383; Bright to John Benjamin Smith, Aug. 28, 1851, Smith MSS, MCL; Cobden to Bright, Aug. 23, 1851, Cobden MSS, BM 43,649; Bright to Cobden, Sept. 25, 1851, Bright MSS, BM 43,383.

(22) Bright to Cobden, Aug. 29, 1851, *ibid.;* Cobden to Bright, Sept. 2, 1851; Sept. 29, 1851, Cobden MSS, BM 43,649.

(23) Bright to Cobden, Sept. 25, 1851; Sept. 26, 1851, Bright MSS, BM 43,383; Bright to Wilson, Sept. 26, 1851, Wilson MSS; Bright to Smith, Aug. 28, 1851, Smith MSS, MCL; *The Times,* Jan. 5, 1850.

(24) Cobden to Bright, Sept. 29, 1851; Oct. 1, 1851, Cobden MSS, BM 43,649.

(25) Bright to Cobden, Oct. 24, 1851, Bright MSS, BM 43,383.

(26) Cobden to Bright, Oct. 29, 1851; Nov. 7, 1851; Dec. 27, 1851, Cobden MSS, BM 43,649.

(27) Cf. *Parl. Deb.,* 158 (June 4, 1860), 2020; Bright to Joseph Sturge, Nov. 26, 1851, Sturge MSS, BM 43,723; Bright to Wilson, Nov. 30, 1851, Wilson MSS, MCL; *The Times,* Jan. 31, 1850; *Parl. Deb.,* 105 (June 5, 1849), 1196ff.; 109 (Mar. 7, 1850), 515–16; 112 (July 9, 1850), 1172; cf. 83 (Feb. 17, 1846), 1131.

(28) *Ibid.,* 105 (June 5, 1849), 1211; *The Times,* Jan. 31, 1850.

(29) *Parl. Deb.,* 102 (Feb. 26, 1849), 1295; 110 (Apr. 10, 1850), 159; Bright to Cobden, Aug. 29, 1851, Bright MSS, BM 43,383; Cobden to Bright, Sept. 2, 1851, Cobden MSS, BM 43,649; *The Times,* Jan. 31, 1850.

(30) *Parl. Deb.,* 107 (July 20, 1849), 779; 108 (Feb. 19, 1850), 1103; Bright to Cobden, Aug. 29, 1851, Bright MSS, BM 43,383; *The Times,* Jan. 31, 1850; Dec. 18, 1851.

CHAPTER FOUR

FOLLY, FOLLY

1851–1853

Although Bright and Cobden disagreed about the feasibility of a parliamentary reform movement, they agreed heartily on one subject that kept cropping up in the early 1850's—the warlike tendencies of their countrymen. The Don Pacifico affair of 1850, they found, was no isolated episode. It was followed the next year by a pro-Hungarian and anti-Austrian outburst, in 1852 by a panic over an alleged French invasion, and in 1853 by a dangerous seizure of Russophobia. (1)

As much as anyone, Bright and Cobden sympathized with the plight of the Magyars under Austrian rule. As much as anyone, moreover, they admired Louis Kossuth (although Bright disliked the excessive praise of the British Constitution expressed by the Hungarian leader in his speeches to British audiences). But sympathy for the victims of Austrian oppression was one thing, and Kossuth's wish to win British military support for the Hungarian cause was quite another. Bright and Cobden feared that some of the wilder Palmerstonians might exploit pro-Hungarian feelings with such success as to cause a war with Austria.

Bright insisted that Britain's task was not to regenerate other countries; there was too much regenerating for the British to do at home and in Ireland. By improving their own institutions and by treating other countries justly, generously, and courteously, they could do far more for humanity than by allowing a Palmerston to despatch troops abroad. Bright stated his views not only to his friends and colleagues but to audiences filled with indignation

52

about Austrian oppression. Even Cobden was impressed by the courage this required. (2)

The anti-Austrian impulse faded, only to be replaced in 1852 by a panic over an alleged French invasion. Bright was horrified that adults could convince themselves of a French plan to attack Britain. The idea was childish and absurd, but there it was— sincerely believed by large numbers of his presumably rational fellow-citizens. In fact, the "Invasionists," led by some Members of Parliament, some circulation-hungry newspapers, and some members of the armed forces, played so effectively on the fears of the country that Parliament passed a totally unnecessary Militia Bill. "We have made a hard fight against it," Bright told Wilson without exaggeration, but the effort was in vain. (3)

Bright held no flattering view of Louis Napoleon. Like Cobden, he regarded him at this time as little more than a "hare-brained adventurer," and he ridiculed the notion that the French leader was planning an attack on Britain. As a result of the panic more money would be wasted on needless defenses, and Anglo-French relations would again worsen. The British government, instead of encouraging the French to reduce tariffs, sponsor freer trade, and work for international peace, was forcing them to increase their military establishment.

Cobden, pondering the spreading militarism in both countries, wondered if reason had any influence on human affairs. He was tempted to grow a beard, hide in a hermit's cave, or migrate to the United States. Although Bright did not go quite that far, he reacted strongly. As usual, he saw a connection between the warlike spirit of his countrymen and the inadequacies of their system of representation. If suffrage reform were achieved, better Members would be returned to Parliament, and the population would not be misled by glory-seeking grandees and the war-mongering newspapers that they controlled. (4)

In the midst of the uproar over the supposed French menace, the Duke of Wellington died, there were elaborate preparations for the funeral, and again Bright raged, but this time in private. He learned the news during another visit to study conditions in

Ireland, but even when he returned to England there was no way of avoiding the news for weeks and weeks. The Duke's body lay in state for what seemed to Bright like an eternity; and the newspapers carried sadistic accounts of how people were injured and even crushed to death in their attempts to have one last look at the hero of Waterloo. Bright could not understand this grief. To him the Duke was nothing but an unthinking servant of the aristocracy. He had never done anything to help the people; what concessions he had made to them were designed simply to avert revolution and preserve as much as possible of aristocratic privilege. Above all, however, Bright deplored the emphasis on martial glory which the Duke's death stimulated; for the British to extol their military heritage was both unwholesome and dangerous. Bright consoled himself with the thought that the death of that real hero Sir Robert Peel had aroused far more general sorrow than that of Wellington. (5)

II

The anti-Austrian fever, the French invasion panic, and the mourning over the death of Wellington all diverted attention from the serious questions with which the British should have been concerning themselves. But at least Bright was encouraged in 1852 by the swift political changes that were taking place. Lord John Russell's Government fell in February; Lord Derby's Tory Government lasted only until December; and then Lord Aberdeen formed a Ministry of Whigs and Peelites. Bright assumed that these changes would do some good: new ministers might bring forward policies about which older ministers had hesitated, and new and healthy expectations could be created in the public. (6)

Bright was particularly pleased to witness the end of Russell's long Ministry. He despised the Whig leader and could not forgive him for the No Popery scandal and for his refusal to improve Anglo-Irish relations through land reform. Furthermore, he found contemptible the puny Reform Bill with which Russell had hoped at the end of his Administration to placate the advocates of parliamentary reorganization. In fact, when Bright met Russell in Scotland, he could not resist telling him that he hoped the bracing air of the North would serve to invigorate his politics in the future. He repeatedly assured him that a real reform bill would be the truest conservatism. (7)

Because Bright was so disillusioned with Russell and his Whigs, he welcomed Lord Derby's Tories. He assumed that they could not be worse than their predecessors; they might even be better because Benjamin Disraeli would be Chancellor of the Exchequer. Although Cobden found Disraeli an unprincipled sycophant of the aristocracy, Bright had a sense of Disraeli's genius. He found him open-minded as well as amusing, and their personal relations were cordial, though Bright was never quite sure when Disraeli was teasing and when he was in earnest. Nor indeed was Disraeli. (8)

To Bright's disappointment the Tories exploited the French invasion scare shamelessly and no less shamelessly capitalized on the death of Wellington. All this was bad enough, but their chief domestic venture was a daring attempt to revise the tax laws for the benefit of the great landowners. These latter-day Tory protectionists were quickly routed; but in order to defeat them, Cobden, George Wilson, and Bright had to revive the Anti-Corn Law League—what Disraeli called their "Jacobin club"—and with much fanfare they gave those who would listen a review lesson on the blessings of economic freedom and the evils of protection. Some of the free traders made such exaggerated claims about the connection between free trade and the material prosperity of the early 1850's that Cobden—a scholar at heart—urged Wilson to encourage speakers to make more cautious statements. After all, the good times were due not only to free trade but to bountiful harvests, railroad construction, and the gold discoveries. Furthermore, as Cobden was aware, even countries with protective tariffs were enjoying prosperity. (9)

With the fall of the Tory Ministry in December 1852, Bright's hopes again ran high. Lord Aberdeen formed a Government of Whigs and Peelites, all committed to free trade, which was certainly a victory for the Manchester School. Furthermore, two Radicals—Charles Villiers and Sir William Molesworth—were asked to join the Government. But Bright was not, and he was both hurt and angry—the more so because the Cabinet was filled with aristocrats. "What a free country we live in after all, where accident of birth is supreme over almost every description and degree of merit," he wrote to a friend. (10)

After almost ten years of service in the House of Commons, Bright had become convinced that only through a cabinet post could he press effectively for the domestic changes he considered vital. Cobden asserted that to join the Government would be corrupting; the members of the Manchester School could hold office only by falsifying their opinions, for the Tories hated them, the Whigs dreaded them, and the Peelites suspected them. Bright, on the other hand, had come to believe that success required boring from within; perhaps as a member of the Government he could get something accomplished. It was small consolation that some of his friends insisted that he could do more good out of the Government than in it. (11)

III

Bright did not have much time to indulge his frustrations, for in the early months of 1853 new difficulties arose. First of all, Cobden decided to give up public life. In the course of his researches for a pamphlet designed to expose the absurdities of the Invasionists, he reached conclusions so favorable to France and so critical of Britain that he saw no point in remaining in Parliament. His was a voice in the wilderness; no one would listen to him and for his trouble he would win only abuse. Since he lacked personal political ambitions, there was no sense in continuing as a public servant.

Cobden had been discouraged before, but not to this extent, and Bright was worried. He begged him to reconsider. If Cobden withdrew, so would he; he could not go it alone. He confessed his dependence on Cobden, recognizing how much he had owed to him in the past, and he protested that he lacked the inner resources to assume Cobden's part as leader of the Manchester School.

Bright had hardly recovered from the fright that Cobden might retire when he received word that his wife was seriously ill. She recovered quickly, but her illness disturbed him profoundly. It made him conscious of how attached he had become to her after almost six years of marriage; and it revived memories of the death of his first wife. He was filled with gratitude when this crisis passed. (12)

Fortified by his wife's recovery and Cobden's decision to remain in public life, Bright devoted himself with renewed energy to the causes he considered important. He gathered and disseminated information about the working of the secret ballot in the United States and elsewhere. He assumed a leading role in the struggle for a free press, insisting on the abolition of the taxes that made newspapers expensive. He argued vigorously for the admission of Jews to Parliament. He worked hard on a parliamentary committee that was investigating the position of tenant farmers. (13) He continued to educate himself about the plight of Ireland and India under British rule. And he spoke up courageously for the overthrow of the Church of Ireland and the East India Company. He even called on Disraeli to discuss the India Question.

Cobden generously told Bright that he was one of only two Members—Gladstone was the other—who gained in stature during the course of the parliamentary session. Much less generously, but more typically, *Punch* ran a poem that began:

John Bright is a pestilent fellow,
    Always ready for making a fight. . . .

But Bright was accustomed to such jibes. (14)

This is not to suggest that his self-doubts had disappeared. It is true that he valued Cobden's praise and approval; once Cobden wrote, "If there be a task of superhuman difficulty, such as fathoming Irish bogs, or clearing Indian jungles, you are sure to undertake it." Nevertheless, whenever Bright spent an extended period with his family in Rochdale, he would question the value of his sacrifices. He enjoyed playing with his children; he loved to read old and new books with his wife and to go walking with her; he enjoyed stopping in and helping out at the family mills. Yet because of the demands of his parliamentary seat he often had to forego these pleasures. He was annoyed, for example, that he had had to read *Uncle Tom's Cabin* alone and away from Rochdale; he wished to be able to discuss this stirring book with his wife. Furthermore, since Members of Parliament were not paid for their services, he estimated that, apart from the countless hours he devoted to his duties, he gave the public about £500 a year of his own income. He was also discovering that after more than a decade of considerable speech-making he no longer relished the role of orator. The thrill of swaying an audience had lessened; and he was more and more impatient with the speakers he had to listen to in the line of duty, speakers who almost invariably used too many words to make their point. (15)

Above all, however, Bright's self-doubts were connected with his sense of estrangement from his countrymen, for in 1853 the war spirit in Britain reached new heights. The Francophobe Invasionists were still trying to spread panic, but increasingly the Eastern Question figured in the news. For all practical purposes this meant hatred of Russia and fear of Russian designs on Turkey. Since Bright wanted the British to mind their own business and let the Russians and Turks settle their differences, he was sickened by the way the British press idealized the Turks and debased the Russians. He was disturbed, moreover, by the glib talk about an Anglo-Russian war. Though a Quaker, Bright was not a pacifist; but he did not believe in entering a war lightly. His reading of British history had convinced him that his country had been involved in many needless wars, and the task of the modern political leader, as he saw it, was not to add to this list of military blunders but to encourage the arbitration of international disputes. (16)

IV

At the close of the parliamentary session, Bright took another short trip to France. Certain that the French government had no sinister designs on Britain, he was intent on discovering evidences of the peaceful intentions of Napoleon III, and he found them without much difficulty. The only depressing part of his stay was

his visit to Cherbourg, where all around were soldiers and fortifications. But if the British would stop their vilification of the French,
he reasoned, these wasteful military precautions would be unnecessary. The French simply wished to protect their country
against "the savage and warlike tribes" across the Channel.

For the rest, peace was in the French air. Bright was delighted
with the strong free trade sentiment that he found. As he wrote
to George Wilson, "What a glorious revolution for England and
France when we scan our mutual imports and exports, instead of
counting up the number of our ships of war!" Nor was the feeling
for free trade all that pleased him. He was also impressed with the
reconstruction of Paris in process. He predicted that if it continued
at the same rate for another ten years Paris would be a far more
beautiful modern city than any other capital in the world, and
Napoleon III would be a leader to remember. He was also struck
by the obvious prosperity of the Parisians. They seemed "well off,
and well dressed, and not at all as if they were living under what
the English papers consider an insupportable tyranny," he confessed to his wife.

Bright recognized the desirability—and necessity—of tolerance on
the part of foreign visitors. Even so, certain things about the Parisians annoyed him. He wished that fewer of them would wear un-
kempt beards, that they would not "jabber" so much, and that their
shops would not charge such outrageous prices. But on the vital
question they were sound—they had no desire for a war with Britain.

In the French countryside Bright also found striking evidences
both of prosperity and a longing for peace. In fact, he thought that
the British rural classes had much to learn from the French, for the
clue to the excellence of French agriculture, he insisted, was the wide
diffusion of land ownership. These French peasants did not want
their thriving agriculture upset by war. (17)

Bright had to cut short his visit because he had been invited to
address a large peace rally in Edinburgh. He would have preferred
to remain in France, urging any influential people he might meet to
work for freer trade and more harmonious relations with Britain,
but he had no choice. The Eastern Question was again becoming

dangerous, and few people in Britain were saying the right things about it. He knew how much was at stake for his country and for himself. He also knew what he was risking in refusing to succumb to the growing war spirit. (18)

For months he had belittled all the chatter about a conflict between Russia and Britain. He considered such talk a defiance of reason and common sense, and to prove his point he collected assurances from anyone he could find who had recently been to Russia. Yet his saying that war would not come did not prevent periodic war scares from turning Britain into "one vast lunatic asylum," and in October 1853, Britain was in the throes of such a scare. Hysterical patriots were eager to put the Russians in their place and teach them a lesson they would not forget. In this atmosphere Bright pleaded for common sense, humility, and restraint, venturing to wish that the British lion, which was an old animal anyhow, would die at last. War was not what it used to be, he warned. Under modern conditions innumerable lives would be lost, great property damage would occur, and the cost of the conflict would burden the British people for years and years. How much more Christian, sensible, and economical it would be for the British and Russians to settle their differences peacefully! Inevitably, to be sure, his enemies seized on his use of economic arguments against war in order to impugn Bright's character, pointing out that sympathy for a righteous cause was being "stifled in cotton-bags." (19)

The prolonged crisis over the Eastern Question impressed Bright with the urgency of parliamentary reform. If the people had the franchise, if they could vote without intimidation, and if seats in the House of Commons were justly distributed, the peace advocates would stand a chance and the warmongers would be powerless to prevent their election. But instead of being governed by a worthy House of Commons, the people were misgoverned by an unworthy one. It infuriated Bright that the Borough of Manchester, with some 90,000 adult males, had only 19,000 voters; that the £10 borough voting requirement, which had been established in 1832 to exclude the working classes, was still in effect; and that some people argued that the £10 householders opposed any lowering of the suffrage requirement. Bright conceded that not everyone merited the right to vote, but he insisted that far more deserved it than had it. Besides, many of the excluded were more worthy of it than some of those who already enjoyed it. (20)

Bright could not ignore the embarrassing fact that some of his fellow advocates of parliamentary reform had joined noisily in the Russophobe and Turkophile campaign. Some of the newspapers that favored an expanded suffrage also favored militant support of what Cobden called "the rights of the Sultan and his 300 wives." In short, the advocates of peaceful arbitration and a democratic suffrage were not always the same. Some of the parliamentary reformers were, in fact, so obsessed with the Turkish cause that they seemed to have forgotten the millions of unenfranchised Britons. By December it dawned on Bright that perhaps the public preferred fighting for the Turkish Empire to agitating for domestic reform. It was also plain to him that people needed a thoroughgoing education in the dangers of meddling in the affairs of other countries. (21)

Worst of all, Bright knew—and Cobden was there to remind him, if he forgot—that a war would stifle any real possibility of reform, and that desirable domestic changes would be postponed for the duration of the conflict. As a student of history, he remembered, moreover, how the French revolutionary wars had delayed reforms for years and then ushered in one of the worst periods of repression in all of British experience.

Christmas in 1853 was not a happy time for Bright. As an opponent of the pledges the British government had given to Turkey, he saw himself in a hopeless minority in the country. And in the approaching Parliament he fully expected to be shouted down as a traitor. As he wrote to Cobden: "How men can prefer the certain and enormous evils of a war to the dim and vague prospect of remote injury from Russian aggrandisement is beyond my understanding. The nation seems little wiser than in 1793, and we may soon be as unpopular as Fox was, and yet be as much right as he was. I feel rather sick of public life, and indeed of the follies of my country." (22)

NOTES

(1) *Parl. Deb.,* 120 (Mar. 29, 1852), 334; Cobden to Wilson, Jan. 3, 1852; Dec. 4, 1852, Wilson MSS, MCL; Bright to Mrs. Bright, Feb. 19, 1853, Bright MSS, UCLL; Bright to Joseph Sturge, Apr. 18, 1853, Sturge MSS, BM 43,723.

(2) Bright to Cobden, Oct. 24, 1851; Nov. 4, 1851, Bright MSS, BM 43,383; Cobden to Bright, Nov. 13, 1851, Cobden MSS, BM 43,649; *Letters,* Oct. 25, 1852.

(3) Franklin Charles Palm, *England and Napoleon III* (Durham, 1948); S. Maccoby, *English Radicalism, 1832–1852* (London, 1935), chap. xxii; *Parl. Deb.,* 121 (May 3, 1852), 176; Bright to Cobden, Sept. 7, 1852, Bright MSS, BM 43,383; Cobden to Bright, Jan. 29, 1852; Oct. 16, 1852, Cobden MSS, BM 43,649; Bright to Wilson, Apr. 13, 1852; Apr. 21, 1852; May 18, 1852, Wilson MSS, MCL.

(4) Cobden to Bright, Jan. 7, 1852, Cobden MSS, BM 43,649; Bright to Cobden, Oct. 19, 1852, Bright MSS, BM 43,383.

(5) Bright to Mrs. Bright, Sept. 16, 1852; Sept. 28, 1852; Nov. 12, 1852; Nov. 15, 1852, Bright MSS, UCLL; Bright to Cobden, Oct. 15, 1852; Oct. 19, 1852, Bright MSS, BM 43,383; Cobden to Bright, Oct. 16, 1852, Cobden MSS, BM 43,649; Bright to Wilson, Nov. 18, 1852, Wilson MSS, MCL.

(6) Bright to Cobden, Sept. 7, 1852, Bright MSS, BM 43,383; Bright to Mrs. Bright, Nov. 24, 1852, Bright MSS, UCLL.

(7) Bright to Cobden, Jan. 3, 1852; Dec. 30, 1852, Bright MSS, BM 43,383; Bright to Mrs. Bright, Feb. 19, 1852; Feb. 21, 1852, Bright MSS, UCLL; Bright to Wilson, Mar. 13, 1852; Aug. 15, 1852, Wilson MSS, MCL.

(8) Cobden to Bright, Jan. 7, 1852; Sept. 9, 1852; Oct. 16, 1852, Cobden MSS, BM 43,649; *Diaries,* Dec. 15, 1852.

(9) Cf. Bright to Thomas Kimber, Jr., Jan. 15, 1852, Charles Roberts Autograph MSS, Haverford College Library; Bright to Mrs. Bright, Nov. 23, 1852, Bright MSS, UCLL; *Parl. Deb.,* 119 (Mar. 19, 1852), 1393; 123 (Nov. 23, 1852), 435ff.; Bright to Wilson, Mar. 4, 1852; Mar. 10, 1852; Apr. 21, 1852; Dec. 13, 1852; Cobden to Wilson, Mar. 19, 1852; Mar. 23, 1852; Aug. 11, 1852; Sept. 11, 1852; Dec. 4, 1852, Wilson MSS, MCL; Cobden to Bright, Aug. 30, 1852, Cobden MSS, BM 43,649.

(10) Bright to Mrs. Bright, Dec. 10, 1852; Dec. 20, 1852, Bright MSS, UCLL; Bright to Cobden, Jan. 3, 1853; Jan. 5, 1853, Bright MSS, BM 43,383; Bright to Wilson, Dec. 21, 1852, Wilson MSS, MCL; Smith to Bright, Dec. 24, 1852; Dec. 27, 1852; Jan. 3, 1853, Bright MSS, BM 43,388; Bright to Smith, Dec. 27, 1852, John Benjamin Smith MSS, MCL; cf. Trevelyan, p. 208.

(11) Cobden to Bright, Jan. 7, 1852; Jan. 20, 1852, Cobden MSS, BM 43,649; Bright to Cobden, Jan. 14, 1853, Bright MSS, BM 43,383; Bright to

Smith, Dec. 27, 1852, John Benjamin Smith MSS, MCL; Smith to Bright, Jan. 3, 1853, Bright MSS, BM 43,388.

(12) Cf. Cobden to Bright, Aug. 28, 1852; Jan. 1, 1853; Jan. 8, 1853; Jan. 14, 1853; Jan. 17, 1853, Cobden MSS, BM 43,649–43,650; Bright to Cobden, Jan. 14, 1853, Bright MSS, BM 43,383; Bright to Wilson, Feb. 24, 1853, Wilson MSS, MCL; cf. Bright to Mrs. Bright, June 11, 1852; Mar. 5, 1853, Bright MSS, UCLL.

(13) *Parl. Deb.*, 125 (Apr. 12, 1853), 1027; 128 (June 14, 1853), 223; Edward L. Pierce to Bright, Sept. 1, 1853, Bright MSS, BM 43,390; *Parl. Deb.*, 125 (April 14, 1853), 1157ff.; 128 (July 1, 1853), 1114ff.; Bright to Cobden, Jan. 3, 1853, Bright MSS, BM 43,383; Bright to Wilson, July 15, 1853, Wilson MSS, MCL; cf. *Parl. Deb.*, 113 (Aug. 5, 1850), 809ff.; 125 (Apr. 15, 1853), 1255ff.; *Speeches,* II, 487ff.; Bright to Mrs. Bright, Mar. 11, 1853; Mar. 12, 1853, Bright MSS, UCLL; Bright to Wilson, May 8, 1853, Wilson MSS, MCL.

(14) Cf. Bright to Charles Gavan Duffy, May 13, 1851, Bright MSS, YUL; Bright to Mrs. Bright, Sept. 24, 1852, Bright MSS, UCLL; Bright to Smith, Oct. 11, 1852, John Benjamin Smith MSS, MCL; *The Times,* Oct. 7, 1852; Oct. 28, 1852; *Parl. Deb.*, 119 (Feb. 10, 1852), 365ff.; 127 (May 31, 1853), 946ff.; cf. Bright to Cobden, Oct. 12, 1850, Bright MSS, BM 43,383; Cobden to Bright, Oct. 18, 1850, Cobden MSS, BM 43,649; Bright to Wilson, Apr. 21, 1852; June 29, 1853; July 5, 1853, Wilson MSS, MCL; Bright to Mrs. Bright, Mar. 9, 1853; Mar. 12, 1853, Bright MSS, UCLL; Bright to Joseph Sturge, Mar. 27, 1853, Sturge MSS, BM 43,723; Bright to unnamed correspondent, Apr. 17, 1853, Bright MSS, National Liberal Club; *Parl. Deb.*, 125 (Mar. 11, 1853), 37ff.; 127 (June 3, 1853), 1169ff.; 128 (June 27, 1853), 870ff.; Bright to Disraeli, June 5, 1853, Disraeli MSS, Hughenden; Cobden to Bright, Aug. 20, 1853, Cobden MSS, BM 43,650; *Punch,* XXV (1853), 93.

(15) Cobden to Bright, Sept. 9, 1852, Cobden MSS, BM 43,649; Bright to Cobden, Jan. 14, 1853; Aug. 18, 1853, Bright MSS, BM 43,383; Bright to Mrs. Bright, Feb. 10, 1852; Sept. 22, 1852; Sept. 24, 1852; Dec. 18, 1852; Feb. 16, 1853; Mar. 14, 1853, Bright MSS, UCLL; Bright to Sturge, Apr. 18, 1853, Sturge MSS, BM 43,723; cf. Bright to Cobden, Sept. 7, 1852, Bright MSS, BM 43,383.

(16) S. Maccoby, *English Radicalism, 1853–1886* (London, 1938), chap. II; Cobden to Villiers, Mar. 30, 1853, Cobden MSS, NYPL.

(17) Bright to Wilson, Sept. 24, 1853, Wilson MSS, MCL; Bright to Cobden, Sept. 29, 1853, Bright MSS, BM 43,383; Bright to Mrs. Bright, Sept. 18, 1853; Sept. 19, 1853; Oct. 2, 1853, Bright MSS, UCLL.

(18) Bright to Cobden, Sept. 29, 1853, Bright MSS, BM 43,383; Bright to Mrs. Bright, Oct. 3, 1853, Bright MSS, UCLL; Bright to Wilson, Oct. 10, 1853, Wilson MSS, MCL.

(19) *Diaries,* July 4, 1853; *Parl. Deb.,* 128 (July 8, 1853), 1425ff.; Bright

to Wilson, July 5, 1853; July 11, 1853; July 13, 1853; July 15, 1853, Wilson MSS, MCL; Bright to Cobden, Aug. 18, 1853, Bright MSS, BM 43,383; *The Times,* Oct. 14, 1853; *Speeches,* II, 359–71; *Punch,* XXV (1853), 227.

(20) Bright to Cobden, Nov. 5, 1853; Nov. 28, 1853; Dec. 16, 1853, Bright MSS, BM 43,383; Bright to Edward L. Pierce, Nov. 16, 1853, Bright MSS, PUL.

(21) Cobden to Bright, Nov. 22, 1853; Dec. 29, 1853, Cobden MSS, BM 43,650; Bright to Cobden, Nov. 28, 1853; Dec. 14, 1853, Bright MSS, BM 43,383.

(22) Cobden to Bright, Nov. 9, 1853; Dec. 29, 1853, Cobden MSS, BM 43,650; Bright to Cobden, Dec. 27, 1853, Bright MSS, BM 43,383.

CHAPTER FIVE

DISASTER
1854–1856

Bright found the idea of fighting a war for the independence and integrity of Turkey stupid, un-Christian, insane. Hence, even in the early months of 1854, when war fever was running high, he tried to do everything possible to avert a conflict. He pleaded with members of the Government and with his colleagues in Parliament to seek a reconciliation with Russia. He wrote and spoke to Lord Aberdeen, imploring him to enable the Tsar to save face. Even at an ultra-aristocratic dinner party at which Aberdeen was a guest, Bright took the opportunity to bring up the Eastern Question; and he was reassured to hear the Prime Minister say that he thought peace might still be preserved. (1)

Bright knew that British pledges to the Turks as well as the warlike utterances of leaders like Lord John Russell had made an Anglo-Russian conflict hard to prevent. Nevertheless, he continued to resist the idea of an irrepressible struggle. Cobden, on the other hand, accepted the war as inevitable—mainly because the Russophobes and the pro-Turks had done their work so well. Indeed, what most distressed Cobden was the fact that David Urquhart, the former Member of Parliament and the most outspoken leader of the Russophobes and pro-Turks, was unbalanced. "What must we say of the public which follows such a leader!" he wrote to Bright. (2)

When the Crimean War began officially in the last week of March, Bright's reactions were confused. His main concern was to bring it to a speedy end, especially because he was alarmed by the irrationality, arrogance, and brutality that had quickly pervaded the country. At the same time, he began to take a malicious delight in each increase in taxation and every business reverse that the war occasioned. These economic hardships, he hoped, would serve as excellent devices by which to teach the British public that neither war nor international meddling was worthwhile. Above all, however, the war disclosed and confirmed Bright's fears of the stern and vengeful God of the Old Testament. He believed that divine punishment was being meted out to the British through the instrument of this shameful and evil conflict. (3)

The war forced Bright to think again of abandoning public service. His wife had just had another baby; he missed his family; and he had an overwhelming sense of failure as a public figure, for he could not recognize as his people the British superpatriots who were clamoring for Russian blood. They were foreigners to him, and he was a foreigner to them. "How little common justice and humanity, not to say Christianity, seem to influence the English public under such an excitement as now prevails," he wrote to his wife. (4)

Just as Bright had feared, the war ended the possibility of early domestic reform, and all the vital issues that he thought Parliament should have been grappling with—the extension of the suffrage, the secret ballot, land reform, the condition of Ireland and India—were postponed indefinitely. Small wonder that he could not find words strong enough to describe his disillusionment, contempt, disgust, grief, shame, anger, and hatred. "Nothing but the most flagrant dishonesty, or the most flagrant imbecility, can have brought on a war out of the materials of a year ago," he wrote to Cobden. "How would you like to be a Cabinet Minister with so much blood on your head and conscience? Tho' I suspect statesmen are not troubled much with conscience—and their heads seem of little use for any good purpose," he wrote to John Benjamin Smith. Bright no longer had any doubt that the British needed to learn about the nature of international relations at the most elementary level. Otherwise the same ignorance and stupidity that were now in the ascendant would continue to endanger Britain's future. (5)

Although Bright never questioned the correctness of his view of the war, he did worry a great deal about the effect that his unpopular

PET OF THE MANCHESTER SCHOOL

"He shall have a little Turk to pull to pieces—that he shall."

☞ Messrs. Bright and Cobden incurred much odium by their persistent opposition to the Anti-Russian feeling of the nation at the outbreak of the Crimean war.—1854.

stand might have on his political future. He was not, in other words, nearly so heroic in wartime as Lord Morley, G. M. Trevelyan, and his other admirers have portrayed him. At one moment he felt confident that Cobden and he would emerge undamaged by their anti-war position; at another he doubted that they could survive politically. More and more he came to believe that they would have to wait for the return of peace for their exoneration. Then the British would know how many lives and how much money they had sacrificed to achieve so little, and he and Cobden would at last be appreciated. In the meantime it was not pleasant to be lashed out at in the press for "eccentric conduct" and "canting imbecility." Nor was it encouraging to be told that one was living in "a state of social isolation and political impotence." (6)

Bright valued every evidence he could find of support for his position. He rejoiced when George Congreve, the ardent Oxford positivist, asked if he might call on him. He welcomed each letter that praised his anti-war stand. A Quaker friend wrote reassuringly: "...whatever amount of present unpopularity may be thy portion, I trust that thou wilt be permitted richly to realise a far more abundant and enduring satisfaction...." (7)

Despite his preoccupation with Anglo-Russian relations in 1854 and 1855, Bright continued to seize every opportunity to call attention to the important subjects with which Parliament should have been dealing. He pointed to the dangers that grew out of the concentration of vast landed estates in the hands of a small number of families and pleaded for the simplification of the purchase and sale of land. He denounced religious bigotry and urged the abolition of the special privileges of the Church of England. He defended and praised the inexpensive American newspapers and worked for the elimination of the preposterous duties—"taxes on knowledge," as they were called—that hindered the growth of an inexpensive British press. He deplored the bribery and corruption that disgraced British elections, insisting that it was nonsense to call the secret ballot cowardly and un-English. Repeatedly he spoke out for better treatment of both India and Ireland. And whenever possible he reminded his countrymen of American progress in the arts of peace, cautioning them that the United States was "the young giant whose shadow ever grows, and *there* [was] the true rival of this country." (8)

II

In 1854 Bright made three important public statements about the war, all of which were attacked savagely in the press. The first was a speech in the House of Commons on March 31; the second, a public letter of late October; and the third, another speech in the Commons on December 22. All were reprinted and widely distributed, a fact that Bright interpreted hopefully but wrongly to mean that there was "an appetite for such aliment as we supply." (9)

Bright's March speech set the tone of his other public utterances about the war. He argued that the interests of Britain were not involved in the Russo-Turkish dispute and that the British aims of preserving Turkish integrity and of curbing Russian expansion were neither attainable nor worth the sacrifices necessitated by a war. Bright saw no way of blotting Russia from the map of Europe; there she was and there she would remain. Nor did he see any way of preventing the decline of the Turkish Empire; indeed, he regarded the promises of aid that Britain had made to this hopelessly decadent power as among the greatest blunders committed in British history. He denounced the idea of the "balance of power" as both vicious and mad, and he maintained that as long as diplomats thought in terms of this balance, peace would be in jeopardy because power was always shifting. Bright's point was that Britain should stop playing the role of "knight-errant of the human race," even if this was a role that appealed to some sections of the public. British intervention in other countries' wars was both needless and disastrous.

In one of his most moving perorations he said:

I believe if this country, seventy years ago, had adopted the principle of non-intervention in every case where her interests were not directly and obviously assailed, that she would have been saved from much of the pauperism and brutal crimes by which our Government and people have alike been disgraced. This country might have been a garden, every dwelling might have been of marble, and every person who treads its soil might have been sufficiently educated. We should indeed have had less of military glory. We might have had neither Trafalgar nor Waterloo; but we should have set a high example of a Christian nation, free in its institutions, courteous and just in its conduct towards all foreign States, and resting its policy on the unchangeable foundation of Christian morality. (10)

Bright's second major public statement was made in his *Letter to Absalom Watkin*. Watkin, a businessman active in Manchester civic life, had invited Bright to a meeting to raise money to aid the dependents of men fighting in the Crimea. In the course of his letter Watkin had justified the war by appealing to the principles of international law set forth in the writings of Emmerich von Vattel, the eighteenth-century Swiss jurist. Bright wrote back, turning down the invitation and decrying Watkin's use of Vattel as an authority. He found it pathetic that Watkin should look no higher than Vattel to discover moral principles; and he found it outrageous that Watkin should invite someone who disapproved of the war to the proposed meeting. Bright's reply was reprinted in *The Times* and other papers and published as a pamphlet. It produced a sensation in Manchester where his critics condemned him roundly and organized to repudiate him. As in the old days of the free trade crusade, Cobden rushed into action, wrote to George Wilson, and gave instructions for the mobilization of Bright's supporters. Nevertheless, T. Perronet Thompson was certainly right when he remarked that on the whole Bright came out poorly in the controversy. (11)

Ever since he began his public career, Bright had contended that the Member of Parliament who spoke his mind was worth any number of cowardly or cautious politicians. Even so, he was startled by the violent reactions to his *Letter*—and mainly, as he rightly told Wilson, because it contained nothing that he had not said in his March speech in the House of Commons. The difference was, however, that the war had been going on inconclusively for many months, and the glorious victory at a Crimean Waterloo that the British expected had not been won. Public frustration over the conduct of the war was vented on Bright and his "pro-Russian manifesto" in a way that he would never forget; some of his constituents burned him in effigy and then condemned him at a number of widely publicized public meetings. He found it hard to believe that after all his efforts the citizens of Manchester should still be so ignorant, and he asked with Milton, "How we are to make *outward* free of *inward* slaves?" But his enemies were saying, "Thank Heaven we are not a nation of Brights and Quakers! If we were, there would speedily be an end of us, and Russia would be free to possess herself, not of Constantinople only, but of Manchester and London." (12)

In the *Letter* Bright took the position that the Crimean War was needless. The British should not have interfered in the quarrel between Turkey and Russia; but, having interfered, they should have forced Turkey to make concessions when the Russians had shown a willingness to do so. Instead, the British had acted "with an imbecility perhaps without example." As a result, they were fighting for the freedom of "the most immoral and filthy of all despotisms." And their ally in this struggle was Napoleon III, that fine friend of liberty who had only recently wiped out a free constitution and legislature. Bright argued that it was absurd to try to uphold Turkish rule in Europe. Furthermore, he condemned the irrational British fear of Russia. He ended his *Letter* in defense of nonintervention with these words:

You must excuse me if I cannot go with you. I will have no part in this terrible crime. My hands shall be unstained with the blood which is being shed. The necessity of maintaining themselves in office may influence an administration; delusions may mislead a people; *Vattel* may afford you a law and a defence; but no respect for men who form a Government, no regard I have for "going with the stream," and no fear of being deemed wanting in patriotism, shall influence me in favour of a policy which, in my conscience, I believe to be as criminal before God as it is destructive of the true interest of my country. (13)

Bright's third important statement on the war was a speech that he delivered in the House of Commons a few days before Christmas. Again he asserted the hopelessness of the Turkish cause—nothing that Britain and France could do would restore the power of the Turks. Again he pointed out that Russia had been willing to settle with the Turks on terms that were deemed satisfactory by Britain and France. Again he proclaimed the war unnecessary. And again he surpassed himself in the eloquence of his peroration:

Let it not be said that I am alone in my condemnation of this war, and of this incapable and guilty Administration. And, even if I were alone, if my voice were the solitary one raised amid the din of arms and the clamours of a venal press, I should have the consolation I have tonight— and which I trust will be mine to the last moment of my existence—the priceless consolation, that no word of mine has tended to promote the squandering of my country's treasure, or the spilling of one single drop of my country's blood.

For two reasons Bright thought that his speech would do some good. First, the difficulty of fighting so far from home was now clear, and the public was learning of the unspeakable suffering of British troops in the Crimea. Second, Lord Aberdeen was eager to conclude the war. So Bright ended the year arranging for the preparation of memorials entreating Aberdeen to seize any suitable opportunity to make peace. Bright was convinced that he and other members of the small group that he liked to call "the peace party" had it in their power to strengthen the position of those leaders of the Government who wanted to end the conflict. As usual, Cobden was less sanguine than Bright. (14)

III

At the end of 1854 the British Expeditionary Force in the Crimea was floundering. As Gladstone's biographer, Sir Philip Magnus, has described it, "More casualties were inflicted by scurvy than by the Russians, and the plight of the sick and wounded, despite Florence Nightingale's efforts, was pitiful." In the last week of January 1855, the Aberdeen Government fell because of its mismanagement of the war effort, and in the first week of February, Lord Palmerston became Prime Minister.

Bright was furious. "What a terrible retribution is brought upon us by this insane war!" he told George Wilson. Although critical of Lord Aberdeen, Bright respected him as a fundamentally decent human being. But now the Government was led by the seventy-year-old aristocrat whom Bright and Cobden regarded as the greatest

charlatan and impostor in public life, the politician who by his outrageous behavior in the Don Pacifico affair had set for the British
people the worst possible standards of international immorality.
"Any fool can plunge a country into a war," Bright told his wife,
"but it requires wisdom and firmness to get creditably out of it";
and Palmerston was not wise. Cobden went so far as to interpret his
appointment as a sure sign that the British were "a used-up nation"
—only a people in their dotage would look to such a man as their
savior. (15)

Despite his hostility to Palmerston, Bright knew that this was
still the man who could determine when the war would end. At the
first possible opportunity, therefore—on February 23—he appealed
to Palmerston in the House of Commons to crown his long public
career by assuming the role of peacemaker. The speech in which
this appeal occurred proved to be the best known and most quoted
that Bright was ever to make.

It was outstanding for its moderation. Bright protested against
neither the war nor the peace terms that the Government was offering the Russians. He did not go into any of the harrowing details
concerning the plight of British troops in the Crimea; nor did he
linger on any of the horrors of the siege of Sebastopol. His purpose
was simply to urge Lord Palmerston to avoid any petty complications
and quibbles that might delay the return of peace, and he pleaded
for a speedy armistice so that as many lives as possible could be
saved. In the words that Bright made famous:

The angel of death has been abroad throughout the land; you may almost hear the beating of his wings. There is no one, as when the first-
born were slain of old, to sprinkle with blood the lintel and the two
sideposts of our doors, that he may spare and pass on; he takes his
victims from the castle of the noble, the mansion of the wealthy, and
the cottage of the poor and the lowly, and it is on behalf of all these
classes that I make this solemn appeal.

Bright knew that his speech was a tour de force, and he engaged
in no false modesty when he wrote to his wife and to George Wilson
about it. "Don't expose me by showing this letter," he begged
Wilson. Bright was pleased with the praise that was heaped on him

by colleagues so different as Cobden and Disraeli; Cobden was even convinced that the speech established Bright's reputation as the most eloquent speaker in the House of Commons. Yet the speech did not fulfill its aim. The Vienna peace negotiations broke down, no armistice was in sight, the siege of Sebastopol went on, casualties grew at an appalling rate, and "the madness for war" and the search for glory and honor continued. The Crimean War, as A. J. P. Taylor has emphasized, "was fought much more against Russia than in favor of Turkey." (16)

Bright did what he could—not much—to press for peace. In March, for example, he was a member of a deputation from Manchester that presented to Lord Palmerston a memorial to end the war. And when the Kingdom of Sardinia joined the allies, he publicly warned the Italian leaders that they were making a terrible blunder. But there was little else that he could find to do. The war party was powerful, and the newspapers endorsed the continuation of the conflict. This was made clear during the wild reception that both press and public extended to Napoleon III when he visited Britain in April. "Festivities here—death in the Crimea!" Bright wrote bitterly to his wife. It infuriated him that the very man who not so long ago was alleged to be planning to invade Britain was now a respectable ally. To Bright he was the same adventurer that he had always been, and he would not do homage to the man who had massacred his fellow citizens to achieve power. By May, Bright was so desperate that he tried to make a curious bargain with Palmerston: he would promise not to speak in the House for the next fifteen years if the Government would end the war. (17)

Week by week Bright's lack of faith in the statesmanship of Palmerston was confirmed, and he feared that the war might go on for years. His hopes for peace depended increasingly on the economic hardships that the war was producing. For this reason there is some truth in the attack on Bright that Tennyson published in 1855 in *Maud*.

> Last week came one to the county town,
> To preach our poor little army down,
> And play the game of the despot kings,

Tho' the state has done it and thrice as well;
This broad-brimm'd hawker of holy things,
Whose ear is cramm'd with his cotton, and rings
Even in dreams to the chink of his pence,
This huckster put down war! can he tell
Whether war be a cause or a consequence?

From Bright's point of view, what mattered was that the political leaders had not ended the war and the people had not clamored for peace. What, then, was the way out? Mounting taxes and alarming business reverses, he thought, might teach the public the virtues of peace in a way that neither political leaders nor casualties had succeeded in doing. (18)

Bright was increasingly upset not only by the incompetence of British political leadership but by the callousness of the public. Like Cobden, he discovered that people did not seem to care about the loss of life in the Crimea; their pride and hunger for glory took precedence over their humanity. In fact, Bright worried about the repercussions that a great British victory might have. Like Cobden, he thought that such a victory would intensify the war spirit and encourage further interference in the affairs of other countries. His hope was that the crushing financial burden of the war might teach the British to esteem peace. (19)

IV

On June 7 Bright delivered another major speech on the war to a crowded House of Commons, but this time his remarks were not conciliatory in tone. He proclaimed Palmerston and Russell the irresponsible and reckless authors of the war, and he condemned them for needlessly prolonging it. He insisted that no objectives that could be gained in the struggle were worth the human and financial sacrifices that the British people had been called on to make. In short, he asserted his resounding lack of confidence in Palmerston's Government.

Once again Bright was gratified by the flattering comments of some of his colleagues, and once again his speech failed to accomplish its purpose. It was clear that for the present there was not the slightest possibility of peace. For days afterward he was in such a state of anxiety that he even forgot his wedding anniversary; for Bright, who had an extraordinary memory for the important dates in his life, this was an ominous lapse. As he apologized to his wife: "...I have been badly bewildered during the recent debate—so disgusted and so saddened...." He was particularly troubled by popular indifference to the loss of life in the Crimea. "In the Clubs and at the House," he told his wife, "men talk of such an one being 'hit' or 'knocked over,' just as if they were discussing a question of sporting at the expense of some dumb animals." Understandably, he turned often for solace and courage to the Bible and John Milton. (20)

For the rest of the year Bright felt bitterness, scorn, anger, and hopelessness. Cobden repeatedly urged him to be philosophical about wartime Britain and its brutish people, to accept conditions as they were, and not to shorten his life in behalf of a lost cause. There was no sense in being stoned, burned in effigy, and martyred. It was better to hide away on an isolated farm among people who had never heard of Sebastopol and hardly knew that a war was going on. Unfortunately for his health, however, Bright was not capable of taking Cobden's advice. He was convinced, on the one hand, that justice and humanity as well as reason and common sense were on his side, and that he had acted consistently and stood firmly by his principles. At the same time, however, he was depressed by his failure to communicate to the public his view that the war was a folly and a crime. He recognized the painful truth that the conflict was widely supported and that Palmerston was an incredibly popular hero. (21)

Bright was also depressed by the savage attacks on him almost everywhere in the country—from *The Times*, the *Manchester Guardian*, and *Punch* to the most obscure provincial newspapers. For speaking what he saw as the truth about the war he was being denounced as a coward, a traitor, a Russian agent—in short, a most unworthy representative of Manchester in Parliament. As *Punch* put it, "JOHN BULL disclaims all and every connection with JOHN BRIGHT, *alias* JOHN *Musco*BRIGHT." Clearly, his career in public life was in danger as it had never been before—and this at the age of forty-four and after thirteen years of parliamentary service. Had he come all the way for this? For *Punch* to tell him that

A Hinglishman's birthright, with sitch a poor sperrit,
Is what chaps like you isn't fit to inherit. . . .? (22)

By the end of 1855, Bright was torn by tensions, humiliations, fears, and conflicts. His attempts to reassure himself that he had much to be grateful for were unsuccessful. The books he turned to— symptomatically, the Book of Job—failed him. His wife, his children, his friends, his status were not enough to bolster him. Early in 1856 he broke down—the victim of frustrated ambition and outraged patriotism. He was as much a war casualty as any English soldier who collapsed during the siege of Sebastopol. The words he had written only recently about a friend applied now to himself: that he had "lived a life of terrible excitement of late years—enough to break down even his iron constitution and frame." (23)

NOTES

(1) *The Times,* Jan. 25, 1854; *Diaries,* Feb. 8, 1854; Mar. 15, 1854; Mar. 22, 1854; Bright to Wilson, Feb. 2, 1854, Wilson MSS, MCL; Bright to Mrs. Bright, Feb. 9, 1854; Feb. 17, 1854; Feb. 18, 1854; Feb. 21, 1854; Feb. 22, 1854; Mar. 21, 1854, Bright MSS, UCLL; Bright to Aberdeen, Mar. 16, 1854, copy, Gladstone MSS, BM 44,112.

(2) *Parl. Deb.,* 131 (Mar. 13, 1854), 675ff.; Cobden to Bright, Jan. 3, 1854, Cobden MSS, BM 43,650; see A. J. P. Taylor, *The Trouble Makers* (London, 1957), chap. II; Bright to Mrs. Bright, May 1, 1854, Bright MSS, UCLL.

(3) *Letters,* Apr. 18, 1854; *Parl. Deb.,* 132 (Apr. 28, 1854), 1012; Bright to Wilson, May 11, 1854; Sept. 9, 1854, Wilson MSS, MCL; *Punch,* XXVII (1854), 39; Bright to Mrs. Bright, May 9, 1854; July 4, 1854; July 17, 1854, Bright MSS, UCLL; Bright to Cobden, Oct. 17, 1854, Bright MSS, BM 43,383.

(4) *Diaries,* Mar. 1, 1854; Bright to Mrs. Bright, Feb. 20, 1854; Mar. 21, 1854; May 1, 1854; May 6, 1854; July 11, 1854, Bright MSS, UCLL.

(5) Bright to W. H. Darby, Apr. 11, 1854, Bright MSS, JRL; Bright to Cobden, Apr. 20, 1854, Bright MSS, BM 43,383; *Parl. Deb.,* 133 (May 29, 1854), 1106ff.; Bright to Smith, Oct. 11, 1854; Oct. 21, 1854, John Benjamin Smith MSS, MCL.

(6) Morley, p. 620; Trevelyan, p. 235; Bright to Cobden, Feb. 25, 1854; Mar. 1, 1854; Apr. 20, 1854; Sept. 4, 1854; Sept. 28, 1854, Bright MSS, BM 43,383; Cobden to Bright, Jan. 5, 1855, Cobden MSS, BM 43,650; *Punch,*

XXVI (1854), 29, 115, 243; *Illustrated London News,* XXIV (Feb. 25, 1854), 162.

(7) Bright to Mrs. Bright, June 9, 1854; Apr. 19, 1855, Bright MSS, UCLL; Cobden to Bright, Sept. 14, 1854; Oct. 1, 1854; Feb. 11, 1855, Cobden MSS, BM 43,650; Bright to Sturge, Sept. 4, 1854; Nov. 11, 1854, Sturge MSS, BM 43,723; Bright to Samuel Haight, Nov. 26, 1855, Bright MSS, Duke University Library; J. B. Braithwaite to Bright, Dec. 23, 1854; Edward L. Pierce to Bright, Dec. 18, 1884, Bright MSS, BM 43,389–43,390.

(8) Bright to Mrs. Bright, Mar. 8, 1854, Bright MSS, UCLL; *Parl. Deb.,* 131 (Mar. 8, 1854), 471ff.; 133 (May 16, 1854), 444ff.; 133 (May 18, 1854), 551; 134 (June 13, 1854), 75ff.; 134 (June 21, 1854), 459; 135 (July 11, 1854), 75ff.; 137 (Mar. 19, 1855), 810ff.; 137 (Apr. 30, 1855), 2006; 139 (Aug. 7, 1855), 1988ff.; *The Times,* Jan. 21, 1854; Dec. 19, 1855; cf. Bright to Cobden, Nov. 29, 1855, Bright MSS, BM 43,384.

(9) Bright to Cobden, Feb. 9, 1855, *ibid.*

(10) *Parl. Deb.,* 132 (Mar. 31, 1854), 243ff.; 267.

(11) Bright to Wilson, Oct. 29, 1854, Wilson MSS, MCL; *The Times,* Nov. 4, 1854; Nov. 17, 1854; Dec. 15, 1854; Thompson to H. B. Peacock, Nov. 27, 1854, Thompson MSS, JRL; successive issues of the *Manchester Guardian,* Nov. and Dec., 1854 and Jan., 1855.

(12) Bright to Wilson, Dec. 10, 1854; Dec. 12, 1854; Cobden to Wilson, Dec. 15, 1854, Wilson MSS, MCL; Bright to Mrs. Bright, Dec. 15, 1854, Bright MSS, UCLL; *The Times,* Dec. 19, 1854; Jan. 22, 1855; *Illustrated London News,* XXV (Nov. 11, 1854), 453; XXV (Nov. 25, 1854), 535.

(13) *Speeches,* I, 529–35.

(14) *Parl. Deb.,* 136 (Dec. 22, 1854), 883ff.; Bright to Sturge, Dec. 28, 1854, Sturge MSS, BM 43,723; Bright to Cobden, Jan. 1, 1855, Bright MSS, BM 43,384.

(15) Magnus, p. 118; Bright to Wilson, Feb. 21, 1855, Wilson MSS, MCL; Bright to Cobden, Sept. 4, 1854; Feb. 9, 1855; Sept. 21, 1855, Bright MSS, BM 43,383–43,384; Bright to Mrs. Bright, Feb. 22, 1855; Feb. 23, 1855, Bright MSS, UCLL; Cobden to Bright, Feb. 11, 1855, Cobden MSS, BM 43,650.

(16) *Diaries,* Feb. 14, 1855; *Parl. Deb.,* 136 (Feb. 23, 1855), 1755ff.; Bright to Mrs. Bright, Feb. 23, 1855; Feb. 27, 1855; Feb. 28, 1855, Bright MSS, UCLL; Bright to Wilson, Feb. 27, 1855; Cobden to Wilson, Feb. 24, 1855, Wilson MSS, MCL; Bright to William Salmon, Mar. 13, 1855, Bright MSS, Cornell University Library; A. J. P. Taylor, "John Bright and the Crimean War," *Bulletin of the John Rylands Library,* XXXVI (1954), 509.

(17) Bright to Mrs. Bright, Mar. 22, 1855; Apr. 19, 1855; Apr. 20, 1855; May 8, 1855, Bright MSS, UCLL; cf. Cobden to Wilson, Apr. 19, 1855, Wilson MSS, MCL; *Parl. Deb.,* 137 (Mar. 26, 1855), 1083; 138 (May 21, 1855), 847.

(18) *The Times,* Feb. 10, 1855; *Parl. Deb.,* 132 (Apr. 11, 1854), 852; 139

(July 19, 1855), 1114; *Diaries,* Apr. 20, 1855; Bright to Mrs. Bright, Apr. 20, 1855; Apr. 22, 1855, Bright MSS, UCLL; cf. James Buchanan to C. L. Ward, Apr. 13, 1855, Buchanan MSS, New-York Historical Society; Bright to Wilson, Feb. 21, 1855; Apr. 23, 1855, Wilson MSS, MCL; Bright to Cobden, Nov. 21, 1855, Bright MSS, BM 43,384; *Maud,* Part I, X, iii.

(19) Bright to Mrs. Bright, Apr. 26, 1855, Bright MSS, UCLL; Bright to Bowring, Apr. 8, 1855, Sir John Bowring MSS, JRL; Cobden to Bright, May 31, 1855, Cobden MSS, BM 43,650; *Parl. Deb.,* 138 (June 5, 1855), 1484.

(20) Bright to Wilson, June 13, 1855, Wilson MSS, MCL; Bright to Mrs. Bright, June 8, 1855; June 11, 1855; June 24, 1855, Bright MSS, UCLL.

(21) Bright to Smith, Oct. 16, 1855; Dec. 31, 1855, John Benjamin Smith MSS, MCL; Bright to Cobden, July 12, 1855; Sept. 21, 1855; Oct. 8, 1855, Bright MSS, BM 43,384; Cobden to Bright, June 26, 1855; Sept. 15, 1855; Sept. 17, 1855, Cobden MSS, BM 43,650; Cobden to Wilson, July 12, 1855; Bright to Wilson, Sept. 12, 1855; Oct. 16, 1855, Wilson MSS, MCL.

(22) *Parl. Deb.,* 139 (July 23, 1855), 1289; Bright to Cobden, Oct. 8, 1855; Nov. 29, 1855; cf. Mar. 17, 1860, Bright MSS, BM 43,384; Bright to Wilson, Oct. 13, 1855, Wilson MSS, MCL; *The Times,* Jan. 30, 1856; *Punch,* XXVII (1854), 203, 237; XXVIII (1855), 13, 62, 103, 246; XXIX (1855), 70, 119, 196, 226, 234, 255, 256; XXX (1856), 60.

(23) Bright to Cobden, Nov. 29, 1855, Bright MSS, BM 43,384; Cobden to Bright, Dec. 3, 1855, Cobden MSS, BM 43,650; Bright to Sturge, Jan. 2, 1856, Sturge MSS, BM 43,723; Bright to Wilson, Jan. 25, 1856; Feb. 9, 1856, Wilson MSS, MCL; Bright to Mrs. Bright, July 22, 1855; Feb. 8, 1856; Feb. 9, 1856; Feb. 10, 1856; Feb. 13, 1856; cf. Jan. 28, 1860; Jan. 27, 1864, Bright MSS, UCLL; Bright to Cobden, Oct. 17, 1854, Bright MSS, BM 43,383.

CHAPTER SIX

OUT AND IN
1856–1857

Bright was no pre-Freudian, pre-Jungian, or pre-Adlerian. He saw his illness as the product of overwork, of too much concentrated mental labor during too many hectic years. He had overexercised his brain and now it refused to work.

Recovery was slow and fitful; and his inability to help himself proved particularly humiliating to a man who had long and eloquently preached the virtues of self-help. Some days he felt fine and ready to resume his parliamentary responsibilities. Other days his head ached so that he doubted he could ever return to his political work or to any other sustained activity. His doctors tried a number of cures, but mostly they recommended complete rest. He was not allowed to read, write, or make speeches, and he had to avoid conversation as much as possible, especially discussions about the war, the peace (that was at last impending), or any other controversial topics. Along with rest his doctors prescribed a change of scene. Yorkshire, Scotland, Wales—Bright went to all of them, and in November he left for an extended stay in North Africa, France, and Italy. Remaining at home in Rochdale had not worked. He longed for his wife and children when he was away from them; but when he was with them he was embarrassed and ashamed to have them see him in his enfeebled condition. (1)

His friends behaved admirably—as he had every reason to suppose that they would. George Wilson consoled and reassured him. John Benjamin Smith reported that the legislative session was so utterly barren that he was lucky to be taking no part in it. Charles Pelham Villiers told him how much he was missed—Parliament was not the same without him. Thomas Milner Gibson, his fellow Member for Manchester and the leader in the struggle to repeal the taxes on knowledge, begged him to take care of himself so that he would soon be able to resume his good work. And Lord Aberdeen invited him to his country house in Scotland. Although Bright usually prided himself on shunning members of "the ruling class," he accepted this invitation. (2)

People he hardly knew showed extraordinary kindness. The author of *Visit to the Exhibition* requested his permission to dedicate the volume to him. Lord Brougham, with whom he had had an ugly controversy back in corn law days, offered him a house on the sea for convalescence. American cousins of his wife urged him to stay with them in the United States. The ocean voyage would do wonders for his health, and so would life in America, they promised, suggesting that he could see for himself how well the secret ballot worked in the approaching presidential election of 1856. Even *The Times*, which differed with him on almost every subject on which he had ever taken a stand, was extremely considerate in its reports of his "indisposition." It went so far as to reprint a poem that he had jotted down in a visiting book at a Scottish inn:

In Highland glens 'tis far too oft observed
That man is chased away and game preserved.
Glen-Urquhart is to me a lovelier glen,
Here deer and grouse have not supplanted men. (3)

Cobden above all others proved his friendship, shielding Bright from every kind of unpleasantness. He gave him medical advice, suggesting that he eat fish and vegetables instead of meat and that he consider bloodletting. He cautioned him about medicines and lotions, venturing the opinion that "*Laissez faire* seems as applicable to the medical profession as to trade." He urged him to go where there was a great deal of sun and light—to a place like Niagara Falls —for there he would sleep well, his brain would get a rest, and he would learn to stop "perorating in bed." And knowing that Bright was not an easy spender, Cobden pleaded with him to seek out the most competent specialists regardless of the outrageous fees they would doubtless demand. Even when Cobden faced tragedy in his own life—the sudden death from scarlet fever of his only son while at a German school—he continued to play a supportive role in Bright's life. (4)

Despite the repeated advice of his doctors and friends, however, Bright could not overcome his obsession with public questions. Indeed, his illness demonstrated how political a man he was and how prominently public affairs figured in his emotional life. At the slightest sign of recovery he would ache for news. He wanted to hear the latest gossip from Westminster and Manchester. He wanted to learn about any new hoaxes that Palmerston might be perpetrating. He wanted to know about the condition of the *Morning Star*, the newspaper he had recently helped to found with the aim of spreading the views of the Manchester School, especially the idea of international arbitration. (5)

Bright's appetite for news reached a high point when he left England in November. He had hardly settled in Algiers when he discovered that no newspaper available there reported what was happening in Britain; he therefore begged Cobden to keep him informed, assuring him that he was well enough by now to hear about how Parliament was "befooling the nation." For months, of course, he had been preoccupied with the effects his illness would have on his career.

Cobden was worried, too. He was in his early fifties, and since he came from a family not notable for longevity, he doubted that he could lead the Manchester party much longer. For years he had regarded Bright as his successor; he had counted on him to conduct the campaigns for all the measures which still had to be carried and which Cobden did not expect to live long enough to see won. He considered Bright even more fit than himself for leadership because of his extraordinary combination of earnestness, honesty, courage, energy, intelligence, and eloquence. There was no one in Parliament, Cobden thought, who could appeal so effectively as Bright to people's minds and hearts. Yet at the age of forty-five this man was a wreck. Cobden had every reason to be worried. (6)

II

Bright was in no condition to enjoy travel. He was, in fact, as homesick and melancholy an Englishman as any who ever visited foreign lands in the nineteenth century. The big event in his life was the arrival of the mail. And in the letters he wrote his central theme was always the same: he was healthy enough to hear the truth about what was taking place at home. He assured his correspondents that reading and writing no longer upset him or made his head feel weak.

When his teenage daughter—Helen, his oldest and the only child of his first marriage—joined him in France in January, his spirits improved considerably. Of all his children he treasured her particularly, among other reasons, because she had never been expected to survive. Like her mother, she suffered from poor lungs, and Bright had frequently feared that she might share her mother's fate. Her gentleness, innocence, sensitivity, and idealism—all helped to cheer him. "Oh! for some of the freshness and the enthusiasm of my dear girl who makes the journey with me!" he wrote understandably to Cobden from Genoa. (7)

In the course of his travels Bright met a number of celebrities, and their flattering comments were good for his low self-esteem. In Nice the Russian Empress invited him to call, and she thanked him for his efforts in behalf of peace and more harmonious Anglo-Russian relations. In Rome he was pleased to discuss American affairs with Mrs. Harriet Beecher Stowe, for whom he had developed a profound admiration; he considered *Uncle Tom's Cabin* one of the most stirring books he had ever read. And in Turin he talked to Count Cavour about the Italian Question, not letting pass a chance to caution him against placing any trust in Palmerston. (8)

Although he was beginning to complain that he had seen too many statues and paintings and too many evidences of Roman Catholicism, it was just as well that in the early months of 1857 he was kept busy as a tourist. For at the end of March came the blow that he had dreaded ever since the beginning of the Crimean War. Despite a moving letter he had sent to the electors of Manchester and despite the efforts of Wilson and Cobden, Bright lost his seat in the House of Commons. Appropriately enough, he had been pre- paring himself for the "ignorance, credulity, selfishness, ingratitude and all the other unpleasant qualities every honest politician must meet with" by reading Bulwer-Lytton's novel *Rienzi*. (9)

The election itself came unexpectedly. Cobden had introduced a motion condemning the Palmerston Government for having be- come involved in a disgraceful and inexcusable war with China. He was agreeably surprised that his motion was carried in the House; he was no less pleased that Parliament was dissolved and a general election held. But the election results were not at all to his liking: they demonstrated that Palmerston and his supporters had the back- ing of the electorate. The *Annual Register* did not exaggerate when it suggested that the "name of that noble Lord was perhaps never more popular in the country than at this time." (10)

The election results also demonstrated that Cobden, Bright, and Milner Gibson, all of whom lost their seats, were by no means heroes to most of the voters of their constituencies. In the blunt words of *Punch*: "The Manchester School has been converted into the School of Adversity. It is to be hoped that this change will con- duce to the improvement of the scholars, who, in consequence of it, will get grounded in a thoroughly English education." No less bluntly the *Economist*, which generally shared the economic ideas of Bright and Cobden but deplored their views on foreign policy, confessed "sincere gratification" at their electoral defeat. Indeed, the *Economist* could not forgive Bright for his recklessness of speech, his disrespectful treatment of his opponents, and his praise of any and all foreigners who insulted the British. Similarly, the *Illustrated London News* moralized that those who aspired to be British states- men had to have British sympathies and had to understand the requirements of national honor. (11)

III

For a man who had only recently been extremely ill, Bright took the humiliation remarkably well. To be sure, he fumed privately at the *Manchester Guardian* and the voters of Manchester, denouncing them as stupid and incompetent. As for the successful candidates, the Palmerstonian Whigs Sir John Potter and James Aspinall Turner, he found them mediocrities and sycophants—"a man who has eaten and dined himself to a knighthood, [and] one whose pompous ignorance and vulgarity are apparent in all he says." Perhaps he was correct in his judgment. Yet what matters is that his defeat by such inferior people helped to liberate him from one of his long-standing fears. The worst had happened, and it turned out to be not nearly so bad as he had anticipated. The Manchester election was a milestone in the rebuilding of his emotional defenses. (12)

All the people who counted said the right things. Even before the election his wife had begged him to give up political life. Now she was delighted—she and the children could have him at home all year round. His brothers were also relieved; they felt that he had done more than enough in public service. And his erstwhile parliamentary colleagues assured him that the House of Commons had rarely been deprived of the services of so valuable a Member.

Bright's defeat infuriated Cobden, who regarded it as a disgraceful instance of ingratitude. His explanation of the debacle was simple but sound. Manchester had grown rich, and the richer it grew, the more snobbish its voters became. They thought like Tories or conservative Whigs, but in any case not like Liberals, much less Radicals, and they were punishing those who had dared to criticize Britain's involvement in the Crimean War. Their voting behavior confirmed Cobden in his belief that Manchester could never be the center of any new agitation. It had succeeded as the headquarters of the anti-corn law campaign mainly because the cotton lords thought that free trade would further enrich them. But any other reform movement would have to come from some other big town. "What so natural as that your genteel people should kick down the ladder by which they rose?" Cobden wrote to Wilson. The old boast of the free traders that the cheap loaf had killed off Chartism was true; but the cheap loaf was also choking off Liberalism and Radicalism. Prosperity was making the age impossible for earnest, reforming politicians. (13)

Cobden had worried that the humiliating election result might give his friend a relapse, but instead it inspired Bright to resume their long-standing political dialogue, which had stopped only because of his health. He assured Cobden that the defeat meant that they were ahead of their time; their political creed and morality were too advanced for their constituents. Despite their years of exertion they had not succeeded very well as teachers of the right kind of foreign policy. In Bright's happy choice of words: "We have taught what is true in our 'School,' but the discipline was a little too severe for the scholars." Unlike their opponents, however, they had

RECOIL OF THE GREAT
CHINESE GUN-TRICK

☞ Mr. Bright was rejected at Manchester on Lord Palmerston's appeal to the country after his defeat by Mr. Cobden on the China Question. He was shortly afterwards returned for Birmingham without opposition.—1857.

not appealed to popular ignorance and prejudice, and of this they could surely be proud. For the rest, they had achieved certain clear results. They were responsible for the widespread acceptance of free trade, for a more enlightened attitude toward colonies, and for the belief in the inevitability of parliamentary reform. These were no small accomplishments in such a short period of time, Bright insisted; therefore it was still too soon to despair of the possibility of reeducating the public about foreign policy. Palmerston, after all, could not last forever, Bright pointed out, not hesitating to express his death wishes for the Prime Minister whose "criminal" behavior had so often enraged him. (14)

A few weeks later Bright again sounded like his old ebullient self. He acknowledged that he was disgusted with the stupidity of the British public in foreign policy, and he confessed that in self-defense he had to "cultivate a callous spirit." At the same time, however, he bluntly told Cobden that "we must try to recover our position again, if we do not mean absolutely to abandon political life." In short, while the fear of defeat had contributed to Bright's breakdown, the reality of defeat helped to restore him to health. Indeed, his friends became increasingly anxious about him, suspecting that he might try to resume political work before he was sufficiently recovered; and they deluged him with letters begging him to be patient and to take care of himself. (15)

IV

Bright did not have much time to adjust to his new-found freedom or to wonder what was to come next. In June 1857, he returned to England. In July the death of one of the Members for Birmingham resulted in his being sounded out on his availability for the vacant seat. In August he was elected without a contest. That he was invited to stand was a triumph for the old peace party in Birmingham. And that he—a peace man—was elected was all the more impressive because his new constituency was the center of the British munitions industry!

Expressions of satisfaction with the Birmingham victory came from the most unlikely sources. "This result was pleasing to persons

of all parties," the *Annual Register* noted with only slight exaggeration, "for, however opinions might differ as to the correctness of
the peculiar views of the 'Manchester School,' it was universally
allowed that Mr. Bright's downright language and plain common
sense was [sic] often of essential service to the interests of the country." Yet even as *The Economist* remarked that it was glad that he
was back in Parliament, it commented on his "mistaken and crotch-
ety" ideas. Even as the *Illustrated London News* congratulated him,
it expressed the hope that he had learned a lesson from his defeat in
Manchester and the regret that he had not spent his youth at Eton
or Harrow, where he would have learned something not only of
independence of character but of deference as well. *The Times*
pointedly reprinted a piece from the *Scotsman* wishing him well
and reminding him that his besetting sin was a lack of toleration
and respect for opinions that diverged from his own.

The victory worked wonders for Bright's morale. After all, the
voters of Birmingham knew that he had been rejected by Manchester. They knew that he had opposed the Crimean War and that
he thought the war had accomplished nothing that could not have
been secured through arbitration. They knew that he opposed meddling in other countries' affairs and that he believed that the less
Britain had of a foreign policy, the better. And they knew that he
detested the Prime Minister. Yet despite all the unpopular stands
he had taken, the people of Birmingham had turned to him to
represent them in Parliament. (16)

Bright's friends also rejoiced over the election result, but they
doubted that he had made a right decision, believing that he would
have done better to avoid public life until he was really well again.
Cobden, in particular, was concerned that a premature return to
politics might cause a relapse in a person with such an "ardent temperament." But apart from his fear that Bright might overtax his
brain before it was fully recovered, Cobden was exuberant over
Bright's victory. How gratifying that the voters of Birmingham
"should have in so handsome a way kicked the posteriors of those
political snobs and fops in Manchester...." (17)

Cobden rightly considered Birmingham a more appropriate

constituency for Bright than Manchester had ever been or ever could be. For Cobden saw Manchester as a fundamentally undemocratic town—with a small number of great capitalists and a large number of mill hands. Birmingham, on the other hand, was a democratic community by its very nature. It had a large number of small and medium-sized business enterprises; owners worked side by side with their workers; and relations between capital and labor were much more cordial than in Manchester. Birmingham, therefore, was a far superior political home for the former Member for Manchester. (18)

Bright, to be sure, felt guilty about his rash behavior, and he was prepared for a scolding from Cobden. His explanation of his action was simple. First, he was feeling much better. Second, he had urged the members of the Birmingham committee that invited him to choose either Cobden or Milner Gibson, but they insisted that they wanted a representative who had spoken out strongly in behalf of parliamentary reform. Third, he believed that his election would be interpreted as a victory for the Manchester School and a defeat for Palmerston. Bright still could not explain his behavior in personal terms; he could not acknowledge that he loved sitting in the House of Commons and that he enjoyed the power, prestige, and status that went with being a Member of Parliament. (19)

There was at least one more conscious reason for his eagerness to return to public life. The Indian Mutiny—"the most hideous occurrence in our history," as Lord Morley was to call it—had recently broken out, and since the Indian Question was a subject to which Bright had given a great deal of thought, he was eager to be in a position to shape the new policy that was at last inevitable. Indeed, several of his friends had been generous enough to tell him in the early stages of the Mutiny that they regarded his absence from the House during this crisis as a national misfortune. (20)

Bright could not understand why so many of his countrymen were shocked by the uprising. To him the remarkable thing was not that it had happened but that it had been so long delayed. He had no doubt that the insurrection would be successfully put down: the natives were docile, they lacked adequate leadership, and they were poorly organized. To be sure, Bright deplored the atrocities that were being committed on both sides, but he recognized that the rebels had a long history of legitimate grievances; the tragedy, as he saw it, was that the British had waited for such an outbreak before they would act to remove these injustices. "In this Country nothing is done but in the pressure of a great calamity," he noted bitterly. (21)

Both Bright and Cobden considered the British role in Indian history as one of almost unmitigated villainy. They accepted the idea that eventually India would be free, and they hoped that that time was not too far in the future. In the short run, however, they believed that the British could do much to atone for their past crimes. But Bright was much more hopeful than Cobden that the right measures would be adopted, and this optimism was one further sign of the resurgence of his old self. "What we want for India is a total change of ideas and policy—no more conquest—no more fraudulent annexations—a prudent use of revenue, with a view to afford relief to the overtaxed cultivators, and some great act which shall give to the people an ownership in the land, and a security in its possession." Bright took it for granted that the British in India were hated as invaders and conquerors—a fact that made it all the more important for them to treat the natives with wisdom, justice, and dignity. (22)

Bright's optimism waned frequently during the last months of the year. As the opening of the parliamentary session, due to take place in February 1858, drew close, he was worried. He wondered whether he had made a mistake in accepting the Birmingham seat. True, he felt better and he was doing what his doctors told him to do—resting, exercising, getting plenty of fresh air. For all that, he knew that he had a long way to go. He was also troubled because Cobden would not be in the House of Commons with him, and now, more than ever, he needed him for emotional support. Bright had not recovered—nor would he ever recover—from his Manchester wound. Indeed, when he met Charles Sumner, the Republican Senator from Massachusetts, he noted bitterly that, unlike his British counterparts, the American leader had not been cast out of Congress because he believed in morality in politics. (23)

Other things depressed him, too. The death of some old friends reminded him that so many of his colleagues in the anti-corn law struggle were disappearing from the scene. Furthermore, the flow of bad news from India—endless atrocities—made him feel less certain about easy answers to the complicated Indian Question. He even decided that for the present he would keep silent about Indian matters—and not only because of his health. He would speak out only when he could talk with his old sense of conviction. (24)

NOTES

(1) *Diaries,* 203–205; *The Times,* Mar. 6, 1856; Mar. 24, 1856; Bright to Mrs. Bright, Feb. 26, 1856; Mar. 17, 1856; June 30, 1856; cf. July 20, 1857, Bright MSS, UCLL; Bright to Joseph Sturge, Mar. 3, 1856, Sturge MSS, BM 43,723; Bright to Smith, Apr. 27, 1856, John Benjamin Smith MSS, MCL; Bright to Cobden, Mar. 6, 1856, Bright MSS, BM 43,384; Bright to Wilson, Mar. 27, 1856; Apr. 2, 1856; Apr. 5, 1856; May 8, 1856; June 11, 1856; July 30, 1856; Nov. 6, 1856, Wilson MSS, MCL.

(2) Smith to Bright, Apr. 30, 1856; Milner Gibson to Bright, Apr. 14, 1856, Bright MSS, BM 43,388; Villiers to Bright, May 18, 1856, Bright MSS, BM 43,386; Bright to Cobden, Aug. 8, 1856, Bright MSS, BM 43,384; Bright to Mrs. Bright, Sept. 15, 1856, Bright MSS, UCLL; Bright to Gordon, Oct. 30, 1856, Lacaita-Shelburne MSS, William L. Clements Library.

(3) Bright to Mrs. Bright, Aug. 31, 1856, Bright MSS, UCLL; Brougham to Cobden, May 5, 1856, Cobden MSS, BM 43,669; Henry D. Gilpin to Bright, June 1, 1856, Bright MSS, BM 43,391; *The Times,* Feb. 19, 1856; Apr. 7, 1856; May 1, 1856; May 5, 1856; June 24, 1856; July 16, 1856; July 25, 1856; Aug. 15, 1856; Nov. 20, 1856.

(4) Cobden to Bright, Mar. 4, 1856; Mar. 8, 1856; Mar. 13, 1856; Mar. 17, 1856; Mar. 21, 1856; Mar. 28, 1856; Apr. 3, 1856; Oct. 30, 1856, Cobden MSS, BM 43,650; Bright to Mrs. Bright, Apr. 12, 1856, Bright MSS, UCLL; Bright to Smith, Apr. 27, 1856, John Benjamin Smith MSS, MCL; Bright to Cobden, May 15, 1856, Bright MSS, BM 43,384; Cobden to Wilson, June 16, 1856, Wilson MSS, MCL.

(5) Joseph Parkes to Bright, Oct. 8, 1856, Bright MSS, BM 43,388; Henry Ashworth to Cobden, July 24, 1856; Aug. 29, 1856, Cobden MSS, BM 43,653; Bright to Cobden, Mar. 18, 1856; Aug. 8, 1856; Sept. 27, 1856, Bright MSS, BM 43,384; Bright to Wilson, May 8, 1856; June 11, 1856; July 17, 1856, Wilson MSS, MCL; Bright to Wilson, Nov. 5, 1856, Bright MSS, National Liberal

Club; Smith to Bright, Apr. 30, 1856, Bright MSS, BM 43,388; Cobden to Bright, Aug. 11, 1856; Oct. 13, 1856, Cobden MSS, BM 43,650; cf. Bright to Sturge, Aug. 23, 1855, Sturge MSS, BM 43,723.

(6) Bright to Cobden, Nov. 30, 1856, Bright MSS, BM 43,384; Bright to Wilson, Dec. 7, 1856, Wilson MSS, MCL; Cobden to Smith, Oct. 3, 1856; Nov. 8, 1856, John Benjamin Smith MSS, MCL; Cobden to Sir John Walmsley, Nov. 10, 1856, Cobden MSS, NYPL; Cobden to Joseph Parkes, Nov. 11, 1856, Cobden MSS, BM 43,664.

(7) Bright to Wilson, Jan. 8, 1857, Wilson MSS, MCL; Cobden to Parkes, Dec. 11, 1856, Cobden MSS, BM 43,664; Bright to Cobden, Jan. 21, 1857; Mar. 21, 1857, Bright MSS, BM 43,384.

(8) Bright to Cobden, Jan. 21, 1857, *ibid.; Diaries,* Jan. 13, 1857; Mar. 10, 1857; Apr. 26, 1857; Bright to Sir James Hudson, Apr. 28, 1857, Lacaita-Shelburne MSS, William L. Clements Library.

(9) *Diaries,* Feb. 20, 1857; Mar. 30, 1857; Cobden to Wilson, Mar. 9, 1857; Mar. 10, 1857; Bright to Wilson, Mar. 22, 1857, Wilson MSS, MCL; Bright to Cobden, Mar. 21, 1857, Bright MSS, BM 43,384; *The Times,* Apr. 10, 1857.

(10) Cobden to Bright, Mar. 6, 1857, Cobden MSS, BM 43,650; Bright to Wilson, Mar. 8, 1857, Bright MSS, National Liberal Club; Donald Read, "The Election of 1857: John Bright's Defeat," *Manchester Guardian,* Mar. 28, 1957; *Annual Register, 1857,* pp. 83–4; for Bright's later denunciations of British treatment of China, see *Parl. Deb.,* 157 (Mar. 16, 1860), 786; 175 (May 31, 1864), 974ff.; Bright to Cobden, Nov. 4, 1863, Bright MSS, BM 43,384; Bright to Sir Louis Mallet, May 17, 1869, Autograph MSS, BPL.

(11) *Punch,* XXXII (1857), 143; *Economist,* XIV (1856), 110–11; XV (1857), 363, 418; *Illustrated London News,* XXX (1857), 303.

(12) *Letters,* Mar. 31, 1857; Bright to Wilson, Mar. 31, 1857; Apr. 19, 1857, Wilson MSS, MCL; Bright to Cobden, Apr. 16, 1857, Bright MSS, BM 43,383; Milner Gibson to Cobden, May 2, 1857; Cobden to Parkes, May 5, 1857, Cobden MSS, BM 43,662–43,664.

(13) Bright to Cobden, Mar. 21, 1857, Bright MSS, BM 43,384; Morley, p. 661; Cobden to Wilson, May 30, 1857, Wilson MSS, MCL; Cobden to William Hargreaves, Apr. 7, 1857; Cobden to Samuel Warren, May 2, 1857; Cobden to Henry Pease, May 2, 1857; Cobden to Sturge, June 15, 1857, Cobden MSS, BM 43,655, 43,669, 43,656.

(14) Bright to Cobden, Apr. 16, 1857, Bright MSS, BM 43,384.

(15) Bright to Cobden, June 7, 1857, *ibid.;* Cobden to Bright, June 30, 1857; Sir James Clark to Cobden, July 7, 1857, Cobden MSS, BM 43,650; Parkes to Bright, June 28, 1857; Mrs. Milner Gibson to Bright, July 18, 1857, Bright MSS, BM 43,388.

(16) *The Times,* June 13, 1857; June 22, 1857; Aug. 12, 1857; *Letters,* Aug. 10, 1857; *Annual Register, 1857,* p. 151; *Illustrated London News,* XXXI

(1857), 159; *The Times,* Aug. 14, 1857; Bright to Sir Austen Henry Layard, Aug. 22, 1857, Layard MSS, BM 38,985.

(17) Cf. Bright to Cobden, July 10, 1857, Bright MSS, BM 43,384; Bright to Joseph Sturge, Aug. 15, 1857, Sturge MSS, BM 43,723; Milner Gibson to Bright, Aug. 13, 1857; Smith to Bright, Aug. 11, 1857, Bright MSS, BM 43,388; Morley, p. 663; Cobden to Sir Joshua Walmsley, Aug. 22, 1857, Cobden MSS, NYPL; Cobden to Bright, Aug. 11, 1857, Cobden MSS, BM 43,650.

(18) Cobden to Smith, Aug. 12, 1857, John Benjamin Smith MSS, MCL; Cobden to Parkes, Aug. 9, 1857, Cobden MSS, BM 43,664.

(19) Bright to Cobden, Aug. 15, 1857, Bright MSS, BM 43,384; Bright to Layard, Aug. 22, 1857, Layard MSS, BM 38,985; Bright to Walmsley, Aug. 22, 1857, Bright MSS, YUL.

(20) Morley, p. 669; see J. B. Harrison, *The Indian Mutiny* (London, 1958) and Ainslie T. Embree, ed., *1857 in India* (Boston, 1963); Cobden to Bright, June 30, 1857, Cobden MSS, BM 43,650; Smith to Bright, June 30, 1857, Bright MSS, BM 43,388.

(21) Bright to Smith, July 1, 1857, Smith MSS, MCL; Bright to Cobden, July 10, 1857, Bright MSS, BM 43,384; Bright to Layard, Aug. 22, 1857, Layard MSS, BM 38,985.

(22) Morley, p. 674; Cobden to Smith, May 19, 1857; Aug. 8, 1857, Smith MSS, MCL; Cobden to Bright, July 6, 1857; Aug. 24, 1857; Sept. 22, 1857, Cobden MSS, BM 43,650; Bright to Cobden, Aug. 15, 1857, Bright MSS, BM 43,384; Bright to Charles Bird, Sept. 10, 1857, Anthony MSS, NYPL; Bright to Sturge, Sept. 19, 1857, Sturge MSS, BM 43,723; Bright to Layard, Oct. 17, 1857, Layard MSS, BM 38,985.

(23) Bright to Wilson, Sept. 20, 1857; Dec. 4, 1857, Wilson MSS, MCL; Cobden to Bright, Dec. 3, 1857, Cobden MSS, BM 43,650; Bright to Sturge, Sept. 24, 1857; Oct. 11, 1857; Oct. 19, 1857, Sturge MSS, BM 43,723, 43,845; Bright to Layard, Oct. 17, 1857, Layard MSS, BM 38,985; Cobden to Wilson, Oct. 30, 1857, Wilson MSS, MCL; Bright to Cobden, Sept. 19, 1857; Nov. 24, 1857; cf. Oct. 24, 1861, Bright MSS, BM 43,384.

(24) Bright to Cobden, Sept. 19, 1857, *ibid.;* Bright to Wilson, Dec. 30, 1857, Wilson MSS, MCL; Bright to Sturge, Nov. 3, 1857, BM 43,845; *Letters,* Dec. 2, 1857; *The Times,* Dec. 4, 1857.

CHAPTER SEVEN

BACK AT WORK
1858

After an absence of two years and despite all his doubts and fears, Bright was sitting in the House of Commons in February 1858. Although he felt awkward about seeing some of his old colleagues, they were kind and cordial. They gave him a rousing reception; they inquired about his health; they gave him well-intentioned advice about getting to bed early and avoiding strain. (1)

He had hardly arrived when Palmerston was again under attack. This time Milner Gibson introduced the critical motion; Bright cheerfully seconded it; the motion was carried. Palmerston resigned and was replaced by Lord Derby as Prime Minister. There could not have been a more auspicious beginning for Bright. He came and Palmerston went. The news of this triumph of "retributive justice" was so gratifying that even Cobden was tempted to consider returning to the House of Commons. At last "the very worst Ministry" that either Bright or Cobden had known was ended; and now the "Impostor" would not be in such a favorable position to work up some new war scare. (2)

Bright took care of himself. He kept good hours, was firm about turning down invitations, walked a great deal. He tried, although with difficulty, to keep his mind off the family's business troubles that had worried him since the eve of the Panic of 1857. Under doctors' orders he continued to defy his temperance background and drink wine to ease his tensions. As much as possible, he stayed away from the Reform Club, agreeing with Cobden that the gossiping there—and the personality clashes—were bad for him. Furthermore, he postponed repeatedly the visit that he felt obliged to pay to the voters of Birmingham who had treated him with immense kindness; the visit, he knew, would be too much of a strain. (3)

He still had occasional outbursts of self-pity. As he confessed to his wife, he was bitter that because of his unpopular views, his future in politics was unpromising; he could not receive the honors and emoluments that far less gifted men obtained. Yet even as he complained he could hear his wife in Rochdale telling him to thank God for the return of his health as well as his other blessings. The fact is that he was grateful. He loved and enjoyed his children, and he appreciated his wife more and more as time went by. After eleven years of marriage, he told her, it was something for them not to be tired of each other. (4)

Already in March and April, Bright was less nervous and more and more self-confident. He spoke up in the House in favor of removing restrictions on travel and simplifying passport requirements. He denounced the East India Company for its irresponsible and immoral behavior, insisting that it was time that Parliament looked at things from the standpoint of "what was best for the people of India." Moreover, he urged what he considered to be the long overdue abolition of church rates, arguing that, despite what Church of England spokesmen said, this would benefit both morality and religion. (5)

There were other signs of Bright's returning self-confidence. He told his wife that the House of Commons "must have been dreadfully dull during the absence of our 'School.'" And he scolded Cobden for being unduly pessimistic about public affairs, suggesting that the intolerant patriotism of the British people was on the decline and that the time had again come to preach the virtues of a mild foreign policy. He recognized, however, that he was not fit to be the preacher. He was flattered to be asked to serve as leader of the small group of liberals in the House of Commons, but he was not strong enough to wage the battles that the role required. He could speak occasionally and briefly without damage to his health, but even then he felt that he was running risks. (6)

During May and June, he was so much better that he spoke up more frequently in the House. He deplored the extremes of poverty and wealth in Britain and lamented what he regarded as a fact—that the poor usually went to the wall, since they had to bear the brunt of the taxes that followed inevitably from the militant foreign policy to which successive British ministries were addicted. "Amity with all nations, justice and courtesy to all, but intimate political alliances with none," that was Bright's policy—one that lacked bravado and boasting. He bluntly warned the landed proprietors who dominated Parliament that their days of misleading the people were nearly over. Soon parliamentary reform would be accomplished; the House would really represent the population; the landlords would lose their tax privileges; and the combative diplomacy that they favored and the war scares that they encouraged would end. (7)

Bright even dared to make three lengthy speeches in the House. In one he argued that the secret ballot was the only real protection for the poor and defenseless in a society marked, as the British was, with such great contrasts of wealth and pauperism. Two other long speeches dealt with India. The second was especially remarkable. One of the greatest he ever made, it was filled with the humility, compassion, and respect for human dignity that characterized Victorian liberalism at its best. It gave no signs whatever that its author had only recently been a very sick man. Nor did it disclose any of the despair Bright frequently felt about the Indian Question because of the power of vested interests. (8)

He argued that the British rule in India had failed and that the Indians had legitimate grievances. They had had neither good nor efficient government nor an adequate administration of justice; their agriculture and industry were shockingly neglected; their usable roads and waterways were few; their tax burden was outrageous. The British in India, instead of undertaking desperately needed public works in the areas they already ruled, spent their time enriching themselves and conquering and annexing further territories to misrule.

Certainly the East India Company needed to be abolished but that was not enough, Bright maintained. Above all, the Governor-Generalship should be eliminated. It was far too dangerous and powerful an office, and no mere human being was adequate to meet its responsibilities in a country so complex because of its many peoples and languages. To replace the Governor-General, Bright suggested the division of British India into at least five Presidencies, each headed by a Governor and a Council, and each serving as a government for its people, and not for British civil servants. Each Council would include as members several natives in whom the inhabitants of the Presidency would have confidence, for it was only by uniting the governed with the government that domestic peace could be assured. All five Governors, to be sure, would correspond directly with the Secretary for India in Britain.

Unlike many of his contemporaries, Bright did not assume that the British rule in India would continue indefinitely. But under his scheme of reorganization, he predicted, the natives would be prepared to prevent anarchy when British sovereignty ended. He believed, moreover, that his proposal would help to improve Anglo-Indian relations. Although the British would always be hated as invaders and conquerors, he insisted that this hatred need not be so profound.

He concluded with a courageous appeal for the abandonment of the campaign of vilification against the natives of India that had been so intense in Britain since the outbreak of the Mutiny; these people were not barbarians and they were not savages. "The less we say about atrocities the better," Bright suggested. For the rest, he urged that an immediate general amnesty be issued; that the Princes be guaranteed the right to adopt heirs; and that the Indian population be assured their religious freedom would be respected. (9)

II

It was one thing for Bright to speak to his colleagues in the House; it was quite another for him to address a large public meeting. Yet he knew he would have to do this before long. His

Birmingham constituents had been patient, understanding, and undemanding, but he was aware that they expected him to visit their town and to talk to them.

In preparation for the ordeal he spent the summer and early autumn resting and relaxing as much as possible. He played with his children in Rochdale, and he fished in Scotland. All this helped; so did the news that the family business was improving. But all the while, he was thinking about the approaching visit. Deciding about the topics of his speeches was easy. He would talk about parliamentary reform and foreign affairs, the subjects about which he felt most strongly. Parliamentary reform was the great need that he had been emphasizing for years, even when the "Rule Britannia" craze had diverted attention from domestic problems. Now he would stress it again, especially since the session of 1858 had at last passed laws admitting Jews to Parliament and abolishing property qualifications for Members. (10)

Bright had no doubt that a reform bill would be enacted soon. But he was concerned that the aristocratic parties—both Whigs and Tories—would make it such a timid and puny measure that it would do more harm than good by once more postponing fundamental changes. The real task, therefore, Bright told Cobden, was to spread so much knowledge and arouse so much feeling that it would be impossible for an unsatisfactory bill to be carried. (11)

At last, after serving for months as Member for Birmingham, Bright visited his constituency at the end of October 1858. The reception he was accorded was extraordinary; and the attention his visit received in the national press was also extraordinary. As the reporter for *The Times* described the scene in the Town Hall at the end of Bright's first speech: He "sat down amid great cheering, which was renewed again and again, the audience rising and waving their hats and handkerchiefs in the most enthusiastic manner." Despite his passion for simplicity, he enjoyed the fuss that was made over him. He even quipped to his wife that perhaps he really was as great a man as everyone said. (12)

But the purpose of the visit was not small talk but speechmaking, and on October 27 he delivered his first public address

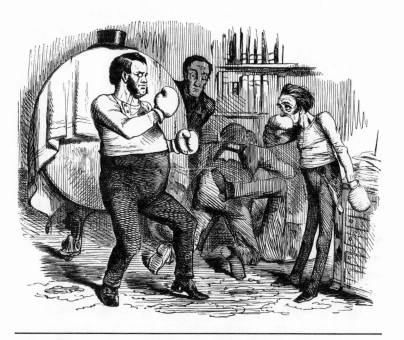

MR. BRIGHT OFFERS TO GIVE SATISFACTION
TO THE LIBERAL PARTY

☞ Mr. Bright rejected the timid Reform proposals of the Whigs, and demanded the widest extension of the franchise.—1858.

in almost three years. Its most striking feature was its candor. He surprised everyone by bringing up delicate matters that he had been expected to ignore. First, he spoke about his illness, describing his deterioration to "a condition of weakness exceeding the weakness of a little child, in which [he] could neither read nor write, nor converse for more than a few minutes without distress and without peril." Second, he referred bluntly to his rejection by Manchester; and then, although he confessed himself insufficiently master of the English language to express his feelings of gratitude, he thanked the voters of Birmingham for having come to his rescue. Third, he did not hesitate to proclaim the Crimean War

a folly and a crime. Correcting the widespread distortions of his
views, he pointed out that he did not believe in peace at any price;
nor did he oppose war under all circumstances. But the Russian
War was a mistake; it could and should have been prevented; and
its results were not worth what they had cost the British in lives
and taxes.

Turning to his main topic—parliamentary reform—Bright predicted that he would be accused of advancing subversive doctrines
and using violent language. As so often in the past, he would also
be attacked for trying to Americanize Britain. Since slavery was
the only American institution which he deplored—and he liked to
point out that it was introduced when the colonies were part of the
British Empire—he did not object to being called an Americanizer.
Just as the British had learned much from the literature, science,
and economics of other countries, so they could learn much from
politics in the United States.

Bright made his position clear: the current state of British
political institutions was splendid only for the landowning oligarchy.
The system of open voting made free elections impossible. The
narrow suffrage disfranchised five out of six adult males. Furthermore, the unequal, unjust, and dishonest distribution of seats in
the House of Commons made representation a sham and a farce.
As for the House of Lords, he confessed that while he had often
heard of its contributions to freedom, he was still unable to figure
out just what they had been.

He belittled the objections of those who opposed political reform. It was wrong to claim that secret voting was cowardly and
unmanly. It was absurd to argue that an enfranchised working class
would threaten property and make it impossible for the rich to
sleep quietly at night. And there could be no justification whatever
for the ridiculous way in which seats in the House of Commons
were allocated. The United States enjoyed a secret ballot, a widespread suffrage, and an equitable distribution of seats in the House
of Representatives. Yet in the United States none of the dreadful
things had happened that British opponents of these changes had
predicted would take place.

Bright cautioned his constituents to be wary of the reform bills that were soon likely to make their appearance. "Let us have a real Bill, a good Bill, or no Bill at all," he insisted, urging the adoption of a measure that would provide for a secret ballot, a widespread extension of the suffrage, and a reallocation of seats in keeping with the distribution of population. For, as long as open voting continued, intimidation would flourish. As long as current suffrage requirements continued, the working classes would be excluded. And as long as the prevailing distribution of seats continued, shocking irregularities would occur: 10 Yorkshire boroughs with a population of 80,000 would return 16 Members, whereas 8 other Yorkshire boroughs with a population of 620,000 would return only 14 Members; and the county of Bucks with a population of 164,000 would return 11 Members, while Birmingham with some 250,000 people would return 2 Members.

Bright concluded with a stirring call to action. He urged his listeners to hold meetings and draw up petitions. Above all he cautioned reformers to be vigilant and make sure that they were not duped by a sham reform bill. For the rest, he promised that as an individual he would do as much as he could: "I feel now sensibly and painfully that I am not what I was. I speak with diminished fire; I act with a lessened force; but as I am, my countrymen and my constituents, I will, if you will let me, be found in your ranks in the impending struggle." (13)

III

Bright did not have much time to rest after his speech. Two days later he made up for his long absence from Birmingham by delivering a second major address to his constituents. This time he was more daring, perhaps even masochistic, for he plunged into the dangerous subject of British foreign policy—the subject that had got him into so much trouble before.

He conceded that he loved peace and hated war and that as much as possible he favored the amicable settlement of disputes between nations. The result was that he had been called unpatriotic and un-English, and he confessed that this kind of name-calling infuriated him. In his best rhetorical style he asked:

How, indeed, can I, any more than any of you, be un-English and anti-national? Was I not born upon the same soil? Do I not come of the same English stock? Are not my family committed irrevocably to the fortunes of this country? Is not whatever property I may have depending as much as yours is depending upon the good government of our common fatherland? Then how shall any man dare to say to any one of his countrymen, because he happens to hold a different opinion on questions of great public policy, that therefore he is un-English, and is to be condemned as anti-national?

Bright placed himself solidly in what he regarded as the best English tradition, and he linked himself with such statesmen as Sir Robert Walpole, Charles James Fox, Earl Grey, and Sir Robert Peel, all of whom had struggled valiantly for peace in their time. And the reason they had to struggle was that ever since the Glorious Revolution other British leaders—mainly aristocrats—were stupidly interfering in the affairs of other countries. Using slogans like "the liberties of Europe" and "the balance of power," they involved Britain in wars that should have been avoided. Indeed, the more Bright studied their meddlesome foreign policy, the more convinced he became that it was "neither more nor less than a gigantic system of out-door relief for the aristocracy of Great Britain."

He decried this interventionist diplomacy because it was costly in both British lives and treasure. Even in times of peace it required ridiculously large expenditures for armaments. "I do not care for military greatness or military renown," he told his audience. "I care for the condition of the people among whom I live." To Bright it made much more sense to abandon foreign meddling and use the money for better purposes—to help, for example, to wipe out the shocking amount of pauperism in the most advanced country in the world.

To be sure, he recognized that the advocates of a militant diplomacy were powerful, and that they had succeeded in producing Chinese wars, Indian troubles, French invasion scares, and the Crimean disaster. But he also recognized that in the past generation several remarkable revolutions in opinion had taken place in Britain—in relation to parliamentary reform in 1832, to the corn laws in 1846, to the treatment of criminals, and to colonial policy. Perhaps, therefore, a revolution in opinion even in relation to foreign policy might be possible. Indeed, Bright would have liked to go down in history as one of those who had helped to effect this revolution; the more so because he was convinced that all sorts of desirable reforms would take place once the British people ceased to be diverted from their domestic problems by an interventionist diplomacy. (14)

The response of his friends and supporters to his Birmingham speeches was everything that Bright could have wished. They told him that he had never been more eloquent or in better form; and after his long absence from public meetings he needed such re-assurances. He was so pleased with the success of the Birmingham visit that he began to see himself once more in the role of a crusader leading the forces of Christian morality against the evil landowning classes. Now if only Cobden would join him! They worked so well together; they trusted each other; and they had such a wealth of experience on which to draw. "If you were with me now, and we had our old fire about us," he told Cobden, "we could do something that would be remembered as a great step for the people in this Country." But Cobden had suffered a series of domestic tragedies since the death of his son; and in any case he had such contempt for both Whigs and Tories that he saw no point in returning to public life. He thought it hopeless even to try to change their views. (15)

Bright was prepared for the attacks that his ideas were certain to provoke. He had a long case history of being denounced in the press, and now that he was feeling better, he could take the kind of treatment that *The Times,* the *Illustrated London News,* the *Manchester Guardian,* the *Economist, Punch,* and a host of lesser publications were meting out. What if the *Economist* treated him like a child who had not outgrown the political passion appropriate to the immature? What if the *Illustrated London News* labeled him "John the infallible, with all the intolerant assumption of a

Pope Hildebrand"? What if *The Times* made fun of him as one who pretended to be able to cure poor old England now that she was "fallen into a feeble and toothless old age"? He was, in fact, reminded of anti-corn law times and the hostility he had met then. Yet there was one striking difference: although he was attacked as before, now at least his speeches were reprinted at length or summarized and therefore publicized in the very papers that condemned him. What Cobden and he would not have done back in the early forties to have had their speeches on free trade made available to the public in this fashion! (16)

IV

The Birmingham visit had such an exhilarating effect on Bright that he felt ready to face even his Manchester enemies, not to mention his friends. His doctor told him not to go back to the town that had been the source of so much suffering to him, but his supporters in Manchester kept urging him to address a large public meeting in the Free Trade Hall with which he had been so closely associated in the past. He consented; George Wilson worked hard to make what was at best an awkward occasion a little less awkward; and in December, Bright gave his first speech in Manchester in almost three years. (17)

Again his subject was parliamentary reform, and what he said to his old constituents in Manchester was essentially what he had just said to his new constituents in Birmingham. What was different was his use of illustrations and striking details. He pointed out that it was bad enough that only one million out of six million adult male Britons had the right to vote; but it was even worse that fewer than 200,000 of those voters returned more than half the Members of the House of Commons. He reminded his audience that rotten boroughs were still very much with them, that the Reform Act of 1832 had not wiped them out (something that scholars have only recently rediscovered). And he emphasized that the one great result of that Act was that it had made possible the entry into the House of about a hundred independent Members who at different points defied the Whig and Tory landowners and won concessions for the people.

Bright took an obvious delight in demolishing some of the misrepresentations of his position. He was not a republican because he admired the United States; nor was he a traitor because he believed that the British should and could learn a great deal from the Americans. Indeed, he enjoyed pointing out what Britain had already received from the United States, apart from cotton, tobacco, and rice: brickmaking machinery, reapers, revolvers for those who wanted to protect themselves against French invaders, printing machines for some of the leading anti-American British newspapers, to say nothing of the works of Bryant, Whittier, Longfellow, Bancroft, Prescott, and Motley. And Bright made it clear that the secret ballot, a widespread suffrage, and a just scheme of representation would be welcome additions to the already impressive list of imports from America. (18)

More than anything else, it was Bright's fervent pro-Americanism that infuriated his critics and enemies, who proceeded to counter his generous praise of the United States with lavish doses of anti-Americanism. The *Illustrated London News* complained bitterly about his "strange hallucinations" about the United States. The *Economist* dwelt maliciously on the activities of American expansionists. *The Times* printed a letter that included the sentence, "He knows nothing at all about America. . . ." *Punch* dreaded the prospect of a House of Commons chosen along the lines of the House of Representatives and added a blunt "no thank you, Mr. Bright."

> Forgive us if your theory we beg to test by fact, JOHN,
> And examine (without spectacles) the Union in act, JOHN;
> With Club-law in its Congress, and Mob-rule in its streets, JOHN,
> Log-rollers in the lobby, when its Legislature meets, JOHN.
>
> With endless floods of Bunkum for useful legislation, JOHN,
> Barnburning, filibustering, wholesale repudiation, JOHN;
> The noblest of the citizens averse from public life, JOHN,
> For those who speak what riles the mob, the tar and feathers rife,
>   JOHN. (19)

Bright's appearance in Manchester convinced his supporters, who did not need to be convinced, that they had lost a first-rate spokesman in Parliament. His enemies were relieved that he no longer bore the name of their constituency and that for all practical purposes he was, as he put it to Wilson, "ostracized from Manchester." He did not reflect their opinions, and they did not want him to associate their community with his detestable doctrines. They had been wary of him from the beginning, and their doubts had been more than confirmed. The £10 borough franchise, enacted in 1832, was designed to exclude working-class voters, and that was a design that they favored and wished to preserve. From their point of view, Bright was a wretched Chartist who would do well to settle in the United States. That was where he belonged. (20)

NOTES

(1) Bright to Sturge, Jan. 8, 1858, Sturge MSS, BM 43,723; Bright to Smith, Feb. 1, 1858, John Benjamin Smith MSS, MCL; Bright to Mrs. Bright, Feb. 10, 1958, Bright MSS, UCLL.

(2) *Parl. Deb.*, 148 (Feb. 19, 1858), 1758; Bright to Mrs. Bright, Feb. 20, 1858, Bright MSS, UCLL; Bright to Cobden, Feb. 20, 1858, Bright MSS, BM 43,384; Cobden to Henry Ashworth, Feb. 27, 1858, Cobden MSS, BM 43,653; Bright to Joseph Cowen, Jr., Mar. 1, 1858, Cowen MSS, Newcastle-upon-Tyne Central Library; *Letters,* Mar. 1, 1858; *The Times,* Mar. 6, 1858; Morley, pp. 682–84.

(3) Bright to Sturge, Feb. 14, 1858; Feb. 27, 1858; Mar. 24, 1858; Apr. 13, 1858; May 5, 1858; May 6, 1858, Sturge MSS, BM 43,723; Cobden to Bright, Feb. 11, 1858; Feb. 20, 1858, Cobden MSS, BM 43,650; Bright to Cobden, Apr. 9, 1858, Bright MSS, BM 43,384; Cobden to William Hargreaves, Apr. 10, 1858, Cobden MSS, BM 43,655.

(4) Bright to Mrs. Bright, May 1, 1858; June 9, 1858; June 10, 1858; July 30, 1858, Bright MSS, UCLL.

(5) Bright to Sturge, Mar. 24, 1858; Apr. 13, 1858; Apr. 23, 1858; Aug. 16, 1858, Sturge MSS, BM 43,723; Bright to Smith, Mar. 31, 1858, John Benjamin Smith MSS, MCL; Bright to Cobden, Apr. 9, 1858, Bright MSS, BM 43,384; *Parl. Deb.,* 149 (Mar. 23, 1858), 599ff.; 149 (Mar. 26, 1858), 843ff.; 149 (Apr. 21, 1858), 1454.

(6) Bright to Mrs. Bright, Apr. 23, 1858, Bright MSS, UCLL; Cobden to Bright, Mar. 31, 1858, Cobden MSS, BM 43,650; Bright to Cobden, Apr. 9,

1858, Bright MSS, BM 43,384; Bright to Sturge, Apr. 23, 1858, Sturge MSS, BM 43,723.

(7) Bright to Mrs. Bright, June 5, 1858; June 9, 1858, Bright MSS, UCLL; cf. *Letters,* Mar. 25, 1858; *Parl. Deb.,* 149 (May 3, 1858), 2148ff.; 150 (May 18, 1858), 872; 150 (June 11, 1858), 1937ff.; 151 (June 21, 1858), 128ff.

(8) *Ibid.,* 150 (June 8, 1858), 1774ff.; *Speeches,* I, 35–84; *Parl. Deb.,* 150 (May 20, 1858), 944ff.; 151 (June 24, 1858), 330ff.

(9) Cf. Trevelyan, p. 267.

(10) *Letters,* May 26, 1858; *The Times,* Aug. 18, 1858; Bright to Mrs. Bright, July 29, 1858; July 31, 1958, Bright MSS, UCLL; Cobden to Bright, Sept. 20, 1858, Cobden MSS, BM 43,650; Bright to Cobden, Sept. 2, 1858; Sept. 26, 1858, Bright MSS, BM 43,384; Bright to Wilson, Oct. 2, 1858, Wilson MSS, MCL; Bright to Sturge, Oct. 25, 1858, Sturge MSS, BM 43,723.

(11) Cf. *Letters,* Feb. 1, 1858; *The Times,* Feb. 4, 1858; Bright to Sturge, Sept. 21, 1858, Sturge MSS, BM 43,723; Bright to Cobden, Sept. 26, 1858, Bright MSS, BM 43,384.

(12) *The Times,* Oct. 20, 1858; Oct. 28, 1858; Oct. 29, 1858; Oct. 30, 1858; *Illustrated London News,* XXXIII (1858), 397; Bright to Mrs. Bright, Oct. 27, 1858, Bright MSS, UCLL; *Diaries,* Oct. 27, 1858; Oct. 29, 1858.

(13) Cf. *Letters,* Sept. 1, 1858; *Speeches,* II, 3–30.

(14) *Ibid.,* 373–99.

(15) Richard Congreve to Bright, Nov. 6, 1858; Bright to Congreve, Nov. 12, 1858, Congreve MSS, BL; William Hunter to Bright, Nov. 30, 1858, Cowen MSS, Newcastle-upon-Tyne Central Library; Bright to Samuel A. Goddard, Jr., Oct. 30, 1858, Bright MSS, Vassar College Library; Bright to Cobden, Nov. 14, 1858, Bright MSS, BM 43,384; Cobden to Bright, Oct. 17, 1858, Cobden MSS, BM 43,650; Bright to Wilson, Nov. 20, 1858, Wilson MSS, MCL.

(16) *Economist,* XVI (1858), 1203; *Illustrated London News,* XXXIII (1858), 419; *The Times,* Nov. 8, 1858; cf. Cobden to Bright, Dec. 26, 1858, Cobden MSS, BM 43,650.

(17) Bright to Wilson, Nov. 20, 1858; Dec. 9, 1858, Wilson MSS, MCL; resolution of congratulations, Manchester, Dec. 10, 1858, RGL.

(18) *Speeches,* II, 31–52; *The Times,* Dec. 11, 1858; cf. Bright to G. H. Moore, Dec. 1, 1858, Bright MSS, NLI.

(19) Henry Drummond, *A Letter to Mr. Bright on His Plan for Turning the English Monarchy into a Democracy* (London, 1858), pp. 11, 22; *Illustrated London News,* XXXIII (1858), 419, 443–44; *Economist,* XVI (1858), 1233–34; *The Times,* Nov. 2, 1858; *Punch,* XXXIV (1858), 67; XXXV (1858), 223.

(20) Cf. Bright to Wilson, Oct. 2, 1858, Wilson MSS, MCL; successive issues of *Manchester Guardian,* Dec., 1858.

CHAPTER EIGHT

DOWN, UP, DOWN
1858–1860

In a phenomenal burst of energy Bright followed his visits to Birmingham and Manchester with short engagements in Edinburgh, Glasgow, London, Bradford, and Rochdale, where he also addressed well-attended rallies on the topic of parliamentary reform. It was clear that he was trying frantically to make up for the time he had lost because of illness. His specific aim was to arouse so much popular interest in reform that when Parliament met in 1859 Lord Derby's Government would be compelled by the pressures of outdoor agitation to introduce a satisfactory bill. A rash of public meetings, petitions, and tracts would produce desirable results, he hoped. (1)

His speech in Glasgow was especially remarkable. Noting that his opponents charged him with being repetitious in his statements and with using the same points and figures over and over, he humbly acknowledged the validity of their complaints. But, he pointed out, the fact remained that about 1/36 of the adult males of the country elected more than half the Members of the House of Commons. It was still a fact that rotten boroughs returned Members who regarded the House as a private club; that the middle classes were being unjustifiably frightened by the prospect of a working-class electorate; that the right to vote would increase the self-respect of workers and encourage social stability (although Bright himself detested the terms "middle classes" and "working classes"); that a more representative House of Commons would rule in the interests of the people, and not in the interests of the great landowners. (2)

For all his eloquence, Bright's public addresses failed in their

"IT WILL SOON BOIL!"

☞ The constituencies at this time were apathetic on the
Reform Question. Mr. Bright had been addressing
numerous Meetings to elicit popular support.—1858.

purpose. Lord Derby's so-called "reform" bill turned out to be unsatisfactory. On the floor of the House, Bright denounced it at the same time that he tried to expose some of the false statements that were being circulated about reform and about himself as a reformer. It was untrue, he insisted, that the voters did not care about reshaping the House of Commons. It was untrue that the working classes were dangerous and untrustworthy. And it was untrue that he was a subversive. Indeed, he insisted, he was a true conservative in his intentions, for it was only through an adequate scheme of parliamentary reform that the future safety of Britain could be assured. This was a point that he would make repeatedly in the next years, but there is no evidence that he won over his enemies. (3)

Although Lord Derby's bill was too timid for Bright, it was too advanced for a substantial number of other Members; it was defeated. Derby resigned, and in June 1859 Lord Palmerston formed his second Government. Fortunately, Bright could not know that this new Ministry would last for almost six and a half years. He was discouraged enough without this knowledge, and discouragement was bad for his health.

Personal matters as well as the course of political events disheartened Bright. He was profoundly saddened by the death of Joseph Sturge, the Birmingham Quaker who had been his friend and loyal supporter in all kinds of political weather. Furthermore, Cobden had gone to the United States to see, as he put it, "the hellish government that Bright is accused of wanting to import into England." And when Cobden was not readily available to consult about dozens of subjects, Bright felt unsure of himself. Cobden, for his part, was concerned about Bright's condition, fearing that he was putting on too much weight and filling up with too much blood. He wrote insistently to him from the United States, begging that he take care of himself. (4)

To be sure, Bright's health was not all that figured in his correspondence. Cobden marveled at the economic development of the United States, and he was certain that much of this progress was due not only to first-rate natural resources but to the exalted status of the American working classes. "It is this universal hope of rising in the social scale which is the key to much of the superiority that is visible in this country," he emphasized. Bright agreed heartily. This was the very point that he had been making for years in his own country. Stop treating British workers as outcasts, help to build up their self-respect, and Britain will be a far healthier and safer country. Ironically, however, Cobden reported that many rich Americans had been urging him to warn Bright about the dangers of too wide an extension of the right to vote. They were very unhappy about their broad suffrage, Cobden dutifully informed Bright—but, of course, with no effect whatever. (5)

Although Bright was saddened by many of the events of the first half of 1859, at least three facts cheered him appreciably: the birth of a son, his seventh child; the growing success of the Manchester School's newspaper, the *Morning Star*; and Cobden's return to the House of Commons. Since it was Bright who had relentlessly pressed Cobden to resume his parliamentary duties and who had arranged for Cobden to be invited to represent Rochdale in the House, he felt properly responsible for the happy ending. (6)

But little else was heartening. He was sickened by the muddle made by Lord Derby. He was depressed by the failure of the British to give greater security of land tenure to the Indian natives and by their failure to understand that the Mutiny was the result of British mismanagement and that the government of India had to be reconstructed. He was worried about the swift deterioration of Austro-French relations over the Italian Question and the possible repercussions. And he was alarmed by the renewed activities of the Invasionists, who were once more spreading the delusion that Napoleon was planning an attack on Britain. It is understandable that for no apparent reason Bright developed trouble with his voice and that even when he spoke in a small room, it would fail him. For, he was again both weary and afraid of public life; he could see no useful results growing out of his efforts. As he put it to John Benjamin Smith: "The world is handed over to the sons of Belial in the shape of Emperors, Kings, Lords, and soldiers, and in our time we cannot hope for any sensible progress towards a deliverance from them." (7)

II

Bright had dreaded another Palmerstonian regime, but ironically it got off to an auspicious beginning: Cobden and Milner Gibson were invited to join the Government. Bright was hurt and resentful that he was not asked, having been led to believe that he might be. But two trusted parliamentary colleagues had been invited, and that was certainly a victory for the Manchester School. Cobden, to be sure, refused; and Bright told himself—and others—that he would have done the same. How could he serve in a Government led by the greatest old sinner of them all? On the other hand, he did believe that, if he were in the Cabinet, he might be able to do some good. At a time when the Invasionists were again stirring up false fears and when the Austro-French War over the Kingdom of Sardinia might involve other countries, he might have been able to work within the Government for both British neutrality and international peace. (8)

Bright knew why he was not asked to join the Ministry. For years he had criticized such Whig leaders as Palmerston and Russell, and for years he had made devastating comments about the aristocracy and the Church of England, both in general and in particular. The wonder, therefore, was not that he failed to be invited to accept a Cabinet post but that he could have envisaged even for a moment the possibility of joining the Ministry. Furthermore, as Cobden was to remark, Bright's tendency in his speeches to exalt the working classes and to denigrate the upper classes had the effect of encouraging the middle classes to range themselves with the upper classes for protection against a suspected common danger. Not only that. As Cobden bluntly explained, Bright's role as a public speaker was damaging to his parliamentary position. For in his public addresses he was constantly lashing out at aristocrats and Anglican bishops; yet these people gave every indication of retaining power for a long time to come. To Cobden the moral was plain. If Bright was ambitious for a post in the Government, he would have to change his ways. He must confine his speech-making as much as possible to the floor of the House of Commons; and he must accept the reality, however painful, that the aristocracy and the Church of England were entrenched and would remain so at least as long as he would live. (9)

III

If Bright was unable to advocate the right kind of foreign policy as a member of the Cabinet, he could do so privately and above all in the House of Commons. He lost no time. In the course of a parliamentary speech on finance delivered in July, he noted gratefully that the Austro-French War had ended quickly; but unfortunately the Invasionists in Britain were still spreading their hatred and fear of France. Insisting that there was no basis for their alarm, Bright pleaded for more cordial Anglo-French relations, and to this end he suggested that steps be taken to encourage freer trade between the two countries. Closer economic ties, he argued, would prepare the way for better diplomatic relations. (10)

Bright's suggestion made sense to Michel Chevalier, the respected and well-connected French economist and the rightful hero of Professor Arthur L. Dunham's classic monograph on the Commercial Treaty of 1860. Through Chevalier's indefatigable efforts, Cobden, who planned to be in France with his family toward the end of the year, was introduced to influential French leaders, and with them he explored the possibilities of an Anglo-French commercial treaty. He was even given the opportunity to discuss the subject with the Emperor; and Cobden appealed to Napoleon's sense of history, telling him how profoundly the memory of Sir Robert Peel was treasured in Britain because of his contribution to freer trade. Of all the arguments that Cobden used, the one that he thought carried most weight with Napoleon concerned the higher standard of living that British workers enjoyed compared with their French counterparts.

Having sworn Bright to secrecy, Cobden kept him informed about the progress of the discussions and negotiations with French leaders; and Bright speedily resumed his old role of morale-lifter. He begged Cobden to be patient and not to let himself become discouraged. He made all kinds of useful technical suggestions. Above all, he kept reminding Cobden of what was at stake: a commercial treaty was the best possible device by which to strike out at the wild patriots in Britain who were spoiling for a war with France. As in the past both Bright and Cobden considered freer trade not an end in itself but chiefly a means by which to promote international peace. Commercial relations would accomplish what the Christian churches had failed to do. (11)

The happy day came in January 1860, when Cobden reported to Bright that he had just signed the Commercial Treaty. To be sure, plenty of work—and irritation—lay ahead. In Bright's words: "The 'services' and the tax-eaters, the courtiers and the war men, are all hard hit by the Treaty and hate it even more than they dare to tell." Ill-tempered discussions took place both in Parliament and the press; individual British businessmen raised strong objections; and further outbreaks of the Invasionist panic added to the difficulties. The strain on Cobden for practically the rest of the year was immense; but it would have been far worse if Bright had not defended the cause in Parliament and if the able Peelite William E. Gladstone had not resisted Cobden's enemies both in Parliament and the Cabinet.

To Cobden, Bright, and Gladstone, the vital thing about the Treaty was not so much its freer trade provisions as the promise it held of better Anglo-French relations. Peace would mean disarmament; fewer military expenditures would mean lower taxes; lower taxes would benefit everybody but in particular the working classes, who bore the heaviest burden of taxation in proportion to their income. This is what Bright had in mind when he told Cobden that he had "done a glorious work—one never to be forgotten or too highly valued." And some contemporaries agreed with him. But Cobden was convinced that nearly all his countrymen regarded the Treaty as a ruse, himself as a dupe, and the Emperor as a diabolical manipulator who could now go ahead with his plans to invade Britain. Indeed, it was a kind of poetic justice that, just as Cobden was bringing his labors to an end in November, Sir Charles Napier, one of the most hysterical of the Invasionists, died; and Bright could not resist hoping that there would "be no French Fleet to disturb his rest in the world to which he is gone." (12)

Because of the pressures of the Invasionists for bigger and better fortifications and the fury of British superpatriots over the French annexation of Savoy as the price of French aid to the Kingdom of Sardinia in the war against Austria, the Commercial Treaty of 1860 was a remarkable victory—much more so than many historians have realized. And at the end of the year it was succeeded by another important measure that augured well for Anglo-French relations. Bright, spending a week with Cobden in France, had an interview with Napoleon in the course of which he suggested that passports were unnecessary evils. Napoleon agreed and proceeded to abolish the passport requirements for Britons visiting France. Not only goods but people would now move more freely between the two countries. Bright was enormously pleased. Good causes did win sometimes, after all; progress sometimes did take place. (13)

IV

The success of Cobden's mission to Paris encouraged Bright and led him to believe that other reforms for which he had worked might prosper. Often he still despaired of being able "to lift up our population into freemen and to bring down the lofty pretensions of the ruling class"; and often he was overwhelmed by what he regarded as aristocratic wickedness and middle-class folly, ignorance, and lackeyism. But now with the prospect of peace with France, perhaps some serious attention would at last be given to important domestic problems. For Bright was outraged—and delighted—by some of the ugly scandals that had broken out late in 1859 concerning corrupt elections in small boroughs, and he hoped that the publicity given to some of the more shocking malpractices would have the effect of demonstrating how right he was: a far-reaching measure of parliamentary reform was urgently needed. (14)

Again Bright miscalculated. Lord John Russell's moderate bill of 1860 quickly joined the growing heap of unsuccessful attempts to reform Parliament. It was plain, in short, that despite Bright's speeches and despite some juicy revelations of electoral corruption, few Members were eager for political reform. Furthermore, only a small portion of the public seemed to care about the condition of Parliament. Many middle-class people were actively opposed to

THE QUAKER AND THE BAUBLE

"It is the Land which the territorial party represents in Parliament. * * * That is the theory of the Constitution: BLACKSTONE *says so. But it is a thing which is not likely to be respected much longer, and it must go, even if involving the destruction of the Constitution."*—MR. BRIGHT, *in his Penny Organ.*

☞ The "Morning Star"—a journal founded to advocate the views of Mr. Bright—met with little support. After an uncertain existence of some years, it was discontinued.—1859.

extending the right to vote to potentially dangerous workers; and affluence was encouraging among all classes widespread indifference to political change. As Cobden frankly told Bright: "I have never had confidence in the zeal of the electoral body for a reform which lessens their power by diffusing it over a lower layer of society. A generous impulse or a sense of danger might give rise to the sudden desire to take the masses into partnership, but in ordinary quiet times this is not the state of feeling." The truth, Cobden added, was that the masses were not pressing for political change. (15)

To Bright it was bad enough that Palmerston would now postpone parliamentary reform to some vague date in the future; but it was even worse that Bright's model of a country—what *Punch* called his "promised land"—was in serious political difficulties in 1860. American governmental institutions, to which he had so often pointed with admiration, and features of which he wished the British to adopt, were rapidly breaking down. He could hardly believe what he read in the papers. For he was so convinced of the genius of American politics that until the Civil War began he thought that it would be averted. (16)

If the course of events in the United States took Bright by surprise, the reasons are plain. He assumed that slavery had reached its culmination as a political question, that increasingly it would be dealt with only as a moral and an economic question, and that on those grounds it would be abolished. Bright had hoped that William H. Seward, in whose judgment he had great faith, would be elected President in 1860 and that he would provide the vigorous leadership needed to eliminate the one great blot on American civilization. (17)

Punch quipped that it was "the blackest hypocrisy" that the United States should pretend to be a land of freedom as long as slavery existed there. Except for slavery, however—and it was for him a big exception—Bright steadfastly considered the United States the finest country in the history of the world. Its people had advantages that no other people had ever had, and they used their advantages brilliantly. Their moral, educational, political, and economic progress demonstrated what a blessed nation they were and how unfortunate the peoples of Europe were in comparison. In particular

Bright marveled at the low level of military expenditures in the United States, which made possible low taxes and a higher standard of living for the masses of the population. He rejoiced in the achievements of the northern states in the field of education. Indeed, he had no doubt that he would have been far happier in New England than in old England—especially when the powerful British "sons of Belial" perpetrated some new outrage on France, on China in the age of the opium wars, or on the incredibly credulous British people. (18)

Bright quickly grasped the implications for Britain of the American political crisis. Now British enemies of the secret ballot, a generous suffrage, and a redistribution of parliamentary seats would point to the United States as a bad example. They would argue that there was nothing that the British could or should learn from the American Republic—what *Punch* now called the "UNTIED STATES"— except to avoid its dangerous and unstable political institutions. "What's now to admire there, JOHN BRIGHT, JOHN BRIGHT? / What's now to admire there, JOHN BRIGHT?," as *Punch* gloated. It is understandable, therefore, that between 1861 and 1865 Bright saw the American Civil War as by far the most important event in contemporary British history. The future of British parliamentary reform would depend on the outcome of the struggle in America. (19)

NOTES

(1) *Mr. Bright's Speeches (Revised by Himself) at Birmingham, Manchester, London, Edinburgh, Glasgow, Bradford, and Rochdale* (London, 1859); *The Times,* Dec. 17, 1858; Dec. 23, 1858; Jan. 29, 1859; Bright to Wilson, Jan. 1, 1859, Wilson MSS, MCL; Bright to William Williams, Jan. 19, 1859, Bright MSS, YUL; Bright to John Richardson, Mar. 17, 1859, Bright MSS, Humanities Research Center, University of Texas.

(2) *The Times,* Dec. 23, 1858.

(3) *Parl. Deb.,* 152 (Feb. 28, 1859), 1029; 153 (Apr. 4, 1859), 1315; 161 (Feb. 5, 1861), 109; *Letters,* Nov. 3, 1860.

(4) Bright to Lord John Russell, June 16, 1859, Bright MSS, Duke University Library; cf. *Economist,* XVI (1858), 1177; Bright to Cobden, Feb. 6, 1859; cf. Oct. 25, 1860, Bright MSS, BM 43,384; Bright to Smith, May 23, 1859, John Benjamin Smith MSS, MCL; Cobden to Henry Ashworth, Jan. 7,

1859; Cobden to Joseph Parkes, Feb. 5, 1859, Cobden MSS, BM 43,653, 43,664.

(5) See Elizabeth Hoon Cawley, ed., *The American Diaries of Richard Cobden* (Princeton, 1952); Cobden to Bright, Apr. 29, 1859, Cobden MSS, BM 43,651.

(6) Bright to Richard Congreve, Feb. 24, 1859, Congreve MSS, BL; Bright to Wilson, Mar. 17, 1859, Wilson MSS, MCL; *The Times,* Apr. 16, 1859; Bright to Joseph Sturge, Apr. 7, 1859; May 3, 1859, Sturge MSS, BM 43,723.

(7) *Parl. Deb.,* 152 (Feb. 4, 1859), 112ff.; 152 (Mar. 7, 1859), 1359ff.; 154 (June 9, 1859), 217ff.; 155 (July 21, 1859), 190ff.; 155 (Aug. 1, 1859), 801ff.; Bright to Abraham Greenwood, May 11, 1859, Bright MSS, Equitable Pioneers Society Ltd. Library, Rochdale; Bright to Smith, April 13, 1859; May 23, 1859, Smith MSS, MCL; Bright to Joseph Cowen, Jr., Sept. 1, 1859, Cowen MSS, Newcastle-upon-Tyne Central Library.

(8) Bright to Wilson, June 15, 1859, Wilson MSS; Bright to Smith, June 28, 1859, Smith MSS, MCL.

(9) Cobden to Bright, Dec. 16, 1859; Dec. 29, 1859, Cobden MSS, BM 43,651.

(10) *Parl. Deb.,* 155 (July 21, 1859), 214; cf. 156 (Feb. 23, 1860), 1619ff.; Bright to Brougham, July 21, 1859, Brougham MSS, UCLL; cf. Bright to Cobden, Oct. 6, 1859, Bright MSS, BM 43,384.

(11) Arthur Louis Dunham, *The Anglo-French Treaty of Commerce of 1860 and the Progress of the Industrial Revolution in France* (Ann Arbor, 1930); Franklin Charles Palm, *England and Napoleon III* (Durham, 1948); J. M. Thompson, *Louis Napoleon and the Second Empire* (New York, 1955) stresses Disraeli's contribution; Cobden to Bright, Oct. 3, 1859; Oct. 17, 1859; Nov. 2, 1859; Nov. 17, 1859; Nov. 20, 1859; Dec. 29, 1859; Jan. 3, 1860; Jan. 16, 1860, Cobden MSS, BM 43,651; Bright to Cobden, Oct. 6, 1859; Nov. 15, 1859; Nov. 16, 1859; Nov. 25, 1859; Dec. 12, 1859; Jan. 12, 1860; Jan. 18, 1860, Bright MSS, BM 43,384.

(12) *Annual Register, 1860,* p. 102; *Parl. Papers,* 1860, LXV; Cobden to Bright, Jan. 23, 1860; Jan. 27, 1860; Jan. 30, 1860; Feb. 10, 1860; Feb. 27, 1860; Mar. 6, 1860; May 25, 1860; June 15, 1860; Aug. 25, 1860; Sept. 11, 1860; Oct. 30, 1860; Nov. 6, 1860; Dec. 7, 1860, Cobden MSS, BM 43,651; Bright to Cobden, Jan. 18, 1860; Feb. 5, 1860; Feb. 8, 1860; Feb. 13, 1860; Feb. 26, 1860; May 20, 1860; Nov. 10, 1860; Nov. 17, 1860, Bright MSS, BM 43,384; James Spence to Cobden, June 2, 1860, Board of Trade MSS 33/2, PRO; Cobden to Jules Le Chevalier St. André, May 29, 1860, Autograph MSS, ULL.

(13) *Parl. Deb.,* 156 (Mar. 5, 1860), 2241ff.; 160 (Aug. 2, 1860), 506ff.; cf. *National Review,* X (1860), 522–44; Cobden to Bright, July 25, 1860; Sept. 18, 1860; Dec. 31, 1860, Cobden MSS, BM 43,651; Bright to Mrs. Bright, Nov. 24, 1860; Nov. 25, 1860, Bright MSS, UCLL; Bright to Cobden, Dec.

20, 1860, Bright MSS, BM 43,384; Smith to Bright, Jan. 15, 1861, Bright MSS, BM 43,388; Bright to Smith, Jan. 18, 1861, Smith MSS, MCL.

(14) Bright to Mrs. Bright, Jan. 30, 1860; Apr. 30, 1860; June 19, 1860, Bright MSS, UCLL; Bright to Cobden, Aug. 21, 1859; Oct. 6, 1859; Feb. 5, 1860; Mar. 17, 1860; May 20, 1860; Nov. 10, 1860, Bright MSS, BM 43,384; cf. Cobden to Bright, Feb. 19, 1861, Cobden MSS, BM 43,651; Bright to Joseph Cowen, Jr., Sept. 1, 1859; Dec. 16, 1859, Cowen MSS, Newcastle-upon-Tyne Central Library; Bright to Smith, Oct. 6, 1859, Smith MSS, MCL; Bright to unnamed correspondent, Dec. 12, 1859, Hope MSS, University of Liverpool Library.

(15) *Parl. Deb.,* 156 (Jan. 26, 1860), 182ff.; 157 (Mar. 23, 1860), 1144; 158 (May 1, 1860), 497ff.; Bright to Cobden, Mar. 7, 1860, Bright MSS, BM 43,384; Cobden to Bright, June 15, 1860, Cobden MSS, BM 43,651.

(16) Bright to Cowen, Aug. 13, 1860, Cowen MSS, Newcastle-upon-Tyne Central Library; Bright to Cobden, June 17, 1860; Dec. 2, 1860; Feb. 6, 1861, Bright MSS, BM 43,384; Bright to Smith, Dec. 6, 1860, Smith MSS, MCL.

(17) Bright to Frederick M. Edge, July 2, 1860, Seward MSS, University of Rochester Library; Bright to Cobden, May 20, 1860, Bright MSS, BM 43,384.

(18) *Punch,* XXXIX (1860), 120; Bright to Cobden, Jan. 12, 1860; June 17, 1860; July 3, 1860; July 25, 1860; Oct. 10, 1860, Bright MSS, BM 43,384; Bright to Mrs. Bright, July 15, 1860, Bright MSS, UCLL; Bright to R. B. Reed, Aug. 16, 1860, Bright MSS, Newcastle-upon-Tyne Central Library; Cobden to Bright, July 27, 1860; Aug. 13, 1860, Cobden MSS, BM 43,651.

(19) *Punch,* XL (1861), 72, 232; XLI (1861), 243.

CHAPTER NINE

WATCHFUL WAITING
1861–1863

Although Bright turned fifty in 1861, he felt a good deal older. Not only had he faced a mass of disappointments, but he had retained little of his old faith in the future, for he saw almost no possibility of winning support for the changes that would make Britain the kind of country he wished it to be. The great landowners were as powerful as they had been in his youth, and the middle classes lacked self-respect and manliness and overflowed with deference and flunkeyism. Palmerston and Russell dominated the political scene and the Foreign Office, and Bright expected them to pursue the same misguided policies in the future that they had followed in the past: "The one is without heart for any good, and the other is so capricious as to be almost without head." And the troubles in the United States would tempt them to display once more their infinite capacity for mischief and evil. (1)

It is true that at the outset Bright regretted the American recourse to violence, but as soon as the war began he saw it plainly as God's instrument for the destruction of slavery. Therefore, he could hardly wait for President Lincoln to take steps to abolish the vicious institution inflicted by the British on colonial America. And long before the Preliminary Emancipation Proclamation of September 1862, Bright implored his American friends to press for such a measure. Certainly he believed that the war was being waged to preserve the Union; but from the beginning he wanted it to be fought explicitly to rid the Republic of its only major evil. As he wrote to Cobden with a clarity that has rarely been achieved by historians dealing with the coming of the Civil War: "Surely the whole question is one of slavery. The North was divided between those who would abolish, those who would control it, and those who would tolerate it for the sake of the Union. The South was and is against its abolition, and against its limitation, and prefers its perpetual existence to the Union itself...." (2)

Bright had no sympathy for those who belatedly discovered that Britain would be faced with a calamitous shortage of cotton. For years he had stressed the dangers of British dependence on the American South as a source of supply; and in the interests of both Britain and the natives he had urged the cultivation of cotton in India. But no one had acted on his suggestions in pre-Mutiny days. Even in the years since the Mutiny nothing of importance had been done to improve and diversify Indian agriculture, to develop communication and transportation facilities, and to raise the standard of living of the native population. It seemed to Bright that the result of this typical British lack of imagination and foresight would be widespread suffering on the part of many innocent people. But Bright had become convinced that only suffering would stir his countrymen to the right kinds of action. Just as the Irish Famine had made the repeal of the corn laws possible, so the cotton famine might make possible the reorganization of Indian agriculture. At least he was hopeful that British textile workers would not experience undue hardships. They had recently been employed at relatively high wages, and even if they had to work at half-time, they could still support their families. (3)

II

It was no surprise that Bright deplored much in British behavior in the early stages of the Civil War. He was enraged by the British Government's issuing of its Proclamation of Neutrality just as the new American minister Charles Francis Adams arrived to assume his duties. Furthermore, Bright was infuriated by the vicious anti-Unionism of *The Times, Punch,* and other influential publications; he could not understand how any honest man could allow *The Times* into his home. And he was appalled by some of the outrageous and gleeful public speeches of the British enemies of the North.

Above all, he was alarmed in late 1861 by the ease and irresponsibility with which people spoke of going to war with the United States at the time of the Trent Affair. Bright had no doubt that Captain Charles Wilkes was wrong to have seized the Confederate agents Mason and Slidell from a British ship. But Bright also had no doubt that this was precisely the kind of international dispute that should be settled by arbitration, not by threats of war, and he wrote to this effect in a series of friendly letters to Charles Sumner, the chairman of the United States Senate Committee on Foreign Relations. He cautioned Sumner about the strength of the "Rule Britannia" forces, and suggested that one war at a time was enough for the North. (4)

Publicly Bright made his position clear in an important address delivered in Rochdale in December 1861. He reminded his countrymen that the Americans were a people mainly of British origins; and for this reason, among many others, the British should sympathize with them in their present distress. He also reminded his countrymen of the meaning of secession. Would the British permit a group of counties to withdraw from the United Kingdom? Would they permit a return to the Heptarchy? The question was patently absurd. Mainly, however, Bright emphasized the urgency of taking a long-range view of the American conflict. While he would not dare to predict how long the struggle would last or who would win, he did predict without hesitation that the wrong kind of British behavior then would have disastrous results for years to come. Since the enmity of the United States was a luxury that the British could not afford, the only proper policy for Britain was one of sympathetic neutrality.

Bright did not let this opportunity escape to praise conditions of life in the United States. He insisted that Americans could teach the world much about education, inventions, the secret ballot, a democratic suffrage, a small military establishment, low taxes, and the humane treatment of criminals. Moreover, he prayed that the speedy end of the war would permit them to return to their laudable peacetime activities. (5)

Bright did not expect his speech to do any harm, but he doubted that it would do much good. The Government's ostentatious preparations for war—in particular, sending troops to Canada—and the martial spirit in the press convinced him that those who determined policy were eager for a fight. Indeed, he urged his old colleague Milner Gibson to withdraw from the Government if it intended to wage war on the United States. At the same time he begged Milner Gibson to use whatever influence he had to press for arbitration and to combat the unreason and passion that were rife in government circles. In Bright's Burkian words: "Magnanimity and not meanness should be our course in regard to a country in such extreme difficulty." Although he did not look for this quality in Palmerston, Russell, the military services, the oligarchy that hated and feared the United States, and "the rich flunkies," he did expect it in Milner Gibson and several other Cabinet members, and he hoped that an occasion would soon arise when British generosity could be useful in preventing war. (6)

Defenders of the Union—both American and British—were delighted with Bright's speech, and they told him so in the most flattering terms. They hoped that God would bless him for his noble performance; they were certain that his speech would produce admirable results; they prophesied that it would go down in history as a major contribution to the cause of freedom and humanity. Weeks after he delivered the speech he continued to receive letters flowing with praise. In fact, his American admirers assured him that no contemporary Englishman was so highly regarded in the United States. (7)

Ironically, however, for many months Bright had again been thinking of abandoning public life, feeling it pointless any longer to "attempt to carry the world on my own shoulders." His brother Thomas was ill and lacked the energy to run the family business; he was accomplishing nothing in public life; and with all the talk of war with the United States, Parliament was now no place for him. The treatment he had received during the Crimean conflict was painfully fresh in his memory; he would never again expose himself to the abuse reserved for those who refused to share in a British war fever. Having suffered enough at the hands of the "knaves and dupes" who were his countrymen, he had no intention of wrecking himself again in an attempt to prove another British war wicked. (8)

An Anglo-American war did not grow out of the Trent Affair because moderate people in both countries made concessions. In Britain Queen Victoria and Prince Albert—then close to death— worked hard for a peaceful settlement of the dispute. In the United States Senator Charles Sumner, present at a famous Christmas Day session of Lincoln's Cabinet, read warm letters from Bright and Cobden pleading for Anglo-American harmony. Shortly afterwards, the Southern commissioners were released. (9)

Bright was pleased to have played a part in promoting international peace, but the amicable settlement of the Trent Affair did not encourage him to believe that similar crises would have the same happy ending. Like Cobden, he feared that the Union blockade was likely to give rise to dangerous incidents, and he expressed this fear repeatedly to Northern leaders. His chief hope was that God would grant such a speedy victory to the North that firebrands in Britain or France would not have the chance to take advantage of the American troubles. (10)

III

Bright was, of course, appalled by the condition of British domestic politics in 1862. Palmerston, "the hoary impostor," was in full control, and Parliament was not dealing with the important subjects—India and parliamentary reform. Bright even wondered what the sense was in holding a parliamentary session in these circumstances. Instead of wasting time in the House of Commons, he would have preferred to be with his wife and children in Rochdale or on vacation in Scotland. At one point he implored his colleagues in the House to abolish church rates so that the session would be memorable for something other than time-wasting. (11)

He followed the course of the American War both intensely and anxiously, looking for signs that the slavocracy was coming to the grief it deserved. Since so much was at stake, he would have paid close attention in any case, but because the domestic political scene in Britain was so bleak, his interest was even keener. He read everything he could find about the war; he saw as many visiting Americans as he could—Cyrus W. Field and Thurlow M. Weed, among others; and he corresponded with a host of influential American leaders, notably Charles Sumner. The result was that Shiloh, Second Bull Run, Antietam, and Fredericksburg were not just names to him. In the light of his love of peace, he was, in fact, ashamed of the interest he took in the military phases of the struggle, as he confessed to Sumner and others. Nevertheless, he saw how relevant the American conflict was to any future reform movement in Britain. Far more important, he saw the war as one of the few in history that had a really righteous aim: Northern arms were blessed because they would liberate some four million Negroes. And Bright felt a compassion for the slaves that rivaled that of the most selfless American abolitionist. "I believe the deliverance of the whole Negro race may come from this terrible strife," he told his wife. "If there be a moral Government of the world, surely this afflicted race will not always be forgotten!" he wrote to Cobden. (12)

He never made the mistake of believing that many of his highly placed countrymen shared his feelings. It pained him that there was more pro-Southern sentiment among statesmen and leading newspapers in Britain than in any other European country, and for this reason he worried about the efforts of Southern agents to win formal British recognition of the Confederacy. He knew that Palmerston and other important members of the Government would have been overjoyed to see the American Republic permanently divided and weakened. When Gladstone in effect joined this group by way of a speech he delivered in October 1862 in Newcastle-on-Tyne, Bright went into a panic and a rage. (13)

For years he had had mixed feelings about this colleague. Sometimes he considered him a fine man—the only great hope of British liberalism—as when Gladstone ingeniously succeeded in his budget of 1860–1861 in abolishing the duty on paper, thus eliminating the last of the taxes on knowledge. At other times Bright found him weak, indecisive, hypocritical, opportunistic, and power-mad. And now Bright had no use for him whatever. How could any Englishman who loved God, Christian morality, and liberty favor recogni-

BRIGHT THE PEACE-MAKER

☞ Mr. Bright took an active part in supporting the repeal of the Paper Duty. He condemned the action of the Upper House in rejecting the Bill, and charged them with usurping the powers properly belonging to the Commons.—1860.

tion of the Confederacy? Bright never forgot or forgave what Gladstone said in his speech—in particular his remarks that Jefferson Davis and other Southern leaders had made not only an army and a navy but a nation and that their success was certain. Although Bright could only conclude that the Gladstone family's slaveholding background had tainted him and deadened his moral sense, it is clear that if the South had won the Civil War Gladstone's speech would have gone down not as one of his greatest blunders but as one of his most masterly strokes of political genius. (14)

Bright was unmoved by Southern appeals to states' rights, free trade, political liberty, or self-determination; and he had long since won Cobden to his position. Nevertheless, his fear of the British defenders of the South made him all the more anxious for the United States to deal boldly with the slavery question. Although he understood the delicacy of President Lincoln's position in relation to the border states, he was certain that emancipation would have healthy effects in Britain and elsewhere in Europe. For, once the slaves were freed, any Briton or European who advocated recognition of the Confederacy would expose himself for what he really was: a champion of slavery. Nor is there any doubt that Bright's reasoning proved to be sound. As Henry Steele Commager has put it: "Public opinion, that newly emerging and still amorphous thing, simply would not tolerate going in on the side of slavery." (15)

In December 1862, Bright delivered another major address on the American Question. He explicitly blamed the British Government for the cotton famine and its hardships, insisting again that if India had been properly developed there would have been no dearth of cotton. For years, however, the British Government had neglected and abused India, and now the result was widespread suffering in Britain. Still, Bright had no doubt that British cotton textile workers, though hard hit, would make sacrifices in behalf of the American Union. Unlike some of their most illustrious political leaders, they knew that the United States was fighting their battle, and hence they opposed the recognition of the Confederacy and its society based on slave labor. Bright granted that not all the British had the good judgment of British workers, confessing his grief that so many prominent people were on the side of the South—more than in any other European country. Even Gladstone, he noted bitterly, was predicting a Confederate victory; at least, Bright rejoiced, while the Chancellor of the Exchequer could make decisions about taxes, he was unable to decide the future of the United States.

Bright was blunt in stating his view of the meaning of sympathizing with the South, of recognizing the South, or of intervening in behalf of the South. The Confederate war aim was to keep four million people—and their descendants—in bondage; people "made black by the very Hand that made us white" were to be enslaved forever. Obviously, the Confederacy was a "great conspiracy against human nature," and the sooner the British people understood this, the better.

At the same time Bright proclaimed his boundless admiration for the Free States—doubtless in response to those who ridiculed his pro-Americanism. Unlike Britain, the Americans did not exclude millions of adult males from the suffrage. Nor did the people have only free votes. They also had free churches, schools, land, and opportunities. To Bright, the Free States were above all "the home of the working man," and he reminded British workers that there would be "one wild shriek of freedom to startle all mankind if that American Republic should be overthrown."

He conceded that perhaps, as Gladstone maintained, the cause of the North was hopeless and the restoration of the Union impossible. But Bright's view of the United States continued to be that of "one people, and one language, and one law, and one faith, and, over all that wide continent, the home of freedom, and a refuge for the oppressed of every race and of every clime." (16)

It is doubtful that any American Unionist could have defended the North more passionately. Bright even dared to include in his speech a section on the *Alabama*, the Confederate raider that was built in Britain and began in 1862 its career of destroying Union ships. And he made it plain that the North had every reason to be furious with the British Government for having permitted the cruiser to be built in Britain, much less to depart from a British port. Small wonder that Bright's British enemies suggested that he ought to move to the United States. In *Punch*'s words:

Of the Old World and New, their wrongs and rights,
　Freedom disowns the picture thou hast drawn,
Thy deepest darks are still her highest lights,
　And what to her seems night thou makest dawn.

Small wonder, too, that his friends, both American and British, overwhelmed him with praise. "A nation greets thee o'er the wave, John Bright!"—so began a poem by an ardent Northerner. His speech, another American told Bright, would give his name "a lustre such as has belonged to that of no British subject since the time of

Chatham." John Greenleaf Whittier, whom Bright respected both as a Quaker and a writer, thanked him profusely for his "eloquent and truthful presentation of the great questions involved in our terrible arbitrament." John Lothrop Motley, whose writings on Dutch history Bright admired, told him that a statue should be erected in his honor in Washington. And Cobden, generous as ever, reported that Goldwin Smith, the tough-minded Regius Professor of Modern History at Oxford, considered Bright the finest modern representative of the style of Demosthenes. (17)

IV

If Bright was, on the whole, more cheerful in 1863—his friends reported that he was looking young and well—the main reason was that the Emancipation Proclamation took effect on January 1. He was aware of the difficulties that surrounded the issuance of the Proclamation, and he knew what a limited emancipation it granted. But the Civil War was at last plainly a struggle over freedom and slavery, and now that it possessed this character unmistakably, Bright was convinced that the possibility of securing British recognition of the Confederacy would be remote. "You will see what meetings are being held here in favor of your emancipation policy and of the North in general," he wrote to Sumner. "I think in every town in the Kingdom a public meeting would go by an overwhelming majority in favor of President Lincoln and of the North." (18)

Bright's improved spirits were reflected in two highly publicized speeches on the American Question. At a public meeting in Rochdale on February 3, he expressed his thanks to a group of New York merchants who had contributed generously to relieve the sufferings of underemployed British cotton textile workers. But he did much more. He emphasized that the British and the Americans were really one people, and that therefore there was no reason for the jealousy and fear of American power to which some Britons were subject. He made it clear that he treasured the cultural ties that linked the two countries. He noted, in fact, that Shakespeare, Milton, and other great British writers had even more readers in the United States than in Britain. The reason, of course, was simple: the twenty million

Americans in the Free States had a far higher rate of literacy than the thirty million people who lived in the British Isles.

Once more Bright praised the American Republic. Its House of Representatives was based on a much fuller, fairer, and freer representation than the House of Commons. Its workers were not designated members of the "lower classes," and even immigrants were speedily and honorably admitted to full rights of citizenship. They were free to buy and sell land. They could send their children to free schools, and they could aspire to whatever careers their talents permitted. Marveling at the progress of social and political liberty in the United States, Bright saw the Republic as a great instrument for good in the world—a "life-boat" for the downtrodden of Europe. And he hoped that the American example would continue to exercise its wholesome influence on Europe.

Just as Bright could not find words flattering enough to describe his feeling for the North, so he could not find words harsh enough to express his hostility to the South. The Confederate leaders were criminals who had tried to break up the freest society in the history of the world. They wanted not only to preserve slavery but to reopen the slave trade. They hoped that the desperate need for cotton would induce Britain to intervene in their behalf. But Bright was confident that British workers would never favor a society based on slave labor, and he pointed with pride to the many meetings taking place all over Britain to celebrate the issuance of the Emancipation Proclamation. (19)

Bright did not hesitate to repeat himself in another speech delivered in March to an immense audience of London trade unionists. Again he blamed Britain for having imposed slavery on the American colonies. Again he proclaimed the Civil War an irrepressible conflict. Again he denounced the privileged classes in Britain for their hatred of the American Republic and for their wish that the American experiment should fail. Again he praised the Free States for honoring labor more than any other country in the world. Again he condemned those British who would use the cotton shortage as an excuse for intervening in behalf of the South. And once more he predicted that the British working classes would take the right side.

Impartial history will tell that, when your statesmen were hostile or coldly neutral, when many of your rich men were corrupt, when your press—which ought to have instructed and defended—was mainly written to betray, the fate of a continent and of its vast population being in peril, you clung to freedom with an unfaltering trust that God in His infinite mercy will yet make it the heritage of all His children. (20)

As a speaker on the American Question, Bright had two chief aims: to encourage the North in its struggle and to contribute to more harmonious Anglo-American relations by demonstrating to Americans that they had at least some friends in Britain. His success in these aims was one of the few satisfactions that he derived from his political career. Having been defeated on so many important issues in the course of his first twenty years of public service, he found it hard to believe that at last he was being recognized as a statesman who was worth listening to. When he absented himself briefly from the House because his wife was having what proved to be their last child, even Cobden begged him to return as quickly as possible: "The fact of your being present with the power of reply exerts a restraining influence on Palmerston and the other speakers on the Treasury bench...." There were additional signs of the esteem in which he was held. When the Speaker of the House made arrangements for a painting of the leading Members of Parliament, Bright was included in the group. And when he interceded in behalf of the young and reckless brother of one of his Birmingham constituents—in the Rubery Case—President Lincoln pardoned the man, even though his acts were treasonable. (21)

The recognition of Bright's stature came less from his countrymen than from Americans, who from President Lincoln down continued to deluge him with praise. But Bright was aware that this was proper. For, as he confessed to Mrs. Harriet Beecher Stowe, he was an American at heart. (22)

NOTES

(1) Bright to Gladstone, Jan. 1, 1861, Gladstone MSS, BM 44,112; Bright to Wilson, Jan. 7, 1861, Wilson MSS, MCL; Bright to Mrs. Bright, Mar. 3,

1861, Bright MSS, UCLL; Bright to Smith, Jan. 26, 1861, Smith MSS, MCL; Cobden to Bright, Mar. 25, 1861, Cobden MSS, BM 43,651; Bright to Cobden, Feb. 6, 1861; Feb. 10, 1861; Mar. 28, 1861; July 29, 1861; Aug. 31, 1861; Sept. 6, 1861; Oct. 3, 1861; Oct. 24, 1861; Nov. 16, 1861; Dec. 9, 1861, Bright MSS, BM 43,384; cf. Bright to W. H. Seward, July 12, 1861, Robert T. Lincoln Collection, LC.

(2) Bright to Mrs. Bright, Mar. 17, 1861; Apr. 26, 1861, Bright MSS, UCLL; Bright to Thomas Hodgkin, May 14, 1861, Bright MSS, YUL; Bradford R. Wood to Bright, Aug. 14, 1861, Bright MSS, BM 43,391; Bright to Sumner, Sept. 6, 1861; Jan. 13, 1862; Feb. 27, 1862, Sumner MSS, HCL; Bright to Robert Hadfield, Nov. 14, 1861, Bright MSS, Buffalo and Erie County Historical Society; Bright to Cobden, May 22, 1861; Oct. 3, 1861, Bright MSS, BM 43,384.

(3) Bright to Frederick Milnes Edge, July 2, 1860, Seward MSS, University of Rochester Library; Bright to Col. Rathbone, Jan. 23, 1861, Misc. MSS, BM 33,963; Bright to Gladstone, Jan. 9, 1861, Gladstone MSS, BM 44,112; Bright to Henry Ashworth, Feb. 14, 1861, Friends Historical Library, Swarthmore College; Bright to Cobden, July 29, 1861; Oct. 24, 1861, Bright MSS, BM 43,384; cf. *Parl. Deb.*, 167 (June 5, 1862), 412.

(4) *Ibid.*, 163 (May 28, 1861), 192; *Punch*, XLII (1862), 2, 10; cf. Bright to Cobden, Jan. 12, 1860; Sept. 6, 1861; Nov. 4, 1861; Dec. 9, 1861; Jan. 13, 1862, Bright MSS, BM 43,384; Bright to Charles Sturge, Dec. 7, 1861, Bright MSS, Friends Historical Library, Swarthmore College; Bright to Thomas H. Dudley, Dec. 9, 1861, Bright MSS, HL; Bright to Sumner, Nov. 29, 1861; Nov. 30, 1861; Dec. 5, 1861; Dec. 7, 1861; Dec. 14, 1861, Sumner MSS, HCL.

(5) Cf. Bright to Wilson, Nov. 15, 1861, Wilson MSS, MCL; *The Times,* Dec. 5, 1861; Dec. 6, 1861; *Speeches,* I, 167–95; Frank Moore, ed., *Speeches of John Bright, M.P., on the American Question* (Boston, 1865) should be reprinted.

(6) Bright to Joseph Parkes, Dec. 9, 1861, Parkes MSS, UCLL; Bright to Cobden, Dec. 9, 1861; Dec. 13, 1861, Bright MSS, BM 43,384; Bright to W. H. Northy, Dec. 23, 1861, Northy MSS, BM 44,877; Bright to Milner Gibson, Dec. 7, 1861, Bright MSS, BM 43,388.

(7) John Bigelow to Bright, Dec. 8, 1861, *ibid.*, BM 43,390; Thomas H. Dudley to Bright, Dec. 6, 1861, *ibid.*, BM 43,391; Cobden to Bright, Dec. 6, 1861, Cobden MSS, BM 43,651; Louis Mallet to Bright, Dec. 6, 1861, Bright MSS, BM 43,389; Neal Dow to Bright, Jan. 6, 1862; Edward Atkinson to Bright, Feb. 6, 1862, Bright MSS, BM 43,391; George Bancroft to Bright, Feb. 25, 1862, Misc. MSS, NYPL; Henry Adams to Charles Francis Adams, Jr., Feb. 14, 1862, Adams MSS, MHS.

(8) Bright to Mrs. Bright, Feb. 5, 1861; Feb. 13, 1861; Apr. 26, 1861; July 16, 1861, Bright MSS, UCLL; Bright to Cobden, Aug. 31, 1861; Dec. 9, 1861,

Bright MSS, BM 43,384; Bright to Sumner, Dec. 5, 1861, Sumner MSS, HCL; cf. *Punch,* XLII (1862), 145.

(9) J. G. Randall, *Lincoln the President* (New York, 1945), II, 49; David Donald, ed., *Inside Lincoln's Cabinet: The Civil War Diaries of Salmon P. Chase* (New York, 1954), pp. 53–55; cf. Cobden to Bright, Dec. 7, 1861, Cobden MSS, BM 43,651.

(10) Cobden to Bright, Dec. 27, 1861; Jan. 3, 1862, *ibid.,* BM 43,652; Bright to Sumner, Dec. 21, 1861; Jan. 11, 1862, Sumner MSS, HCL; Bright to Motley, Jan. 9, 1862, copy, Seward MSS, University of Rochester Library; Bright to Smith, Jan. 13, 1862, Smith MSS, MCL; Bright to Mrs. Bright, Mar. 5, 1862; Apr. 6, 1862; Apr. 14, 1862, Bright MSS, UCLL.

(11) Bright to Bradford R. Wood, Apr. 10, 1862, American Academy of Arts and Letters Collection, LC; Cobden to Bright, July 12, 1862, Cobden MSS, BM 43,652; Bright to Mrs. Bright, Feb. 6, 1862; Feb. 8, 1862; Feb. 14, 1862; Mar. 15, 1862; Mar. 16, 1862; July 1, 1862; July 24, 1862, Bright MSS, UCLL; Bright to Cobden, Aug. 6, 1862; Aug. 30, 1862; Oct. 8, 1862, Bright MSS, BM 43,384; *Parl. Deb.,* 166 (May 14, 1862), 1715; cf. Bright to T. H. Green, Mar. 19, 1861, Bright MSS, PUL.

(12) *Diaries,* Feb. 14, 1862; Feb. 21, 1862; Mar. 29, 1862; Bright to George Bancroft, Mar. 29, 1862, Bancroft MSS, MHS; Bright to W. H. Seward, July 12, 1862, Robert T. Lincoln Collection, LC; Bright to Mrs. Bright, Feb. 14, 1862; Feb. 18, 1862; Mar. 15, 1862; June 29, 1862; July 20, 1862; July 27, 1862; Sept. 24, 1862, Bright MSS, UCLL; Bright to Helen Clark, May 7, 1862; May 20, 1862; July 25, 1862, Bright MSS, S; Bright to Sumner, July 12, 1862; July 14, 1862, Sumner MSS, HCL; *Parl. Deb.,* 165 (Feb. 17, 1862), 387; *The Times,* Feb. 5, 1862; Feb. 6, 1862; Bright to Cobden, Jan. 6, 1862; Jan. 13, 1862; Aug. 6, 1862; Aug. 30, 1862, Bright MSS, BM 43,384.

(13) Bright to Cobden, Aug. 30, 1862; Oct. 8, 1862, *ibid.;* Cobden to Bright, Oct. 7, 1862; Dec. 7, 1862, Cobden MSS, BM 43,652; Bright to Sumner, Oct. 10, 1862, Sumner MSS, HCL.

(14) Bright to Wilson, Aug. 4, 1855, Wilson MSS, MCL; *Parl. Deb.,* 149 (Apr. 21, 1858), 1465ff.; Bright to Cobden, Sept. 2, 1858; Nov. 16, 1859; July 15, 1860; Dec. 20, 1860; Aug. 31, 1861, Bright MSS, BM 43,384; Bright to Mrs. Bright, Apr. 19, 1860, Bright MSS, UCLL; *Diaries,* p. 262; Bright to Thomas H. Dudley, Oct. 18, 1862, Bright MSS, HL; Cobden to Bright, Dec. 29, 1862, Cobden MSS, BM 43,652; cf. Magnus, p. 152ff.

(15) Bright to Cobden, Jan. 20, 1862, Bright MSS, BM 43,384; Bright to Wilson, June 27, 1862, Wilson MSS, MCL; Bright to Mrs. Bright, July 21, 1862, Bright MSS, UCLL; Bright to Sumner, Jan. 11, 1862; Dec. 6, 1862, Sumner MSS, HCL; Henry Steele Commager, "How 'The Lost Cause' Was Lost," *New York Times Magazine,* Aug. 4, 1963.

(16) *Speeches,* I, 197–225; *The Times,* Dec. 19, 1862; Dec. 20, 1862.

(17) *Punch,* XLIV (1863), 3; New York *Evening Post,* Jan. 13, 1863; James A. Pike to Bright, Dec. 21, 1862, Bright MSS, BM 43,391; Whittier to Bright, Jan. 21, 1863, Whittier MSS, Berg Collection, NYPL; Motley to Bright, Feb. 9, 1863, Bright MSS, BM 43,391; Cobden to Bright, Dec. 29, 1862, Cobden MSS, BM 43,652.

(18) Bright to Mrs. Bright, Jan. 4, 1863, Bright MSS, UCLL; see John Hope Franklin, *The Emancipation Proclamation* (New York, 1963); Bright to Sumner, Jan. 30, 1863, Sumner MSS, HCL.

(19) *Speeches,* I, 227–43.

(20) Bright to Helen Clark, Feb. 27, 1863, Bright MSS, S; *The Times,* Mar. 27, 1863; *Speeches,* I, 245–53.

(21) Bright to Theodore Tilton, Mar. 9, 1863, Gluck MSS, Buffalo and Erie County Public Library; Bright to Lewis Tappan, Apr. 2, 1863, Tappan MSS, LC; Cobden to Bright, Apr. 22, 1863, Cobden MSS, BM 43,652; Bright to Mrs. Bright, Feb. 27, 1863; Feb. 28, 1863; June 26, 1863, Bright MSS, UCLL; Bright to Sumner, May 15, 1863; June 27, 1863; Nov. 20, 1863; Jan. 22, 1864, Sumner MSS, HCL.

(22) Cobden to Bright, Apr. 1, 1863, Cobden MSS, BM 43,652; Bright to Mrs. Bright, Feb. 27, 1863; May 1, 1863, Bright MSS, UCLL; Lewis Tappan to Bright, Mar. 5, 1863; Cyrus W. Field to Bright, Aug. 3, 1863, Bright MSS, BM 43,391; Bright to Lorenzo Sherwood, Mar. 16, 1863, Bright MSS, Rochester Public Library; Bright to R. J. Walker, July 27, 1863, Bright MSS, New-York Historical Society; Bright to Mrs. Harriet Beecher Stowe, Mar. 9, 1863, Bright MSS, Chicago Historical Society.

CHAPTER TEN

END AND BEGINNING
1863–1866

Bright saw the Emancipation Proclamation as a decisive step in the right direction as well as the turning point of the Civil War. He was certain that now that the American Government had made clear its intentions concerning the Negro, God would reward the North with the speedy victory it deserved. At the same time, however, Bright's guilt about the past treatment of the Negro remained profound. As he told a Northerner: "You will derive much satisfaction from your labors on behalf of the Negro. To have lifted from his back only a portion of the burden under which he has groaned will be a blessing to you in a day to come, more than can be derived from the results of successful ambition. I wish you every success, and all the consolation and recompense which God gives to those who act justly by the suffering ones of His creatures." (1)

To Bright's distress the war showed no signs of ending in 1863, and like many of his countrymen he found himself immersed in the details of Vicksburg and Gettysburg—so much so that he confessed to his wife his inability to give himself to any other public issue until the American conflict ended. Once the North achieved victory —and Palmerston died—he did not doubt that the British parliamentary reform movement would take on unprecedented importance; but for the present what mattered was winning the war. At times his anxiety was so acute that he dreamed about the United States, "seeing telegrams that [he] could not read, and worried by a sense of the desperate struggle there impending." He did not exaggerate when he told Sumner that Cobden and he discussed American affairs endlessly and with an interest so intense that they might just as well have been members of the Senate. (2)

Despite Bright's hopes, the Proclamation did not end the attempts of some of his countrymen to press for recognition of the Confederacy. On the contrary, it made them all the more eager to help the South before it was too late. John Roebuck, the Member for Sheffield and a notorious xenophobe, introduced his motion to recognize the Confederacy as late as June—months after the issuance of the Proclamation. Naturally, Bright was furious, and his attack on Roebuck's motion was one of the most devastating that he made in the course of his career—the more so because he despised Roebuck as a vain, jealous, and spiteful man. He ridiculed Roebuck's efforts to enlist the diplomatic cooperation of Napoleon III, the same despot whom the Member for Sheffield had so irrationally condemned in the past. He made it clear that to recognize the Confederacy was to nullify the Emancipation Proclamation and to restore slavery where it had been abolished. And he elaborated on the horrors that marked slavery as an institution. (3)

In one respect Bright's speech on Roebuck's motion was unusual. It was one of the few in which he referred to his private life. In deploring the fate that awaited children born to American slave parents, he burst into a eulogy of domesticity; and he confessed that the greatest joys he had ever known, or hoped to know, came, and would continue to come, from his associations with his children. The reference was meaningful because the sixteenth anniversary of his marriage had just been celebrated, and Bright was even more happily married than in 1847. Furthermore, his eighth and last child had just been born, and he enjoyed thoroughly the new infant. Playing with him even made Bright wonder why, since infants were so appealing, adults were "so much less charming." (4)

II

Although the failure of Roebuck's efforts in behalf of the Confederacy came as a great relief, Bright was not like those modern historians who regard 1863 as the year when, for all practical purposes, Southern diplomacy collapsed. He remained on the alert, still fearing that Palmerston, Napoleon III, the men of *The Times*, the members of the Southern Independence Association, and other "secesh people" who wanted the United States permanently dismembered might bring on a conflict with the North. He was particularly concerned because the British press seemed to go out of its way to spread false views of the United States. And since he had an overpowering sense of the role of contingency in human affairs, he constantly resisted any tendency to overconfidence concerning the American Question. A tactless speech by Palmerston, the building of a Confederate ship in Britain or France, or a ridiculous episode at sea exploited by the press could lead to a flaring up of tempers and an Anglo-American war—fundamentally because of British jealousy of the growing power of the United States.

Not only that. Just as in 1860–1861 Bright had feared that in order to prevent civil strife the North might arrange a disgraceful compromise with the South, so in 1863–1864 he was worried that in order to secure peace the North might make disgraceful concessions in relation to slavery and perhaps repudiate the Emancipation Proclamation. For this reason he welcomed every sign of Lincoln's firmness that appeared. Indeed, as 1863 ended and 1864 began, Bright was increasingly anxious about the presidential election due in November. What if Lincoln were not reelected? What if someone who would permit a restoration of slavery became president? (5)

All the while the carnage continued, for 1864 was the year of the Wilderness, Spotsylvania, Cold Harbor, Petersburg, and the March through Georgia. Still the war failed to end. Bright could not avoid the conclusion that the United States was being punished for having tolerated slavery for such a long time—the sins of their fathers were being visited on Americans to the third and fourth generations. Although he did not doubt that the North would win, he was repeatedly impressed with the idea that Americans were being forced to atone for their past crimes against the Negro by way of a protracted and bloody war. (6)

Although Bright saw Americans as sinners discovering the wrath of God, they saw him as one of the authentic saints of the modern world. President Lincoln continued to admire his noble character. Horace Greeley dedicated *The American Conflict* to him with the words "TO JOHN BRIGHT, BRITISH COMMONER AND CHRISTIAN STATESMAN: THE FRIEND OF MY COUNTRY, BECAUSE THE FRIEND OF MANKIND." Frank Moore, the editor of the *Rebellion Record,* sought his permission to publish a volume of his inspiring speeches on the American Question. Charitable organizations requested his autograph so that they could raise money for the widows and orphans of Union soldiers. Northern audiences burst into wild applause any time a speaker mentioned his name. Writers sent him copies of their publications inscribed with moving tributes. And both eminent and obscure Americans begged him to visit the United States, assuring him that his reception would be the warmest ever accorded to a foreign dignitary. (7)

The American response was fully justified, for Bright rivaled the most idealistic immigrant in his passion for the Republic and his faith in the promise of American life. As he wrote to an American historian: "I have been a friend of your country from a belief that on your continent and with your institutions our race seems to have a chance of a better time, and I live in the expectation that from you much will be learned that will advance the cause of freedom: not in Europe only, but throughout the world."

Furthermore, it was not only that his speeches on the American Question dealt with American affairs from an enthusiastically American point of view. Even on those occasions during the Civil War years when he spoke about British domestic matters, he would often include some flattering references to the United States. In January 1864, for example, he delivered a spirited address on the unsound and unjust distribution of land in Britain, warning that the concentration of ownership in the hands of a small number of proprietors menaced the safety of Britain. The model society which he hoped his countrymen would emulate was the United States, whose recently enacted Homestead legislation he could not praise highly enough. Similarly, when he spoke in May in favor of a motion to abolish capital punishment in Britain—a subject about which he had long felt concerned—he drew admiringly on the experiences of Rhode Island, Wisconsin, and Michigan, contrasting the merciful treatment of criminals in these Free States with the barbarities that marked the punishment of crime in the United Kingdom. These Americans regarded human life as sacred, and they recognized that capital punishment undermined reverence for human life. (8)

Unlike most of his countrymen—and many Americans—Bright appreciated President Lincoln while he was alive. Even Cobden had found Lincoln unequal to the demands of his office, intellectually inferior, and prone to surround himself with mediocrities. But practically from the outset Bright sensed Lincoln's moral stature, which more than compensated for any of his inadequacies. Indeed, the most memorable event of 1864, as Bright saw it, was the American election. Since he regarded a vote for Lincoln as a vote for unity and freedom, he hoped that Lincoln would win many votes, as he wrote to Horace Greeley in a public letter that appeared in the New York *Tribune* and was widely reprinted—even in *The Times* (London). He was not unduly optimistic about the election results, for his fears of the strength of Copperheadism were profound. As he told an American in September, "I hope there is virtue enough in the North to support the Administration in its efforts to restore the Union and to purge the Country from the curse and guilt of Slavery." And as Cobden wrote to him on Election Day, "Let us hope the vote today for Lincoln will be so overwhelming as to extirpate Copperheadism." (9)

III

By the time the news of Lincoln's victory arrived—news that Bright awaited impatiently—he and his wife had suffered the greatest disaster of their married life. In November their son Leonard, not quite six, died suddenly of scarlet fever. Bright, who had recently consoled Cobden, Milner Gibson, and his brother Jacob when they had undergone similar tragedies, was now the one to be consoled; but he discovered that there was no consolation. All he could do was to trust in God's wisdom and try to keep busy. Cobden begged him not to make the mistake that he had made—seclusion was not the answer. Instead, he urged him to keep himself and his wife in society—to be among people as much as possible. (10)

Bright had hardly begun to cope with the reality of the loss of his son when he suffered another disaster. At the age of sixty-one Cobden died, in April 1865, five months after Leonard's death and shortly before word arrived of Lee's surrender at Appomattox Court House. In a sense Bright was prepared for this blow. For years Cobden had harped on the fact that his family was undistinguished for longevity, that the absence of sunshine in Britain would ruin him, and that in any case he had damaged his lungs and throat during his years as an active agitator. Bright had repeatedly been concerned about the state of his friend's health, but the plain fact of Cobden's death was impossible for him to accept. "I have been so disturbed for three days past," he told his wife, "that I have feared I should break down and be ill in some serious way." His hands shook, his head ached, and he felt like a very old man. To make matters worse, April also saw the death of his brother-in-law, Samuel Lucas, the staunchly pro-Union editor of the *Morning Star*. Bright's life had become a journey from one funeral to another. (11)

Of course, he welcomed the news of the Union victory over what he often called "the rebel conspiracy." As he wrote to his wife on April 23: "What a grand result! White and black are henceforth alike free on the American Continent! I seem to have more reason to rejoice than most others, for I have had more anxiety and more faith. It is another proof that He who made the world still rules it, and will not forsake it." But his private trials in April kept Bright from relishing the victory as he would otherwise have done. And then at the end of the month came more grief—over the assassination of President Lincoln. It was hard for Bright to go on; to get through a day was a triumph. His head ached so much that he was constantly reminded of his experience in 1856 when he had had his breakdown. (12)

IV

Like Cobden, he tried to convince himself that the way to deal with sorrow was through useful work, and now there was less and less reason for inaction. For he had been insisting for a long time that two events had to precede any effective agitation for parliamentary reform in Britain, and both occurred before the year ended: the triumph of the American Republic in April and the death of Lord Palmerston in October. Bright now had to prove that the end of the Civil War and the end of the career of his archenemy would mark the beginning of a successful movement to change Parliament. The time had come for Dr. Bright—as *Punch* called him—to present the "Franchise Pill" which he had discovered after some twenty years of research in America and which he regarded as a positive cure for a great variety of disorders. (13)

He had looked forward for so long to "the close of the official life" of Lord Palmerston that he could hardly believe that he was "out of the way." He regretted that Cobden was not alive to hear the welcome news, for Cobden's hatred of Palmerston had been as intense as his own. To be sure, Cobden felt guilty about his hostility to a man who had made all kinds of generous offers to him; nevertheless, he had held Palmerston responsible for corrupting and degrading British politics. But at least Cobden was spared the sickening eulogies that were appearing in the obituary notices of the Prime Minister. Bright, on the other hand, had to listen to praise of the man who for him symbolized everything that was wrong with the British way of life. It was bad enough that Palmerston had been filled with eighteenth-century notions and prejudices; but worse still he had appealed shamelessly to the ignorance, credulity, and passion of the British public. For this Bright could not forgive him, and throughout the rest of his life he could never hear his name mentioned without a feeling of revulsion. He could no more understand what he viewed as Palmerston's disgusting superpatriotism than Palmerston could understand what he regarded as Bright's shocking lack of patriotism. (14)

Bright's growing preoccupation with domestic reform did not mean that he ceased to be concerned about the course of events in the United States. Quite the contrary. He continued to urge Britons planning to visit the United States to study educational institutions in the New England states and to discover "what Englishmen in

America have done to make instruction as universal as air and water are." He worried about the spread of protectionist fallacies among Americans. Moreover, he took an active interest in the problems of reconstruction, discussing them at length with Senator Sumner and other American leaders.

He had strong opinions about two subjects with which the United States had to deal. In the first place, he thought that the leaders of the Southern conspiracy should be banished permanently —that would be punishment enough for them, for he condemned capital punishment for any crime, whether political or social. For the rest, he believed that as much magnanimity as possible should characterize Northern treatment of the South. As he put it to Sumner: "One of the great objects of your Government now should be to change the character of the South, to root out the brutality and cruelty which have sprung from slavery, to create a reverence for human life, and to prove the mercy no less than the justice of your Federal Government." In the second place, Bright favored vigilance as well as legislation to guarantee the rights of Negroes; otherwise their freedom would be largely fictitious. Specifically, he considered it dangerous to restore the Southern states to full power and leave the Negroes at the mercy of their old masters. He had no doubt that the ex-slaves needed special protection, especially since he worried about President Johnson's pro-Southern tendencies. (15)

Just as Bright did not forget postwar America, so postwar Americans did not forget him. They flattered him so much that he feared for his modesty. George Bancroft wrote to him about a speech that he delivered to an audience including such luminaries as President Johnson, Senators, Congressmen, Supreme Court Justices, and high-ranking army and navy officers. When Bancroft mentioned Bright's name, "these grave men broke out into the most vehement and enthusiastic and long continued applause." Schuyler Colfax, the Speaker of the House of Representatives, told him that he knew his face well because he had often looked at his portrait in President Lincoln's reception room; and he assured him that every loyal American knew, honored, and esteemed him. And many Americans, including Sumner, Salmon P. Chase, and John

Greenleaf Whittier, wished him well in his efforts to extend the suffrage. (16)

V

On resuming in 1866 his campaign for political reform, Bright knew that he had certain marked disadvantages. He felt much older than a man in his mid-fifties, he was sad and dispirited much of the time, he resented having given so much of his life to public service, and he lacked the energy that public speaking and attendance at meetings demanded. Besides, he was, as he rightly called himself, "an 'outsider' and a 'pariah' among politicians," and except for a handful of Members, he had no followers on whom he could count in the House. He had a powerful group of enemies among the great landowners—both aristocrats and squires—who saw him as a latter-day Robespierre. With good reason *Punch* proposed the toast "Bright and the British aristocracy," and with equally good reason quipped that he would probably be made a peer. "I am the great 'terror' of the squires," he told his wife without exaggeration. Since the great landowners dominated the House of Commons, their hatred of him was an important political fact; and the truth was that he despised them with such intensity that when he reviled them he became, as the *Economist* suggested, "absolutely blind to the drift of his own words." Many members of his own class were also hostile to him because of his ardent defense of working-class rights. Shortly before his death, even Cobden had begged him not to alienate the middle classes and to strive for middle-class and working-class cooperation. And John Benjamin Smith repeatedly appealed to him to surprise his enemies by being mild and moderate in his demands for change. Finally—and this was the disadvantage that Bright felt most keenly—Cobden was no longer available to restrain him, encourage him, give him advice, argue with him, and force him to clarify his thinking. (17)

Bright also recognized that in pressing for reform he now had advantages that he had not enjoyed before. He could point to the Union victory to prove that political democracy meant strength, not weakness; and he was certain that the restored American

DR. BRIGHT AND HIS PATIENT

DOCTOR *"Do you get good wages?"*
PATIENT *"Yes."*
DOCTOR *"Have you plenty to eat and drink?"*
PATIENT *"Yes, as far as that goes."*

DOCTOR *"Do you do as you like?"*
PATIENT *"Yes."*
DOCTOR *"Do you pay taxes?"*
PATIENT *"None to hurt me much."*

DOCTOR *"Ah! We must change all that. We must go in for* REFORM!*"*

☞ This colloquy gives a not unfair summary of Mr. Bright's address to his constituents in the preceding month.—1865.

Republic would exert a wholesome influence on all good causes in Europe. Also, he could remind his countrymen of the admirable behavior of the British working classes during their recent hardships, and he could insist that these were people who had earned full rights of citizenship. As he said in a parliamentary speech as early as 1862: "Depend upon it, that in the short and simple annals of the poor there is to be found a heroism not less than that for which often the thanks of Parliament are given; and I trust that hereafter, when we come to look back upon the abundant compliments which hon. Members now pay to that population, there may be some who will change their opinion of them, and think that they are not improper subjects for admission to political power." Furthermore, he could capitalize on the state of confusion among the Whigs in the post-Palmerston era, and he could try to persuade them that to survive they would have to extend the suffrage. Much as Bright distrusted Gladstone because of his conduct during the Civil War, he heartily approved of the position that the Chancellor of the Exchequer had taken publicly since 1864 on the justice of parliamentary reform. (18)

As Bright foresaw, Russell headed the Government after Palmerston's death; and as Bright anticipated, he was not asked to join the Ministry. Having been rebuffed several times before, however, he was less upset about being passed over than were some of his friends and relatives. "It is better that men should ask why I am *not* in the Ministry than why I am in it," he wrote to his wife. "The chief reason why men fear me in a Government is that I should not stand such disgraceful and helpless imbecility as we too often witness," he told John Benjamin Smith. (19)

In the spring of 1866 Gladstone led the fight in the House of Commons for the Ministry's reform bill. Bright consulted frequently with him and with Russell; he pledged his cooperation to them; he hoped that they would not yield to cowardice and indecision; and he defended their bill vigorously on the floor of the House. As Bright feared, the measure was lost because of a coalition of Tories and Whigs who were alarmed at the prospect of arming working-class people with the franchise. And as Bright expected,

THE POLITICAL "WALL-FLOWER"

MISS BRIGHT. *"Nobody asks* ME; *and if they did, I should certainly decline."*

☞ Lord Russell's Whig prejudices were too strong to permit his offering Mr. Bright a seat in the Cabinet —though none had better deserved it.—1865.

Lord Derby formed a new Government in 1866 even though the Tories were a minority in the House. (20)

Bright believed that now the great task was to arouse so much public enthusiasm for reform that Tories and "Whig traitors" would be compelled to yield to the clamor. He recognized that the parliamentary reformers lacked the financial resources of the Anti-Corn Law Leaguers, and this was certainly unfortunate. Nevertheless, he found a few hopeful signs. He was delighted with the large public meeting that took place in Trafalgar Square in early July, and he hoped that it would be followed by bigger and better ones. He was pleased when the Tory Government in effect condemned itself by trying to prevent a Hyde Park meeting of reformers. Above all, he was encouraged by the persistence of such organizers of the outdoor agitation for reform as George Wilson, George Howell, and Edmond Beales, and he kept in constant touch with them. (21)

But he regretted the part he had to play. For it was plain that he had to become a platform man again, making speeches, speeches, speeches. It depressed him that this should have been necessary since the case for parliamentary reform was so strong and the case against it so feeble. Yet several points had to be made clear by means of public meetings: that many people who already enjoyed the right to vote were *not* opposed to its extension to others; that workers were *not* indifferent to their lack of political rights; and that they were *not* irresponsible, untrustworthy, and inferior human beings. This last point took on particular importance for Bright. For increasingly it struck him that many opponents of suffrage reform spoke of British workers in the same way that Southern planters spoke of Negroes. (22)

NOTES

(1) Bright to Lewis Tappan, Apr. 2, 1863, Tappan MSS, LC; Bright to Sumner, June 27, 1863, Sumner MSS, HCL; Bright to Edward L. Pierce, Sept. 26, 1863, Bright MSS, PUL.

(2) Bright to Helen Clark, June 14, 1863; Oct. 9, 1863, Bright MSS, S; Bright to Mrs. Bright, Feb. 9, 1863; Mar. 25, 1863; June 22, 1863; June 27, 1863; June 29, 1863; July 19, 1863; July 22, 1863; May 12, 1864, Bright MSS, UCLL; Bright to Sumner, Apr. 4, 1863; May 2, 1863, Sumner MSS, HCL; Bright to Thomas H. Dudley, Apr. 27, 1863, Bright MSS, HL.

(3) Cf. Bright to Cobden, Aug. 31, 1861, Bright MSS, BM 43,384; Bright to Sumner, Apr. 24, 1863, Sumner MSS, HCL; Charles Francis Adams, Jr., *Charles Francis Adams* (Boston, 1900), pp. 332–33; *Parl. Deb.* 171 (June 30, 1863), 1826ff.; *Speeches,* I, 267–83.

(4) Bright to Mrs. Bright, Apr. 30, 1863; May 2, 1863; June 5, 1863; June 10, 1863; cf. Apr. 18, 1864; Apr. 23, 1865; July 20, 1867; Aug. 27, 1867, Bright MSS, UCLL.

(5) Cf. Bright to Thomas H. Dudley, Jan. 26, 1863, Bright MSS, HL; Bright to Mrs. Bright, July 22, 1863; Jan. 26, 1864, Bright MSS, UCLL; Bright to J. B. Smith, Dec. 24, 1863, Smith MSS, MCL; Bright to Cobden, Oct. 14,

1863, Bright MSS, BM 43,384; Bright to Sumner, Apr. 4, 1863; July 31, 1863; Sept. 11, 1863; Nov. 20, 1863, Sumner MSS, HCL; Bright to Sumner, Nov. 6, 1863, enclosed in letter to Seward, Seward MSS, University of Rochester Library; Bright to Thomas H. Dudley, July 9, 1863; Sept. 2, 1863; Sept. 5, 1864, Bright MSS, HL; Bright to unnamed correspondent, Oct. 28, 1864, Lee Kohns Collection, NYPL; cf. Bright to Frank Moore, Jan. 1, 1865, Bright MSS, New-York Historical Society.

(6) Bright to Helen Clark, Feb. 25, 1864, Bright MSS, S; Bright to Dudley, Apr. 27, 1864, Bright MSS, HL; Cobden to Wilson, May 25, 1864, Wilson MSS, MCL; Bright to Mrs. Bright, July 24, 1864; July 27, 1864, Bright MSS, UCLL; cf. *Letters,* Mar. 8, 1882.

(7) J. K. Hosmer to Bright, Dec. 27, 1863; Simeon Whiteley to Bright, Feb. 10, 1864; S. Montgomery Bond to Bright, Apr. 4, 1864; Edmund C. Bittinger to Bright, Apr. 15, 1864; Horace Greeley to Bright, July 13, 1864, David A. Wells to Bright, Sept. 8, 1864; Frank Moore to Bright, Nov. 28, 1864; Feb. 6, 1865, Bright MSS, BM 43,391; Bright to Mrs. Bright, Feb. 9, 1864; Mar. 9, 1864, Bright MSS, UCLL; Bright to Frank Moore, Jan. 11, 1864, Bright MSS, New-York Historical Society; Bright to Benjamin Moran, Feb. 4, 1865, Bright MSS, University of Kentucky Library; Bright to Z. Eastman, May 23, 1865, Eastman MSS, Chicago Historical Society.

(8) Bright to James Kendall Hosmer, May 4, 1864, Hosmer MSS, Minnesota Historical Society; *Speeches,* II, 333-58; 445-59; Bright to Mrs. Bright, Feb. 3, 1850; Apr. 19, 1864, Bright MSS, UCLL; *Parl. Deb.,* 97 (Mar. 14, 1848), 577; 104 (May 1, 1849), 1084; 112 (July 11, 1850), 1279; 174 (May 3, 1864), 2092ff.; Bright to James Y. Smith, Mar. 4, 1864, Bright MSS, PML; James Smith to Bright, Mar. 21, 1864; Arthur Blair to Bright, Mar. 23, 1864; James T. Lewis to Bright, Mar. 29, 1864, Bright MSS, BM 43,391.

(9) *Diaries,* June 1, 1864; Bright to Mrs. Bright, May 4, 1865, Bright MSS, UCLL; Bright to Ticknor and Fields, Jan. 2, 1867, Bright MSS, PML; Cobden to Bright, Mar. 25, 1861; Oct. 7, 1862; July 10, 1863; Nov. 7, 1864, Cobden MSS, BM 43,651-652; Cobden to Wilson, July 16, 1863, Wilson MSS, MCL; Bright to Horace Greeley, Oct. 1, 1864, Bright MSS, YUL; *The Times,* Nov. 7, 1864; Bright to Sumner, Sept. 2, 1864; Sept. 3, 1864, Sumner MSS, HCL; Bright to Mrs. E. C. Ogden, Sept. 19, 1864, Bright MSS, Illinois State Historical Library.

(10) Bright to Cobden, Nov. 8, 1864; Nov. 17, 1864, Bright MSS, BM 43,384; Cobden to Bright, Nov. 10, 1864; Nov. 19, 1864, Cobden MSS, BM 43,652.

(11) Bright to Mrs. Bright, Mar. 1, 1865; Mar. 4, 1865; Apr. 1, 1865; Apr. 2, 1865; Apr. 3, 1865; Apr. 4, 1865; Apr. 6, 1865, Bright MSS, UCLL; Cobden to Bright, Feb. 24, 1864; Dec. 14, 1864, Cobden MSS, BM 43,652; Bright to Sumner, Jan. 26, 1865; Apr. 14, 1865, Sumner MSS, HCL; Bright to Bradford

R. Wood, Apr. 14, 1865, Bright MSS, HSP; Bright to Wilson, Apr. 19, 1865, Wilson MSS, MCL.

(12) Bright to Mrs. Bright, Feb. 11, 1865; Apr. 23, 1865; June 12, 1865, Bright MSS, UCLL; *Parl Deb.,* 178 (Apr. 3, 1865), 677; *Diaries,* Apr. 29, 1865; Bright to John Benjamin Smith, May 15, 1865, Smith MSS, MCL; Bright to Sumner, May 16, 1865, Sumner MSS, HCL; Bright to Mrs. Cobden, May 23, 1865, Bright MSS, D.

(13) Bright to Wilson, Dec. 28, 1863; May 14, 1865, Wilson MSS, MCL; Bright to Thomas B. Potter, Mar. 21, 1864, Bright MSS, Duke University Library; Bright to Cobden, July 17, 1864, Bright MSS, BM 43,384; Bright to Thomas H. Dudley, July 10, 1865, Bright MSS, HL; Cobden to Bright, Jan. 7, 1864; Jan. 12, 1865, Cobden MSS, BM 43,652.

(14) Bright to Cobden, Dec. 14, 1853, Bright MSS, BM 43,383; *Letters,* May 15, 1865; *The Times,* Sept. 19, 1865; cf. Cobden to Bright, Jan. 16, 1863; Aug. 16, 1864, Cobden MSS, BM 43,652; Bright to Sumner, Oct. 20, 1865, Sumner MSS, HCL; Bright to Seward, Oct. 21, 1865, Seward MSS, University of Rochester; Bright to John Benjamin Smith, Oct. 28, 1865, Smith MSS, MCL; Herbert C. F. Bell, *Lord Palmerston* (London, 1936), II, 135–36, 233, 418.

(15) Bright to Henry Vincent, July 19, 1866, Bright MSS, YUL; Bright to Cyrus W. Field, Mar. 13, 1867, Field MSS, PML; Bright to Joseph Aspinall, June 10, 1865, Burton Collection, Detroit Public Library; Bright to Thomas H. Dudley, Aug. 18, 1865; Nov. 27, 1865, Bright MSS, HL; Bright to Cyrus Field, Sept. 10, 1865, Field MSS, NYPL; Bright to George Bancroft, Mar. 8, 1866; July 3, 1866, Bancroft MSS, MHS; Bright to Egerton Leigh, Aug. 16, 1865, Bright MSS, Brotherton Library, University of Leeds; Bright to Seward, Oct. 21, 1865, Seward MSS, University of Rochester; Bright to Sumner, May 16, 1865; Oct. 20, 1865; July 3, 1866, Sumner MSS, HCL; cf. Bright to Helen Clark, Feb. 23, 1865, Bright MSS, S; Bright to Frank Moore, Mar. 5, 1866, Bright MSS, New-York Historical Society; Bright to Elihu Burritt, Nov. 28, 1866, Bright MSS, New Britain Public Library, Conn.; Bright to C. Edward Lester, Jan. 9, 1867, Bright MSS, LC.

(16) Cf. John Greenleaf Whittier to Walker Jubb, Feb. 19, 1892, Whittier MSS, Friends Historical Library, Swarthmore College; Union League Club to Bright, May 8, 1865; Frank Moore to Bright, Aug. 10, 1865; Benjamin Moran to Bright, Aug. 21, 1865; Charles Francis Adams to Bright, Oct. 5, 1865; George Peabody to Bright, Oct. 18, 1865; George Bancroft to Bright, Feb. 20, 1866; Lewis Tappan to Bright, Apr. 17, 1866; Schuyler Colfax to Bright, May 20, 1866; Salmon P. Chase to Bright, Oct. 1, 1866; Whittier to Bright, May 18, 1867, Bright MSS, BM 43,391; Bright to Mrs. Bright, Mar. 4, 1866; May 4, 1867; May 8, 1867, Bright MSS, UCLL.

(17) Bright to Field, Sept. 10, 1865, Field MSS, NYPL; Bright to Smith,

Oct. 28, 1865, Smith MSS, MCL; Robert Curzon to Walter Sneyd, Dec. 30, 1865, Sneyd MSS, University of Keele; *Punch,* L (1866), 181, 216; Bright to Mrs. Bright, Feb. 18, 1866, Bright MSS, UCLL; *Economist,* XXII (1864), 131ff.; *The Times,* Jan. 29, 1864; Jan. 30, 1864; Bright to W. H. Northy, Feb. 20, 1866, Northy MSS, BM 44,877; Cobden to Bright, Oct. 19, 1861; Mar. 30, 1864, BM 43,651–652; Smith to Bright, Nov. 4, 1865, Bright MSS, BM 43,388; *Diaries,* Apr. 8, 1865.

(18) Bright to James L. Claghorn Nov. 15, 1865, Dreer Collection, HSP; *Parl. Deb.,* 166 (May 9, 1862), 1506; Milner Gibson to Bright, Nov. 14, 1865, Bright MSS, BM 43,388; *Diaries,* May 11, 1864; Magnus, pp. 160, 164; Bright to Mrs. Bright, May 12, 1864, Bright MSS, UCLL; Bright to Seward Oct. 21, 1865, Seward MSS, University of Rochester.

(19) Bright to Sumner, Oct. 20, 1865, Sumner MSS, HCL; Bright to Mrs. Bright, Feb. 7, 1866; Feb. 11, 1866, Bright MSS, UCLL; E. Perry to Bright, Jan. 4, 1866, Bright MSS, BM 43,389; Bright to Smith, Jan. 7, 1866, Smith MSS, MCL.

(20) Bright to Wilson, Feb. 2, 1866; Apr. 30, 1866, Wilson MSS, MCL; Bright to Gladstone, Feb. 10, 1866, Gladstone MSS, BM 44,112; Bright to George Bancroft, July 3, 1866, Bancroft MSS, MHS; Bright to Mrs. Bright, Feb. 5, 1866; Feb. 10, 1866; Feb. 17, 1866; Mar. 14, 1866; Apr. 13, 1866; Apr. 14, 1866; May 13, 1866; May 31, 1866; June 2, 1866; June 6, 1866, Bright MSS, UCLL.

(21) Bright to Wilson, June 23, 1866; July 10, 1866, Wilson MSS, MCL; Bright to Sumner, July 3, 1866, Sumner MSS, HCL; Bright to Mrs. Bright, July 3, 1866, Bright MSS, UCLL; Bright to W. H. Northy, July 21, 1866, Northy MSS, BM 44,877; Bright to George Howell, June 27, 1866; July 19, 1866; Dec. 22, 1866, Howell MSS, BI.

(22) Cf. Bright to Arthur Albright, Nov. 3, 1864, Wilson King MSS, BPL; Bright to Wilson, June 27, 1866, Wilson MSS, MCL; Bright to George Howell, July 26, 1866, Howell MSS, BI; cf. J. B. Smith to Bright, Nov. 18, 1865, Bright MSS, BM 43,388; Bright to unnamed correspondent, May 19, 1866, Bright MSS, FHL; *Letters,* May 19, 1866.

CHAPTER ELEVEN

FROM VICTORY TO VICTORY
1866–1868

The speeches on parliamentary reform that Bright delivered in the last months of 1866 were a triumph of duty over inclination. What he wanted to do was to spend as much time as possible with his family and enjoy his wife and children while he had them. He was tired of being forced to imagine that he heard them singing "Rock of Ages"; he wanted to be there with them, having had his fill of daydreaming. Weary of public life, he felt that despite his years of effort he had accomplished little. Since the House of Commons was a "horrid place" where good causes languished, there was no sense in continuing the struggle for changes that should have been achieved long ago. Let other—and younger—reformers assume the part that he had tried to play for almost a quarter of a century. At fifty-five he was ready to become an obscure manufacturer who attended to his family and his business and who did not have to warn his wife against opening his mail for fear that she might see the threatening letters addressed to him. In short, Bright was a reluctant agitator in 1866. But what an agitator! His heart may not have been in the campaign; his oratorical genius was, as he delivered speech after speech in town after town—Birmingham, Manchester, Leeds, Glasgow, Dublin, London. Usually he consoled himself with the thought that when his cause triumphed he would give up both speechmaking and politics for good. (1)

Since Bright was the chief spokesman of the agitation, it was no surprise that opponents of parliamentary reform filled their speeches, pamphlets, newspapers, letters, and conversation with fierce denunciations of him. The attacks were so many and so standardized that he suspected orders must have gone out from Tory headquarters to cover him with as much dirt as possible and always with the same kind. In the words of one typical anti-Bright outburst:

Who is it, against the Quaker vow,
Which such proceedings don't allow,
Is always kicking up a row?
    Our Johnny.
Who ever more the charges rings
On working men and makes 'em kings,
Then in the mob his cap up flings?
    Our Johnny.
Who to delight that darling mob
Both truth and fact alike would rob,
And patriot so style "a job"?
    Our Johnny.
Who, as he many a time hath shown,
Loves every country but his own,
Sees all her faults and hers alone?
    Our Johnny.
Who when corrected and set aright,
Answered, exposed, confuted quite,
Repeats false charges in despite?
    Our Johnny.
Who when we fain must disagree
With all his stout absurdity,
Says it's because we will *not* see?
    Our Johnny.
Who choked with demagogic lust,
His spleen down all our throats would thrust,
Because with power we will not trust?
    Our Johnny. (2)

Some of his opponents charged that, far from being a friend of the working classes, Bright was an inveterate enemy of labor. They pointed gleefully to his hostility to factory legislation, and maintained that workers were shamelessly maltreated in his own family's business. But this latter charge quickly backfired. Representatives of workers in both the cotton and the carpet departments of his factories issued a moving statement declaring the Bright family to be model employers who attended not only to the economic but to the moral, spiritual, and intellectual needs of their labor force. (3)

At the same time that Bright was being widely attacked, he was also being widely hailed. Reformers from every part of the United Kingdom—including Ireland—thanked him profusely for his efforts and begged him to honor their community with a speech. The compliments showered on him left no doubt about the admiration that his supporters felt for his earnestness, courage, integrity, outspokenness, and independence of mind. Few things were so gratifying to him as to be recognized for the independent that he was, for he liked to see himself as a member of no party—as an individualist who examined all questions for himself. Indeed, he thought that if he had had to shape his views in keeping with a party's creed, he would have destroyed his self-respect. In this sense he had not changed since 1849 when he had said of his great hero Adam Smith that his opinion was worthy of the greatest respect but neither Smith's opinion nor that of "any other Adam should be held to be an absolute rule in this country." (4)

Bright had defended parliamentary reform so long and so often that his arguments came easily. The House of Commons was a travesty of a representative body. It was elected by a ridiculously small portion of the adult males of the Kingdom, and its seats were distributed most inequitably. Consequently, the great landowners dominated the House and pursued policies representing the interests not of the nation but of their narrow-minded and selfish class. The working classes enjoyed the franchise in many countries but, ironically, not in Britain, the home of the Mother of Parliaments. People who questioned the competence of workers to vote were doing a great injustice to the class constituting the bulk of the nation, and workers should make it clear through petitions and meetings that they resented their inferior political status as well as "the Botany Bay view" of them presented by antireformers. Only when they were granted real political rights would Britain be safe from the revolutions and disorders that occurred in other countries. Furthermore, the sooner workers were admitted to full rights of citizenship, the

THE BRUMMAGEM FRANKENSTEIN

JOHN BRIGHT. "*I have no fe—fe—fear of ma—manhood suffrage!*"

MR. BRIGHT'S Speech at Birmingham

☞ The unwillingness of Parliament to accept any measure of Reform had aroused a wide-spread discontent amongst the working classes. A monster gathering was held at Birmingham in August.—1866.

sooner would policies be pursued that took into account the needs of the whole nation.

Ironically, however, the two literary masterpieces that grew out of the struggle for parliamentary reform prove that Bright's extraordinary powers of persuasion sometimes failed: Matthew Arnold's *Culture and Anarchy* (1869) and the revised edition of Walter Bagehot's *The English Constitution* (1872). Perhaps the explanation is that Bright knew workers and therefore did not fear them, while Arnold and Bagehot did not know them and therefore feared them. (5)

Time and again in his speeches Bright outdid himself in his choice of quotable words:

I say that the accession to office of Lord Derby is a declaration of war against the working-classes.

Stretch out your hands to your countrymen in every part of the three kingdoms, and ask them to join you in a great and righteous effort on behalf of that freedom which has been so long the boast of Englishmen, but which the majority of Englishmen have never yet possessed.

The rich find everything just as they like. The country needs no reform. There is no other country in the world so pleasant for rich people as this country. But I deny altogether that the rich alone are qualified to legislate for the poor, any more than that the poor alone would be qualified to legislate for the rich.

The class which has hitherto ruled in this country has failed miserably. It revels in power and wealth, whilst at its feet, a terrible peril for the future, lies the multitude which it has neglected. If a class has failed, let us try the nation. That is our faith, that is our purpose, that is our cry—let us try the nation.

There is no greater fallacy than this—that the middle classes are in possession of power. The real state of the case, if it were put in simple language, would be this—that the working-men are almost universally excluded, roughly and insolently, from political power, and that the middle class, whilst they have the semblance of it, are defrauded of the reality.

So, now, it is not I who am stimulating men to the violent pursuit of their acknowledged constitutional rights. We are merely about our lawful business—and you are the citizens of a country that calls itself free, yet you are citizens to whom is denied the greatest and the first blessing of the constitution under which you live. If the truth must be told, the Tory party is the turbulent party of this nation. (6)

II

As the parliamentary session of 1867 approached, Bright was painfully uncertain about what might happen. At one moment he considered the reform cause doomed because the middle classes were hopelessly deferential to the great landowners; therefore, only the prospect of revolution would force concessions from those in power. At another moment he thought that the massive public demonstrations in behalf of reform would have a wholesome influence on Parliament, and that it might still be possible to achieve change peacefully. His constant fear was that Lord Derby's Tory Government might favor a very tame reform measure that would do more harm than good because it would delay for years the widespread extension of the franchise. (7)

The parliamentary session of 1867 was a difficult one for Bright. He expected the worst from the Tories. Instead, Lord Derby and Disraeli ("*the mystery man*," as Bright called him) surprised him by carrying through Parliament a reform bill that went much further than Gladstone's abortive measure of the previous session. In the months before this Reform Act of 1867 was passed, however, there were complicated intrigues, maneuvers, compromises, and concessions, and as a result Bright was frequently a wreck. On some days he would brim over with good cheer, congratulating himself and others on their prospects of success. On other days he would be so depressed by what he regarded as the foolishness, cowardice, and treachery of his colleagues that he would pray to God to protect him from both his enemies and his "friends"; he would immerse himself in the poetry of John Milton—as he had done, and would continue to do, for many years—to overcome his disgust with the pettiness, meanness, and unreliability of people. Also, he would be grateful when there was some fine weather, over which, happily, neither Tories nor Whigs had any control. (8)

As the parliamentary struggle over reform proceeded, Bright was invited to speak at a public breakfast in honor of William Lloyd Garrison, then on a visit to Britain. He found it easy to be eloquent in his praise of the American abolitionist leader, and he predicted that the name Garrison would become "the synonym of good to millions of men who will dwell on the now almost unknown continent of Africa." But he was so preoccupied with British domestic questions that he could not let them rest even for a morning. He asked how any great change—not just abolition—was accomplished, and he answered unequivocally: "By love of justice, by constant devotion to a great cause, and by an unfaltering faith that what is right will *in the end* succeed." Bright found the words easy to say, and he believed them; but the difficulty lay in the phrase "*in the end.*" For Bright was an impatient man, and, like Garrison, he wanted to see the changes he considered necessary accomplished in his own lifetime. (9)

Since the measure that was finally passed in 1867 provided for a generous enfranchisement of urban workers—the introduction of the household suffrage in boroughs—Bright was overjoyed. He could hardly believe that after so many years of unsuccessful agitation he had finally won. As he saw it, the most important single influence in the victory had been the great meetings arranged by Edmond Beales's Reform League; and he was grateful that Lord Derby and Disraeli had at last shown some sense and yielded to the inevitable. Nevertheless, he was repelled by the opportunism and hypocrisy that permitted the Tories to abandon their traditional political posture and flaunt themselves now as tribunes of the people. (10)

Despite his satisfaction with the Reform Act, Bright did not consider the struggle for political change ended. Now a secret ballot was essential, and he strongly urged Beales not to disband the Reform League until this was won. Bright contended that free elections were impossible without a secret ballot. As long as open voting remained, influence, intimidation, corruption, and disorder would continue to discredit and disgrace British elections. (11)

III

Bright's contempt for the Tories was due not only to their erratic and opportunistic behavior in relation to parliamentary reform; it was due also to their treatment of the Irish Question. For in 1866 and 1867 the Irish were again very much in the news, and Bright felt even more strongly about Ireland than about India. For years—more years than he cared to remember—he had called for Irish reforms, but no one listened to him, much less acted on his recommendations. Now that the Irish republicans known as Fenians were engaged in their violent anti-British activities in England, Ireland, Canada, and

DR. DULCAMARA IN DUBLIN

☞ Mr. Bright visited Dublin, by request, in October. His speeches were mainly devoted to the discussion of Irish questions.—1866.

the United States, the Irish Question was attracting the attention of Parliament—but again in the wrong way. For Tories—and also Whigs—were intent on putting the Fenians in their place. Bright had no doubt that the use of force would succeed temporarily, but he also had no doubt that in the long run coercion was no answer. Ireland would be peaceful—and the Fenians would lose their appeal—only when Irish grievances were removed. Bright felt as guilty about the Irish as any American abolitionist felt about the Negroes. He saw Ireland as Britain's greatest humiliation, and he feared that Britain would be punished for its treatment of the Irish just as the United States had been punished for its treatment of Negroes. It infuriated him that the British Government had to wait for an insurrection, or the threat of one, before moving into action. (12)

Because Bright had expressed his guilt about the Irish for years, no English Member of Parliament was so admired as he in the Ireland of the late 1860's. When, for example, the posthumous memoirs of an Irish patriot were published, his widow sent Bright a copy, with a covering letter that overflowed with gratitude. Even when the English dread of Fenianism was at a high point, late in 1866, Bright dared to accept an invitation to speak publicly in Dublin—in favor of the Union with Britain—without fear of being assassinated. (13)

Despite what his enemies said about him, Bright detested the Fenians and what they stood for—violence and Irish independence. He was particularly anxious about their activities in the United States, where they were trying to do everything possible to embitter Anglo-American relations. If the Irish in America were Americans, as Bright supposed they were, that was one thing, and they should act like Americans. If, on the other hand, they were Irish and not Americans, then Britain had a responsibility to prevent them from engaging in acts of violence directed against the United Kingdom and Canada (which country, Bright assumed, would in any case inevitably join the United States). Always, however, he stressed that Fenianism was a symptom, insisting that the sooner action was taken to get at its underlying causes, the sooner it would disappear. (14)

As so often in his career, Bright was tempted to cry "I told you so"—and not infrequently he yielded to the temptation. Still, he recognized that now more than ever before statesmanlike behavior was needed in Anglo-Irish relations, and that, among Tory and Whig leaders, statesmen were hard to find. Almost all of Parliament had joined in the hysteria induced by Fenianism, and the political atmosphere hardly favored the kind of wisdom, magnanimity, and remedial legislation that the Irish Question required. (15)

More and more Bright saw Gladstone as the only prominent politician who might grapple successfully with Irish difficulties. He discussed with him repeatedly in 1867 and 1868 the importance of disestablishing the Church of Ireland and of effecting land reforms that would improve the position of Irish tenant farmers in a country dominated by absentee landlords. Bright never underestimated the opposition that such changes were certain to arouse, but his argument was that only justice to Ireland could undermine Fenianism. If Parliament failed to legislate wisely, Ireland would be the scene of countless insurrections and embarrassments for years to come. Coercion alone would not ensure Irish domestic tranquillity. (16)

As long as Tories headed the Government, Bright had little hope for the right kind of pacification of Ireland. They were too committed to the idea of a state church, to the interests of the great landowners, and to the practice of coercion. Indeed, as the Fenian panic spread in late 1867 and 1868, the Tories responded in their traditional way—with force, not with remedial legislation. Bright, for his part, feared that coercion would simply add to the long list of Irish heroes and martyrs and further embitter Anglo-Irish relations. Unfortunately, it was clear that the party that looked back to Edmund Burke had forgotten the wise things that Burke said about magnanimity. (17)

When Disraeli served as Prime Minister (February to December 1868)—final proof to Bright of the decadence and decrepitude of the British aristocracy—Bright continued to plead the Irish case as often and as vigorously as possible. Any time he met an influential figure, whether it was the Prince of Wales, Lord Russell, or Gladstone, he brought up the Irish Question. He still hoped that it was not too late

for Britain to act decently—the damage done during several centuries
of misrule might yet be undone. He called for immediate steps to rid
the Irish of their "alien church," and while he admitted that this
might seem a revolutionary act, he insisted that in reality it was not.
For the number of Anglicans in Ireland was small, and the fact that
after so many centuries the Church of Ireland had won so few ad-
herents was the clearest sign that it had failed in its mission to convert the Roman Catholic population. Why not recognize this failure,
disestablish the Anglican Church in Ireland, and remove one of the
profound sources of Irish Catholic resentment and hostility? (18)

Just as the Established Church should go, so, too, the traditional
land system should be abandoned, Bright argued. Since he sympathized fully with Irish tenants, he favored laws that would bolster
their legal rights in their dealings with their landlords. Not only
that, however. Bright wanted legislation that would encourage and
enable tenants to buy their land on easy terms, establish themselves,
in effect, as independent Jeffersonian proprietors, and become bul-
warks of social peace in the Irish countryside. Such proprietors would
transform the conditions of Irish rural life by giving tenants new
motivations and aspirations, and all the countryside would feel the
wholesome effects of their status. In an Ireland of satisfied small
proprietors the voice of the Fenian would be the voice of the mad-
man or the drunkard. In such an Ireland coercion and the suspension
of personal liberties would be memories from an unbelievable
past. (19)

Disraeli did not take Bright's advice on the Irish Question. He
was having trouble enough in 1868 with his Tory colleagues, who
were still furious with him over what they regarded as the detestable
Reform Act; to antagonize them further by striking out at the
Church of Ireland and the great Irish landowners was unthinkable.
For the hostility among old Tories to any further changes was profound. As one of them put it typically, "All these reforms and
improvements look bad for poor old England. What with strikes,
Fenians, reform, and other leagues, etc., there is no security
left." (20)

IV

At last, in December 1868, Gladstone formed his first Ministry, and *Punch* marked the event with some revealing words:

> Gone is Dizzy;
> From the busy
> Cares of State repose he can.
> In comes Gladdy,
> Who of Paddy
> Means to make a loyal man.

Bright was not so sure, however; he was not overly optimistic that Irish affairs would be dealt with properly. For, as he correctly described the situation, many of the Whig leaders agreed with the Tories when it was a question of Ireland; nor was Gladstone's position sufficiently strong for him to be able to impose his views on his followers. (21)

Still, it encouraged Bright that Gladstone was willing to listen to him. For the first time in his career Bright was offered a cabinet post, and while he did not feel sturdy enough at fifty-seven to function in the demanding office of Secretary of State for India, he did consent to serve as President of the Board of Trade.

> This sitter 'neath the gangway moved
>   Up to the Treasury Bench!
> A Member of the Cabinet, he
>   Who erst made Cabinets blench!

Thanks to Gladstone, he would at last be able to help shape the policies of the Government. For the present at least he could overlook the resentment he felt toward Gladstone because of his support of the Crimean War and his sympathy for the South during the American Civil War. (22)

Bright's appointment made many people happy: Americans like Charles Francis Adams and his young son Henry, who saw a new era in Anglo-American harmony dawning and who could not help contrasting the present with the miserable Age of Palmerston; Frenchmen like Michel Chevalier, who looked to more cordial

Anglo-French relations as well as the furtherance of freer trade all over the world; Indians who regarded Bright as their most informed, reliable, and eloquent spokesman in Britain; Irish who knew that he had been their outspoken friend from pre-Famine times; and a variety of domestic reformers who counted on him to press for the causes they favored. (23)

Bright tried hard to be casual and humble about his membership in the Ministry, and he kept mentioning how reluctantly he had accepted office and power.

> "I sought them not: they came to me,"
>   He says—and says what's true:
> So *Punch* can vouch—whose baton oft
>   Hath beat him black and blue.

However true the second part of *Punch*'s description was, the first part was not true. Bright was enormously pleased and flattered and at the same time ashamed to be so pleased and flattered. He certainly was happy that the unpopular positions he had adopted on so many occasions were no longer being held against him. On the contrary, it was as if he were being rewarded for having spoken the unpleasant truth for so many years. Even in the world of politics honesty *was* the best policy, after all. He had been trying to convince himself for years that this was really so, and his powers of self-persuasion had often failed him, but now the traditional ethic in which he wanted and needed to believe was exonerated. (24)

Bright was particularly happy about Queen Victoria's conduct toward him. For years she had viewed him as a subversive and an incendiary who would corrupt her Privy Council. Now she was most gracious in making any number of concessions to him. Because of his religious scruples, he would not have to kneel during the required ceremonies, nor would he have to wear formal court dress. Clearly the reasons for Victoria's change of attitude were personal. Bright had admired the Prince Consort for his conciliatory behavior during the crisis over the Trent Affair. And after Albert's death Bright, as a good family man, could understand the grief that drove the Queen into seclusion. Having been a widower himself, he could sympathize with a widow—even if she happened also to be a queen.

Indeed, when a speaker at a public meeting that he attended referred harshly to Victoria's withdrawal from public life, Bright spoke bluntly to his London audience: "I think there has been by many persons a great injustice done to the Queen in reference to her desolate and widowed position. And I venture to say this, that a woman, be she the Queen of a great realm or the wife of one of your labouring men, who can keep alive in her heart a great sorrow for the lost object of her life and her affections, is not at all likely to be wanting in a great and generous sympathy with you." Victoria saw to it that Bright was told by Gladstone how touched she was by his statement; and she herself made sure to tell him so. (25)

In certain respects Bright's new status made his life more difficult. As a member of the Cabinet, he had frequent meetings to attend; and as President of the Board of Trade, he could not avoid certain departmental duties even though he had two outstanding civil servants—Shaw Lefevre and Thomas Henry Farrer—on whom to rely. Yet his new status also simplified his life, and in a way that he liked. Now he was no longer in a position to make public speeches as in the past; they might easily be misinterpreted as official statements and be given undue importance. Therefore, since he could not speak with his traditional freedom, the best policy was as much silence as possible, and this Bright relished. He had had more than his fill of speeches and of playing the part of a "public instructor." (26)

Bright's elevation to the Cabinet was his most notable personal victory, but he was recognized in other gratifying ways between the passage of the Reform Act of 1867 and the beginning of Gladstone's Ministry at the end of 1868. His brother Jacob was elected Member of Parliament for Manchester, an event that he rightly interpreted as a personal vindication. Macmillan brought out a substantial edition of his speeches, the Oxford political economist James E. Thorold Rogers serving as editor. Americans continued to tempt him with heartwarming invitations to visit the United States. Irish patriots repeatedly begged him to return to Ireland, and when he did so he discovered what it meant to be lionized. The citizens of Edinburgh gave him the freedom of their city. Even within England he was being invited to the kinds of dinner parties—with "Dukes and Lords and Archbishops and Bishops abundant"—that showed that he was becoming "respectable," as he told his wife. (27)

Despite the signs that he was no longer a pariah—or at least that he was much less an outsider than he had been—Bright did not forget the humiliations to which he had been subjected for years. It was typical of him that when he was complimented by some of his colleagues for a speech he delivered in the House in 1868, he told his wife that he would try to stand up to their praise as he had tried to stand up to their abuse; the point is that he remembered the abuse. It was also typical of him that when members of his family complained in their letters that they had nothing new to report, he assured them that this in itself was good news. For he was convinced by years of experience that news was mostly bad, and the heartening events of 1867 and 1868 did not undermine this conviction. The cheerful, buoyant, and resilient crusader of anti-corn law days had long ago lost his cheerfulness, buoyancy, and resiliency. The effects of years of disappointments and frustrations were not to be erased. (28)

NOTES

(1) Bright to Mrs. Bright, Apr. 13, 1866; Apr. 14, 1866; June 4, 1866; June 14, 1866; Oct. 27, 1866; Mar. 11, 1867; Apr. 1, 1867, Bright MSS, UCLL; Bright to John Oxford, Aug. 8, 1866, Bright MSS, PUL; Bright to Sumner, Aug. 16, 1866, Sumner MSS, HCL; *Diaries,* Feb. 7, 1867.

(2) *Punch,* LII (1867), 31; Bright to Northy, Dec. 29, 1866, Northy MSS, BM 44,877; Bright to Sumner, Dec. 14, 1866, Sumner MSS, HCL; *The Press and St. James's Chronicle,* Sept. 1, 1866.

(3) *Letters,* Jan. 3, 1867; Field House Mills, Rochdale, Jan. 25, 1867, Document "signed in behalf of the hands in your employ," RGL.

(4) Richard Congreve to Bright, Sept. 27, 1866, Bright MSS, BM 43,389; Bright to Mrs. Bright, Oct. 29, 1866; Nov. 2, 1866, Bright MSS, UCLL; Bright to W. H. Arnold, Dec. 25, 1866, Bright MSS, National Liberal Club; Bright to Thomas Gee, Dec. 27, 1866, Bright MSS, NLW; Address to John Bright from the Scottish National Reform League, Glasgow, Oct. 16, 1866, RGL; Bright to T. H. Barton, Oct. 31, 1866, Brotherton Library, University of Leeds; *Parl. Deb.,* 103 (Mar. 23, 1849), 1221.

(5) Cf. Bright to John Hamilton, Nov. 23, 1857, Bright MSS, Trinity College, Dublin; *Letters,* Mar. 25, 1866; May 19, 1866; Feb. 16, 1867; *Speeches on Parliamentary Reform, etc., Delivered during the Autumn of 1866, to the*

People of England, Scotland and Ireland, at Birmingham, Manchester, Leeds,
Glasgow, Dublin, and London (Manchester).

(6) *Speeches,* II, 192, 197, 208–9, 211, 216, 235.

(7) Bright to Horace Greeley, Nov. 28, 1866, Horace Greeley MSS, NYPL;
Bright to Sumner, Dec. 14, 1866, Sumner MSS, HCL; Bright to Northy, Dec.
25, 1866, Northy MSS, BM 44,877; Bright to Greeley, Dec. 28, 1866, Bright
MSS, PML; Bright to C. Edward Lester, Jan. 9, 1867, Bright MSS, LC; cf.
Bright to John Benjamin Smith, Aug. 9, 1866, Smith MSS, MCL.

(8) Cf. John Benjamin Smith to Gosling, May 28, 1867, Smith MSS, MCL;
Bright to Arthur Albright, Dec. 25, 1866, Wilson King MSS, BPL; Bright
to W. S. Nichols, Feb. 16, 1867, Bright MSS, Bradford Central Library; Bright
to Mrs. Bright, Mar. 3, 1867; Mar. 4, 1867; Mar. 21, 1867; Mar. 31, 1867;
April 1, 1867; May 8, 1867; May 11, 1867; May 12, 1867; Aug. 8, 1867, Bright
MSS, UCLL; Bright to R. D. Webb, May 18, 1867, Bright MSS, YUL; Bright
to Gladstone, July 31, 1867, Gladstone MSS, BM 44,112; *Diaries,* Feb. 25, 1867;
Mar. 1, 1867; Mar. 4, 1867; Mar. 12, 1867; Apr. 8, 1867; Apr. 13, 1867; May
9, 1867; July 15, 1867; Bright drew more heavily on Milton than any other
nineteenth-century political figure, but he is not mentioned in James G.
Nelson, *The Sublime Puritan: Milton and the Victorians* (Madison, 1963);
cf. Bright to Joseph Parkes, Dec. 9, 1861, Parkes MSS, UCLL.

(9) Bright to Mrs. Bright, June 22, 1867; June 26, 1867, Bright MSS,
UCLL; *Diaries,* June 29, 1867; *Speeches,* I, 285–92.

(10) Bright's suggestions to Disraeli are reprinted in Trevelyan, pp. 381–
82; Magnus, p. 185; Bright to Mrs. Bright, May 5, 1867, Bright MSS, UCLL;
see Home Office MSS, 41/20, PRO; Bright to Edmond Beales, Mar. 5, 1867,
Bright MSS, FHL; Robert Curzon to Walter Sneyd, Apr. 30, 1867; July 10,
1867, Sneyd MSS, University of Keele; Bright to Sumner, Oct. 26, 1867, Sumner MSS, HCL.

(11) Bright to Edmond Beales, July 26, 1867, Bright MSS, FHL; *Letters,*
Aug. 18, 1867; Sept. 29, 1867.

(12) Bright to T. H. Barton, Oct. 31, 1866, Bright MSS, Brotherton Li-
brary, University of Leeds; Home Office MSS, 41/20, PRO; Bright to Greeley,
Nov. 28, 1866, Greeley MSS, NYPL; Bright to Northy, Dec. 26, 1867, Northy
MSS, BM 44,877.

(13) *Parl. Deb.,* 173 (Mar. 11, 1864), 1879ff.; 174 (Apr. 13, 1864), 955ff.;
Bright to the Knight of Kerry, July 23, 1866, Bright MSS, NLI; Bright to J. B.
Smith, Aug. 9, 1866; Oct. 7, 1866, Smith MSS, MCL; Fanny Byrne to Bright,
Jan. 14, 1866, Bright MSS, BM 43,389.

(14) Bright to Thomas H. Dudley, Feb. 22, 1866, Bright MSS, HL; Bright
to Sumner, Aug. 16, 1866; Dec. 14, 1866, Sumner MSS, HCL; Bright to
Greeley, Sept. 2, 1866, Bright MSS, Friends Historical Library, Swarthmore
College; Bright to Ernest Jones, Oct. 4, 1867, Northy MSS, BM 44,877; *Parl.*

Deb., 186 (May 3, 1867), 1930; for Bright's views on Canada, see *Speeches,* I, 123–63; cf. Bright to Smith, Apr. 14, 1865, Smith MSS, MCL.

(15) Bright to Sumner, Jan. 11, 1868, Sumner MSS, HCL; Bright to H. Dix Hutton, Jan. 27, 1868, Bright MSS, PUL.

(16) Bright to Mrs. Bright, July 24, 1867, Bright MSS, UCLL; *Diaries,* July 24, 1867; Nov. 30, 1867; Bright to Gladstone, Dec. 9, 1867, Gladstone MSS, BM 44,112.

(17) Home Office MSS, 41/20 and 41/21, PRO; *Diaries,* May 3, 1867; Nov. 21, 1867; Nov. 24, 1867; *Letters,* Nov. 11, 1867; Jan. 27, 1868.

(18) Bright to Dr. John Brown, Mar. 2, 1868, Bright MSS, Friends Historical Library, Swarthmore College; Bright to Sumner, Mar. 7, 1868; Aug. 1, 1868, Sumner MSS, HCL; *Diaries,* Mar. 9, 1868; Mar. 12, 1868; Apr. 22, 1868; Bright to Mrs. Bright, Mar. 12, 1868; Mar. 15, 1868; Apr. 21, 1868; Apr. 23, 1868; May 3, 1868, Bright MSS, UCLL; Bright to Aubrey De Vere, Mar. 22, 1868, De Vere MSS, NLI; Henry Earl Grey, *Letter to John Bright, Esq., M. P., Respecting the Irish Church;* Grey to Bright, Mar. 27, 1868, Bright MSS, BM 43,389.

(19) *Letters,* Nov. 11, 1867; *Speeches,* I, 349–437.

(20) Bright to Lord Grey, Apr. 1, 1868, Grey of Howick MSS, The Prior's Kitchen, The College, Durham; Robert Curzon to Walter Sneyd, Apr. 22, 1868, Sneyd MSS, University of Keele.

(21) *Punch,* LV (1868), 258; Bright to H. Dix Hutton, Jan. 27, 1868, Bright MSS, PUL.

(22) Cf. *Economist,* XXVI (1868), 381; Bright to Mrs. Bright, Dec. 4, 1868, Bright MSS, UCLL; Bright to Gladstone, Dec. 5, 1868, Gladstone MSS, BM 44,112; *Punch,* LVI (1869), 14.

(23) Granville to Bright, Dec. 6, 1868; Charles Francis Adams to Bright, Dec. 4, 1868; Henry Adams to Bright, Feb. 3, 1869; Chevalier to Bright, Dec. 10, 1868, Bright MSS, BM 43,387, 43,391, 43,389; Bright to Walmsley, Mar. 25, 1869, Bright MSS, University of Kansas Library.

(24) Bright to Jaffray, Dec. 6, 1868, DeCoursey Fales MSS, NYPL; Bright to Margaret Leatham, Dec. 6, 1868; Bright to Mrs. Bright, Dec. 13, 1868, Bright MSS, UCLL; Bright to Sumner, Dec. 25, 1868, Sumner MSS, HCL; *Punch,* LVI (1869), 14.

(25) *Diaries,* Dec. 9, 1868; Dec. 30, 1868; Bright to Mrs. Bright, undated letter marked "Very Private"; Dec. 9, 1868; Feb. 8, 1869; Feb. 23, 1869; Mar. 3, 1869; July 8, 1869; Nov. 21, 1869, Bright MSS, UCLL; Granville to Bright, Dec. 17, 1868, Bright MSS, BM 43,387; Granville to Gladstone, Dec. 31, 1868; Gladstone to Granville, Jan. 6, 1869, Ramm; Bright to Gladstone, Feb. 8, 1869, Gladstone MSS, BM 44,112; Elizabeth Longford, *Queen Victoria: Born to Succeed* (New York, 1964), p. 374.

(26) Bright to Mrs. Bright, Dec. 13, 1868, Bright MSS, UCLL; Gladstone

to Granville, Dec. 14, 1868, Ramm; Memorandum signed by Bright and dated Jan. 14, 1869, Board of Trade MSS, 13/4, PRO; Bright to William Fenton, July 26, 1868, Bright MSS, BPL; Bright to Charles Holland, Jan. 9, 1869, Misc. MSS, BM 37,772; Bright to A. J. Mundella, Sept. 19, 1869, Mundella MSS, University of Sheffield Library.

(27) Jacob Bright to George Jacob Holyoake, Dec. 5, 1867, Holyoake MSS, Cooperative Union Ltd., Manchester; Bright to Northy, Dec. 6, 1867, Northy MSS, BM 44,877; John Bigelow to Bright, May 5, 1868; Cyrus W. Field to Bright, July 3, 1868, Bright MSS, BM 43,390, 43,391; Bright to Dudley, Dec. 15, 1868, Bright MSS, HL; Bright to Mrs. Bright, Mar. 23, 1868; May 1, 1868; May 3, 1868; June 25, 1868; June 27, 1868; July 7, 1868; July 12, 1868; July 13, 1868, Bright MSS, UCLL.

(28) Bright to Mrs. Bright, Mar. 12, 1868; Mar. 15, 1868; Mar. 28, 1858; July 1, 1868, *ibid.*

CHAPTER TWELVE

A FRIEND IN POWER
1868–1874

It is nonsense to claim, as some historians have done, that Bright found his new office a prison. He was, of course, unaccustomed to being a member of the group in power, but he adjusted rapidly and enthusiastically to his new status. He had hardly learned of the sweeping Liberal-Whig electoral victory in November when he wrote to Gladstone about the measures for which he thought the Government should press. "In my view of the future there is plenty of work for you," he pointed out. Those Tories who interpreted the election results to mean that British institutions would be shaken up were proven altogether right. (1)

Occasionally Bright had a profound sense of the difficulties that reform necessarily entailed in a country like Britain. As he once wrote to an American: "We have many evils coming down from past times, which nobody in England would think of establishing or defending if he had not found them here, but which many well meaning men are afraid to touch, not knowing how much may fall with them." The reassuring truth was, after all, that when the British departed from Britain, they did not "set up Peerages, and State Churches, and Land Laws for privileged classes, and refuse to provide for the education of the people." The trouble, therefore, grew out of the superstitions and prejudices inherited from the past, and the great problem was this, as Bright saw it: Could the British "make such changes gradually and without violence, as have been accomplished in other nations for the most part by war and revolution?" (2)

Bright placed legislation for Ireland at the head of his list of vital changes. But he was also intent on securing the secret ballot and educational reform. To justify the abandonment of open voting, he pointed out to Gladstone some of the glaring instances of intimidation and corruption that had taken place in the recent elections. Educational reform hardly needed any justification, for Bright, like Cobden, regarded British educational backwardness as both a disgrace and a threat to the Kingdom, and he did not hesitate to press for state action to correct it. As he had said repeatedly: "We may have a great monarchy, aristocracy, Church, etc.—symbols it may be of greatness—but if the millions are poor and ignorant and degraded, there is a rottenness in the fabric which threatens its overthrow." Indeed, his hostility to the Anglican hierarchy was due, among other things, to its failure to use its immense political influence and power to wipe out illiteracy. (3)

There were other important subjects on which Bright wished the Government to act. Expenditures for the armed forces required drastic cutting. Furthermore, the troublesome *Alabama* claims, about which he had corresponded for years with Sumner and other American leaders, needed to be settled in the interests of Anglo-American friendship. As Bright cautioned Lord Clarendon during one of the frequent crises over the claims: "There is a great temptation to say what is smart and cutting, but there is great danger in it,—and troubles and even wars have sprung from indulging in it." At any rate, once these matters were dealt with properly, Bright thought that he would be able to withdraw from public life with the feeling that he had met his responsibilities. Other reformers would then have to carry on the liberal tradition that Cobden and he had tried to establish, maintain, and foster. (4)

Bright favored immediate attention to what he considered the critical problem—Anglo-Irish relations. Fortunately, Gladstone had come to agree with him, and the result was that the Church of Ireland became the main subject of public and parliamentary discussion in the first half of 1869. Supporters of the Irish State Church moved into action on a grand scale, raising the cry of the "Church in danger." They argued that if the Church of Ireland were disestablished, the Church of England would speedily suffer a similar fate, and other institutions—aristocracy, monarchy, property—would also be doomed. Understandably, the defenders of the Church of Ireland singled out Gladstone and Bright for special abuse, and their attacks on them often smacked more of the sixteenth century than of the nineteenth. One Tory Member of Parliament was tamer than many of his like-minded contemporaries when he addressed Gladstone in this fashion:

> You've kept me here both day and night
>   To hear you bully, brag, and blunder,
> While helping Beelzebub and Bright
>   To quarrel o'er the sacred plunder. (5)

Since Gladstone had the votes in the Commons, the fate of the Irish Church Bill depended on the Lords, who were subjected to pressures from many sides to accept the measure. Prominent among those who cautioned the Lords of the dangers of resistance was Bright. In a tactless—and typical—public letter he predicted that if the Lords remained out of harmony with the nation, they might "meet with accidents not pleasant for them to think of." Bright's statement did not have the useful result he intended. It was quickly interpreted as a threat, and, instead of helping the Government, embarrassed it. By a fortunate coincidence, word had just reached England that Charles Sumner had made a speech in the United States in which he criticized Bright for his John Bullism. Since Sumner had emerged as Britain's arch-enemy in the United States because of the extravagant demands he was making for the settlement of the *Alabama* claims, his criticism of Bright's patriotism was invaluable to the Government. Gladstone urged Lord Granville to make use of the remark in the House of Lords in dealing with Bright's critics, and this Granville did with the desired effect. (6)

Bright's bluntness with the Lords failed, but more subtle pressures succeeded, and in the summer the Irish Church Bill was enacted. Bright was elated. What he called "the Church of conquest" had at last lost its privileged status, and what he regarded as the worst violation of the principles of the Reformation was undone. Bright saw the Irish Church Act not only as a sound and wise law in itself but as a symbol of a new era in Anglo-Irish relations. At last Parliament was meeting its responsibilities to the Irish people.

At last steps were being taken to form a true and sturdy union between Britain and Ireland. At last it was plain that Ireland was an integral part of the United Kingdom. Now if Parliament would only continue to act in the way that it did on the Church Bill, Irish memories of centuries of oppression might still be erased. (7)

II

While the controversy over the Irish Church was proceeding, Bright was telling Gladstone that the Irish land question must be dealt with as soon as possible, for every delay made it more complicated. Bright was concerned about the increasingly radical proposals that were gaining currency in Ireland, and he wisely argued that what could now still be a satisfactory remedy would in a short while be unsatisfactory. His preference was for a generous scheme of land purchase that would create a loyal class of Irish farmer proprietors, and his expectation was that land reform, as an economic matter, could be achieved more easily than Church reform, which inevitably aroused so much unreasonable passion. (8)

To Bright's disappointment, Gladstone and other members of the Cabinet kept telling him how complex and baffling land reform was, something he had known much longer than they. And it was increasingly plain to him that they were mainly concerned with improving the status of the tenant farmers and that they were wary of his proposal to place the Government in the real estate business in order to create farmer proprietors. He found himself in the awkward position of having to announce that he still adhered to the principles of a "sound" political economy but that the Irish case was exceptional and justified a bold kind of state intervention in economic life. (9)

Bright's confidence in the feasibility of his own scheme was shaken. At times he despaired of ever winning the support of either the Cabinet or Parliament. Other times he thought it better to go down fighting than to accept an inadequate dose of land reform. He marveled at the number of new farms being taken up in the United States under the generous provisions of the Homestead Act, and he prayed for a miracle that would bring something similar to this to Ireland and thus put an end to the Irish Question. (10)

THE BILL OF FARE

Mr. Gladstone (the "Chef") *"Irish stew first, Mrs. B., and then—"*
Mrs. Bright (the Cook) *"Lor bless you, Mr. G., the Irish stew's quite as much as they'll get through, I'll be bound!"*

☞ Commenting on the difficulty of passing several important measures in one Session, Mr. Bright had said, "It was not easy to drive six omnibuses abreast through Temple Bar."—1870.

Since Bright believed in the supreme importance of action—of some statute dealing with the land—he backed the proposals discussed in the Cabinet to strengthen the position of Irish tenant farmers. He also appealed to Gladstone to look ahead to the next critical step: the freeing of Fenian prisoners. His point was that such an act, in combination with Church and land reform, would do wonders for Anglo-Irish relations, since many Irish who condemned the Fenians regarded them, nevertheless, as patriots. To show mercy to them would, therefore, have wholesome results. (11)

In January 1870, shortly before Parliament was to meet, Bright addressed his constituents in Birmingham. He confessed that he did not like to look backward, but he could not resist the temptation to take pride in the work of the last parliamentary session, especially in the Irish Church Act and what it had done to remove any legitimate basis for religious grievances among the Irish. But there were other grievances to be eliminated in the near future. Bright explained what he considered to be the main difficulty of the Irish land question: since agriculture was by far the most important Irish industry, the competition for land was intense, and tenants were necessarily at a disadvantage. Even so, he insisted, much could be done to improve the status of tenants without serious injury to landlords, and he urged his constituents to be patient and understanding as the Government proceeded to grapple with the Irish land question.

But Parliament also had to consider other important questions: the establishment of an adequate national system of elementary education, the introduction of a secret ballot, and the reduction of government expenditures. Bright could offer no timetable to his audience, pointing out that it was hard "to drive six omnibuses abreast through Temple Bar." But he assured his constituents that important questions would be dealt with soon. (12)

III

When Parliament met in February 1870, Bright was not present to defend Gladstone's Land Bill: he was in the throes of another breakdown. All the alarming symptoms of 1856 had returned—unsteadiness, dizziness, weakness, an inability to read, write, or work. In a sad note to Gladstone, Bright apologized that he could not be with him in Parliament to continue the struggle in behalf of Ireland; and he offered to resign as President of the Board of Trade. Gladstone refused to consider such a possibility, assuring him that when he was well again his post would be waiting for him. (13)

Bright's illness was publicly explained as the result of overwork, and he himself ascribed it to the excessive demands of official life. There is doubtless some truth in this explanation—just as there is doubtless some truth in the present-day explanation that emphasizes changes in body chemistry as a source of mental illness. Nevertheless, what brought on Bright's illness in 1870, and not before, remains unexplained. He had feared that he might go under a number of times in the sixties, most notably when both his son and Cobden died. Moreover, he had been under almost unbearable strain during the American Civil War and during the fierce agitation that preceded the Reform Act. Yet he survived those crises. His breakdown occurred at a time when things were going relatively well for him.

How, then—however inadequately—to "account" for it? Partly it seems to have been linked with his anxieties over the battles for Irish land reform and educational reform that were about to take place; illness was a way of escaping from them and from some of the ugly fights and sickening compromises that would arise. Partly it seems to have been related to his anxiety over his advancing age and the speed with which his life was ending; his hair was very white, and while he liked to hear people say that he looked much younger than he was, he was close to sixty and painfully conscious of the fact. And partly his breakdown seems to have been connected with his loneliness in London away from his family. In the early stages of his illness he snapped at his wife: "I told thee something would happen, and that we should not always be so much separated." (14)

This time, as in 1856, Bright rested and rested. As much as possible his family shielded him from anything unpleasant, especially in the newspapers. Some days he was certain that he would never recover and that his usefulness was over; but other days he had hopes that he might still be able to do some good in the world. As before, people behaved admirably. Queen Victoria and Gladstone inquired repeatedly about the state of his health, as did a host of other contemporaries. If Bright wanted and needed to be reassured that he was wanted and needed, he received such reassurances on a grand scale. Even *The Times* and the *Manchester Guardian* wished him well and noted how much he was missed. (15)

On his good days he occasionally wrote to Gladstone about his views of public affairs. He still felt strongly about freeing the Fenian prisoners, and he begged Gladstone to consider the wholesome consequences that would follow such an action. He also felt strongly about keeping Britain neutral in the potentially dangerous Franco-German War that had broken out during the summer of 1870. When he learned that Gladstone's Ministry was making commitments for the military defense of Belgium, he immediately submitted his resignation. He could not remain a member of a Government that might provoke a war by meddling in the affairs of other countries. Although Gladstone did not expect to succeed, he begged him to reconsider his decision. Bright consented to stay on so as not to embarrass the Government; he also made it clear that if his health did not improve soon, he would prefer to resign for reasons of illness, instead of differences over policy. (16)

Although Bright opposed British intervention in behalf of Belgium, he urged Gladstone to use his powerful position to improve Franco-German relations. Gladstone should be kind and helpful to France in her humiliation, and he should avoid giving offense to the Germans. At the same time, he should advise the Germans to take no territory from France; to do so would only provide the basis for a later war of revenge, Bright predicted. For the rest, he rejoiced over the speedy German victory. Like many of his contemporaries, he saw it as a triumph for Protestantism, peace, and liberalism; and he was glad that Europe would no longer have to be concerned about the aggressive inclinations of Napoleon III. While Bright admired Napoleon for what he had done for freer trade, the beautification of Paris, and the lifting of restrictions on passports, he approved of little else. He detested him for his role in the Crimean War, for his Mexican adventure, for his pro-Southernism during the American

Civil War, and for his use of French troops to keep Rome from joining the Kingdom of Italy. (17)

In November 1870, Bright and Gladstone again disagreed about foreign affairs—this time about Anglo-Russian relations. Bright wanted Britain to yield to Russian demands concerning its position as a Black Sea power; but the Cabinet would support no such step. Bright submitted his resignation, bluntly reminding Gladstone that the Crimean War was the worst blot on the reign of Victoria, and that the Government should do everything to avoid another such disgraceful conflict. The big danger, Bright maintained, came from the British military services, which were constantly asking for increased appropriations and creating a warlike atmosphere. (18)

Bright insisted that his resignation be ascribed entirely to his poor health, for he was eager not to appear to differ with the Prime Minister. Even more important, however—and this has rarely been understood—he did not want his action to be interpreted by the newspapers as an indication that the Cabinet was warlike. On the other hand, while it was true that he felt better, he was still far from well; it was not right, therefore, for him to retain his Presidency of the Board of Trade and his membership in the Cabinet. What he called his "broken-down head" still needed a great deal of rest as well as relief from the excitement of official life. Whenever he tried to write or talk about public affairs, his head still ached. (19)

The people who mattered to Bright—Queen Victoria, Gladstone, Lord Granville, officials at the Board of Trade, colleagues in Parliament, and his relatives and friends—all said the right things about his resignation. Victoria wrote to him directly, expressing her wishes for his complete recovery. Lord Granville, the Foreign Secretary, told him how much he would be missed and how invaluable his advice on Anglo-American affairs would have been. And Louis Mallet, the ardent Cobdenite at the Board of Trade, hoped that he would soon be able to resume "a public life which is becoming every year more precious and more indispensable in the eyes of those ... who believe that the principles of which you are the chief representative are essential to the happiness and greatness of the country." (20)

IV

In 1871, the year he reached sixty, Bright continued to spend most of his time resting and much of his time wondering about his future. A few events cheered him. He was elated over the conclusion of the Treaty of Washington, which provided for the submission to an international tribunal of all outstanding Anglo-American differences, for he hoped that the Treaty would set a healthy precedent that would be widely imitated in the settlement of international disputes. He was flattered by the continuing interest of Queen Victoria in the state of his health, and he was overwhelmed to receive an invitation, which he dared not accept, to visit her at Balmoral Castle. Moreover, he was pleased that Gladstone kept pursuing him to rejoin the Ministry. Indeed, Gladstone could not have acted more admirably, assuring Bright that the vigor he had brought to the Government in its early stages could now be matched by the dignity that he would give it in its old age. (21)

Along with the good news went the usual complement of sad news. George Wilson, who had played such an important part in the making of Bright's career, died at the end of 1870, and at the beginning of the new year Bright's mother-in-law, with whom he got along well, also died. His daughter Mary seemed to be turning into a chronic invalid. And he himself, as during his earlier breakdown, continued to have some very bad days.

Public affairs still upset him unduly. He was annoyed that the Government had not emphasized economy sufficiently, especially now that a small band of republicans was criticizing the expense of maintaining the British monarchy. He was disturbed that Gladstone did not seem to recognize the importance of renewing the Anglo-French Commercial Treaty even at the cost of generous concessions to the French. Above all, he was angry that the Ministry had rushed through an Education Act that was much too generous to the Church of England. In fact, he repeatedly scolded Gladstone in 1871 for having backed a measure that was such a mass of blunders and so unsatisfactory to the non-Anglicans in the British population.

Gladstone was decent and well-mannered enough not to remind Bright that initially he had raised no objections to the Education Bill and that his opposition came belatedly. In any case, Gladstone was grateful that at least for the present Bright was not expressing publicly his strong feelings about the measure. (22)

Although Bright did not rage publicly over the Education Act, many other Nonconformists did. Since Gladstone needed their support to remain in power, he intensified his efforts in 1872 to bring Bright, a hero to many Nonconformists, back into the Government. Gladstone assured him that he would not have much work. He praised and flattered him. When, for example, the bill providing for the adoption of the secret ballot was at last being enacted, he told him that the measure was really his. But despite Gladstone's appeals, Bright was still afraid to expose himself to the pressures, strains, and controversies that would accompany a Cabinet post. Furthermore, he was concerned about what people would say if he did rejoin the Ministry. For he was convinced that, if he resumed his office before he could fully meet its responsibilities, his action would be interpreted as a shameless bid for power and glory. He felt guilty enough about not having resigned his seat in Parliament at the time he took ill; he was not disposed to add to his guilt feelings by assuming further obligations that he could not fulfill. (23)

Whenever he thought about the future—which was often—he grew confused, and to bolster his spirits he tried to persuade himself that he was simply not a political animal and that political life was not natural to him as it was to someone like Gladstone. He dreaded what he called "the turmoil of elections"—a survival, clearly, of his traumatic Manchester experience. Worse still, he doubted his ability to do good. He recognized that there were still many worthwhile changes to be accomplished. The land laws had to be basically reformed; the right to vote had to be extended to agricultural laborers; seats in the House of Commons had to be redistributed more equitably; the Education Act had to be revised and expanded; government expenditures had to be cut drastically; and the Church of England had to be disestablished. But each of these changes would involve fierce battles with the great landowners, and Bright lacked the necessary physical and emotional resources. However much he had insisted through the years that he had no objection to "the use of hard words in debate," the truth was that he had become increasingly thin-skinned; he could no longer take criticism in his stride. (24)

Although he did not rejoin the Government in 1872, he ventured to speak out in a number of public letters on some of the issues that were attracting attention. He denounced the idea of Irish home rule, insisting that it would be "an intolerable mischief" to have two legislative assemblies in the United Kingdom; one was bad enough sometimes, he had found. He called attention to the need to lessen public expenditures and to eliminate the taxes that added to the price of tea, coffee, and sugar. He ridiculed the notion of abolishing the monarchy and of establishing a republic in Britain, making it clear that he was no candidate for the presidency of a British Republic. His contention was—and he repeated it in 1873—that it made more sense to work to improve the government, as reformers had been trying to do for the past forty years. Because of the folly and crimes of Charles I, the British had tried republicanism; the aftermath had been a century of unsettled government. And he supported the new Anglo-French Commercial Treaty, although he would have preferred to see its freer trade provisions much more generous than they were. (25)

Bright risked giving only one public speech in 1872, in response to a persistent deputation from the Staffordshire Potteries. "The first orator of his day," as the *Illustrated London News* now called him, was nervous at the outset. Once he began to talk, however, the words flowed much more easily than he had anticipated, and they were authentic Bright. He used the occasion to review some of the beneficent legislation that had been enacted in the course of his thirty years of public life: the repeal of the corn laws, the repeal of the Navigation Acts, the repeal of the taxes that had impeded the growth of cheap newspapers, the Reform Act of 1867, the Irish Church Act, the Irish Land Act, and the Ballot Act. The moral he drew was clear: Just as these wise measures had made it possible for Britain to avoid the revolutions that took place in other European countries, so similar legislation in the future would again enable Britain to escape revolution. As for foreign affairs, Bright once more inveighed against the Crimean War as the greatest blot on the Victorian Age, and he hoped that the British people and their political leaders had learned something from that blunder as well as from the mistaken policies pursued in the period of the American Civil War. A truculent diplomacy did not suit the conditions of the nineteenth-century world. Peace should be the grand aim of British foreign policy. (26)

V

When the parliamentary session of 1873 began in February, Bright was not feeling "quite well," but he resumed his place in the House of Commons. He had had doubts about how much work he could do, and he found public life distasteful, but he was guilt-ridden about any further extension of his three-year absence from Parliament. He was touched by the cordial reception his colleagues and the press gave him, and he was flattered that Gladstone continued to urge him to rejoin the Ministry. After countless pleas, he consented, and in the fall he became Chancellor of the Duchy of Lancaster but again with Gladstone's assurances that his departmental duties would be undemanding. Ironically, this was an office he had criticized many years before, pointing out that it could advantageously be abolished. (27)

When Bright reentered the Cabinet, he knew that a general election would take place soon, but he was confident about the results. The Government, after all, had a remarkable record of achievement: the Irish Church Act, which proved that religion could prosper without state support; the Irish Land Act, which introduced a dual concept of property, improved the legal position of tenants, limited the rights of landlords, and which by its "Bright clauses" facilitated the creation of proprietors by authorizing government loans to tenants who sought to buy their holdings from their landlords; the Education Act of 1870, which, despite the uproar it created, was an important step in spreading literacy, and which Bright praised because it embodied the principle that the "education of the children of the country is henceforward to be provided for by the State"; the extension of civil service examinations; the abolition of religious tests at Cambridge and Oxford; the reorganization of the British army and the elimination of the corrupt practice of purchasing commissions; the adoption of the secret ballot, which at last made possible free elections; and the settlement of the *Alabama* claims, despite the difficulties caused by Sumner and despite the fury of British superpatriots who argued that Britain was yielding too much to the United States. (28)

To be sure, Bright disapproved heartily of some of the Gladstone Ministry's actions. There had not been nearly enough empha-

A FRIEND IN NEED

MR. GLADSTONE. *"My dear John, I congratulate you! Just in time to settle accounts with our black friend yonder!"*

JOHN BRIGHT. *"H'm! Fighting is not quite in my line, as thee knowest, friend William; nevertheless—!"*

☞ Several important changes had been made with the view of strengthening the Cabinet. Amongst others, Mr. Bright again accepted office as Chancellor of the Duchy of Lancaster. The Ashantee War was now in progress.—1873.

sis on the reduction of expenditures. The Education Act should have been discussed longer and more thoroughly, and it should have discouraged denominational schools. The Government, moreover, should not have permitted the War Office and the Colonial Office to involve the country in the shameful Ashanti War of 1873–1874. In fact, Bright saw no reason whatever for Britain to be on the Gold Coast, and he urged prompt withdrawal from the area. (29)

Despite Bright's strong misgivings about a few of the deeds of the Gladstone Ministry, he was convinced that its worthy actions far outstripped its blunders, and he was certain that it would stand out as one of the great administrations in British history. Indeed, once the Government was returned to power by the electorate, it could continue its remarkable performance. It could extend to agricultural laborers the right to vote. It could improve the land laws by abolishing primogeniture, limiting entails, facilitating the purchase and sale of land, and eliminating legal encouragements to great estates. It could redistribute seats in the House of Commons. It could improve the Education Act. It could cut expenditures and taxes. It could better the legal status of workers. It could work for international peace. Above all, it could again demonstrate to the world the lofty standards of the British liberal tradition—a tradition that encouraged reform and deplored revolution. (30)

NOTES

(1) Trevelyan, p. 395; R. A. J. Walling, ed., *Diaries,* p. 338; Bright to Gladstone, Nov. 27, 1868, Gladstone MSS, BM 44,112; Lord Lytton to Mrs. Schüster, Nov. 10, 1868, DeCoursey Fales MSS, NYPL.

(2) Bright to C. Edward Lester, Jan. 9, 1867, Misc. MSS, LC.

(3) Bright to Gladstone, Nov. 27, 1868; cf. Jan. 1, 1870, Gladstone MSS, BM 44,112; Bright to A. J. Mundella, Mar. 25, 1869, Mundella MSS, University of Sheffield Library; Cobden to E. Alexander, Dec. 20, 1864, Cobden MSS, BM 43,676; Bright to Rev. John Allen, Nov. 21, 1868, Bright MSS, PUL; cf. Bright to E. R. Humphreys, Mar. 23, 1853, Autograph MSS, University of Rochester Library.

(4) Bright to Charles Holland, Jan. 9, 1867, Misc. MSS, BM 37,772; Bright to Seward, Oct. 21, 1865, Seward MSS, University of Rochester Library; Bright

to Sumner, Mar. 7, 1868; Dec. 25, 1868, Sumner MSS, HCL; Bright to Field,
Aug. 24, 1869, Cyrus Field MSS, PML; Bright to Clarendon, Mar. 25, 1869;
Mar. 27, 1869; Dec. 22, 1869, Clarendon MSS, BL; Bright to Gladstone, July
30, 1869, Gladstone MSS, BM 44,112.

(5) Cf. Edward Cheney to Ralph Sneyd, July 28, 1869, Ralph Sneyd MSS,
University of Keele; MS poem, dated July 14, 1869, Davenport MSS, JRL.

(6) Edward Cheney to Ralph Sneyd, July 28, 1869, Ralph Sneyd MSS,
University of Keele; *Letters,* June 9, 1869; *Parl. Deb.,* 196 (June 15, 1869),
1794; 197 (June 17, 1869), 1ff.; Gladstone to Granville, June 15, 1869; June 17,
1869; Granville to Gladstone, June 17, 1869, Ramm; *Annual Register, 1869,*
pp. 71, 82–3, 92; cf. Clarendon to Bright, Mar. 22, 1869; Henry Adams to
Bright, May 30, 1869, Bright MSS, BM 43,387, 43,391.

(7) *Parl. Deb.,* 194 (Mar. 19, 1869), 1881–82, 1894; 195 (Apr. 29, 1869),
1863; 195 (Apr. 30, 1869), 2016; 196 (May 6, 1869), 291–2; 197 (July 15, 1869),
1934, 1980; 198 (July 16, 1869), 86, 92.

(8) Bright to Gladstone, May 21, 1869, Gladstone MSS, BM 44,112; cf.
William Joseph O'Neill Daunt, *Why Is Ireland Discontented?, A Letter to
John Bright* . . . (Glasgow, 1869); *Parl. Deb.,* 195 (Apr. 30, 1869), 2010;
Bright to Northy, Dec. 27, 1869, Northy MSS, BM 44,877.

(9) Gladstone to Granville, May 21, 1869; May 24, 1869; May 27, 1869;
Granville to Gladstone, May 26, 1869, Ramm; Clarendon to Bright, Oct. 8,
1869, Bright MSS, BM 43,387; Bright to Clarendon, Oct. 14, 1869, Clarendon
MSS, BL.

(10) Bright to Gladstone, Oct. 15, 1869; Jan. 5, 1870, Gladstone MSS, BM
44,112.

(11) MS memorandum, dated Dec. 1, 1869, Bright MSS, D; Bright to
Gladstone, Nov. 29, 1869; Dec. 3, 1869; Jan. 1, 1870, Gladstone MSS, BM
44,112; Gladstone to Granville, Sept. 22, 1869; Granville to Gladstone, Nov.
21, 1869; Dec. 23, 1869, Ramm.

(12) Cf. *Letters,* Dec. 22, 1864; *Addresses,* pp. 170–87.

(13) Bright to Gladstone, Feb. 8, 1870, Gladstone MSS, BM 44,112.

(14) Bright to Wilson, Aug. 3, 1869; Jan. 11, 1870, Wilson MSS, MCL;
Bright to Gladstone, July 30, 1869, Gladstone MSS, BM 44,112; Bright to
Thomas Simpson, Apr. 16, 1869, Bright MSS, FHL; Bright to Mrs. Bright,
Mar. 18, 1868; June 17, 1868; June 20, 1868; Feb. 4, 1870; Feb. 8, 1870, Bright
MSS, UCLL; *Diaries,* Nov. 16, 1870; Nov. 16, 1871.

(15) Albert Bright to Gladstone, Feb. 12, 1870; Feb. 16, 1870; Feb. 18,
1870, Gladstone MSS, BM 44,424, 44,425; Helen Clark to Northy, Apr. 25,
1870, Northy MSS, BM 44,877; Bright to Gladstone, Mar. 16, 1870; May 2,
1870; July 3, 1870; Sept. 29, 1870, Gladstone MSS, BM 44,112; Mary Bright
to Mrs. Patching, Sept. 20, 1870, Bright MSS, PUL; Bright to Thomas H.
Dudley, Sept. 22, 1870, Bright MSS, HL; Bright to H. G. Calcraft, Dec. 5,

1870, Friends Historical Library, Swarthmore College; *The Times* and the *Manchester Guardian* printed very frequent reports on his health.

(16) Bright to Gladstone, July 4, 1870; Aug. 3, 1870; Aug. 5, 1870; Aug. 10, 1870; Sept. 29, 1870, Gladstone MSS, BM 44,112; Granville to Gladstone, Aug. 4, 1870; Gladstone to Granville, Aug. 7, 1870, Ramm.

(17) Bright to Gladstone, Sept. 11, 1870; Sept. 29, 1870, Gladstone MSS, BM 44,112.

(18) Gladstone to Granville, Nov. 16, 1870; Nov. 19, 1870, Ramm; *Diaries,* Nov. 17, 1870; Dec. 20, 1870; Bright to Gladstone, Nov. 17, 1870; cf. Dec. 3, 1873, Gladstone MSS, BM 44,112, 44,113.

(19) Bright to Gladstone, Nov. 17, 1870; Nov. 18, 1870; Nov. 20, 1870; Nov. 28, 1870; Dec. 14, 1870, Gladstone MSS, BM 44,112.

(20) Queen Victoria to Bright, Dec. 29, 1870, Bright MSS, RGL; Bright to Gladstone, Jan. 1, 1871, Gladstone MSS, BM 44,112; Granville to Gladstone, Nov. 21, 1870, Ramm; Granville to Bright, Dec. 18, 1870; Nov. 21, 1870, Bright MSS, BM 43,387; Louis Mallet to Bright, Dec. 21, 1870, *ibid.,* BM 43,384; *Economist,* XXVIII (1870), 1545–46.

(21) Granville to Bright, June 4, 1871; Dec. 14, 1871; Lord Ripon to Bright, June 26, 1871, Bright MSS, BM 43,387, 43,389; Granville to Gladstone, June 3, 1871; Nov. 26, 1871; Nov. 27 1871; Gladstone to Granville, Nov. 4, 1871; Nov. 15, 1871; Nov. 25, 1871, Ramm; Gladstone to Bright, Nov. 17, 1871, copy; Bright to Gladstone, Dec. 6, 1871; Dec. 19, 1871, Gladstone MSS, BM 44,112; *Diaries,* Nov. 14, 1871.

(22) Cf. Bright to Mrs. Bright, Feb. 23, 1869; Mar. 1, 1869, Bright MSS, UCLL; *Diaries,* Dec. 29, 1870; p. 345; Bright to J. W. Hurrell, July 14, 1871, Bright MSS, FHL; Bright to Sumner, Aug. 10, 1871, Sumner MSS, HCL; Bright to Gladstone, Oct. 27, 1871; Oct. 31, 1871; Nov. 24, 1871; Nov. 28, 1871; Dec. 3, 1871; Dec. 6, 1871; cf. July 4, 1870, Gladstone MSS, BM 44,112; Bright to Northy, Dec. 25, 1871, Northy MSS, BM 44,877; Gladstone to Granville, Sept. 10, 1871; Nov. 29, 1871, Ramm.

(23) Gladstone to Granville, July 27, 1872; cf. Sept. 3, 1873; Granville to Gladstone, July 28, 1872, *ibid.;* Gladstone to Bright, Mar. 26, 1872, Bright MSS, BM 43,385; Bright to Gladstone, Feb. 4, 1872; Feb. 20, 1872; July 30, 1872, Gladstone MSS, BM 44,113; *Diaries,* July 26, 1872; Bright to Thomas H. Dudley, Sept. 2, 1872, Bright MSS, HL; Bright to Cyrus Field, Nov. 19, 1872, Field MSS, PML; *Letters,* Jan. 29, 1872.

(24) Bright to R. H. Inglis Palgrave, Jan. 29, 1872, Foxwell Collection, Baker Library, Harvard University; Bright to Field, Mar. 3, 1872, Field MSS, PML; Bright to Gladstone, Apr. 5, 1872, Gladstone MSS, BM 44,113; Bright to Sumner, Sept. 17, 1872, Sumner MSS, HCL; Bright to Northy, Nov. 18, 1872; Dec. 27, 1872, Northy MSS, BM 44,877; *Parl. Deb.,* 198 (July 16, 1869), 119.

(25) *Letters,* Jan. 20, 1872; Mar. 4, 1872; Apr. 7, 1872; Nov. 22, 1872; *Annual Register, 1873,* pp. 48–49; cf. *Economist,* XXXI (1873), 587–88.

(26) *Illustrated London News,* LX (1872), 374; *Diaries,* July 11, 1872; *Addresses,* pp. 188–96.

(27) Bright to Mrs. Cobden, Feb. 28, 1873, Bright MSS, D; Bright to Joseph Chamberlain, Mar. 5, 1873, Chamberlain MSS, University of Birmingham Library; Sir William Harcourt to Bright, Aug. 8, 1873, Bright MSS, BM 43,388; Gladstone to Granville, Aug. 19, 1873; Aug. 28, 1873; Granville to Gladstone, Aug. 19, 1873, Ramm; Bright to Gladstone, Aug. 25, 1873, Gladstone MSS, BM 44,113; Bright to Mrs. Bright, Sept. 14, 1873, Bright MSS, UCLL; *Diaries,* Apr. 1, 1873; Aug. 4, 1873; Aug. 6, 1873; Sept. 30, 1873; *Annual Register, 1873,* p. 83; *Parl. Deb.,* 117 (June 26, 1851), 1276–77.

(28) *Addresses,* pp. 197–214; *Illustrated London News,* LXIII (1873), 403; Bright to Field, Mar. 1, 1872, Field MSS, PML; Bright to Sumner, Sept. 17, 1872, Sumner MSS, HCL; Allan Nevins, *Hamilton Fish: The Inner History of the Grant Administration* (Rev. Ed., New York, 1957), pp. 529–30.

(29) Cf. Bright to Wilson, Aug. 3, 1869, Wilson MSS, MCL; Bright to Mrs. Bright, June 22, 1873, Bright MSS, UCLL; Bright to Gladstone, Apr. 2, 1873; Apr. 16, 1873; Aug. 12, 1873; Sept. 17, 1873; Oct. 7, 1873; Oct. 28, 1873; Nov. 18, 1873; Feb. 6, 1874, Gladstone MSS, BM 44,113; *Diaries,* Oct. 3, 1873; Nov. 21, 1873; Louis Mallet to David Wells, Dec. 21, 1873, Wells MSS, LC.

(30) Bright to Joseph Chamberlain, Mar. 5, 1873; Apr. 10, 1873; Aug. 19, 1873, Chamberlain MSS, University of Birmingham Library; *Letters,* Mar. 19, 1873; Nov. 2, 1873; *Addresses,* pp. 215–27; Bright to Northy, Jan. 2, 1874, Northy MSS, BM 44,877; Bright to Edward L. Pierce, June 28, 1874, Bright MSS, PUL.

CHAPTER THIRTEEN

THAT MAN IN DOWNING STREET
1874–1878

To say that Bright was pained by the Tory triumph in the General Election of 1874 would be inaccurate: he was horrified. He saw Tories as backward-looking people who spent their lives blocking forward-looking measures. However, they now enjoyed what amounted to a mechanical majority in the House of Commons—and this as a result of the first General Election held since the adoption of Bright's beloved secret ballot.

Bright attributed their victory to their superior party organization and their skill as liars. Like Gladstone, however, he acknowledged that angry Nonconformists and Roman Catholics as well as disgruntled Tory liquor interests had much to do with the outcome of the election. Bright recognized that in the future Liberals would have to be less self-confident and give more attention to informing the public about what they stood for. For the present he consoled himself with the thought that the past could not be undone and that British liberalism was "too firmly built up to suffer material injury from those who have always done their utmost to obstruct the Builders." (1)

Disraeli's Ministry lasted from February 1874 to April 1880—six hard years for Bright. It was difficult enough to be a sexagenarian; but he found it intolerable to have to spend what he was sure were his last years with Disraeli as the head of the Government. For, especially since 1866–1867, he had come to view Disraeli as hopelessly opportunistic, untrustworthy, and immoral—therefore thoroughly dangerous. Six years of his Government convinced

Bright that his estimate was sound. They also proved to Bright what an ineffectual teacher he had been. For it was clear that the lessons he had been trying for more than a generation to drive home to the British public had been poorly learned. (2)

Bright was unprepared for the jingoism that came to pervade the Britain of the late seventies, because the Tory Ministry got off to a quiet start. Indeed, his complaint in 1874 and 1875 was that nothing of moment was happening in the world of British politics; there was a lull in the country, and as so often in the past, important subjects were being ignored. To be sure, Bright was furious with Isaac Butt's Irish Home Rulers in Parliament because, by pursuing their separate course, they had the effect of weakening the Whig-Liberals; but he doubted that they could do much damage because they lacked cohesion as well as respect for one another, and they had little faith in Butt. At the same time Bright was candid enough to recognize that the Whig-Liberals also had themselves to blame for their plight. For after Gladstone's retirement from leadership, the party was afflicted with personal squabbles and bickerings. Lord Hartington's lot as party leader was not a happy one. (3)

The time would have been perfect for Bright to visit the United States, and a number of his American admirers suggested that he make the trip. Cyrus Field, John Greenleaf Whittier, and President Grant, among others, urged him to come. "We should give thee such an ovation as never man had before," Whittier promised. But Bright had grown increasingly afraid of distant travel, and he doubted that he could endure the strain to which he would be subjected in the United States. As much as ever, however, he appreciated the kindnesses that Americans showed him. Williams College offered him an honorary degree. The Union League Club of New York commissioned a bust of him. American writers sent him copies of their books, and American visitors to Britain constantly sought him out, feeling that unless they could meet him they would not have seen England. Nor were his American admirers wrong to feel about him as they did. He was, after all, one of the few Victorian luminaries who in a letter on July 4 would note, "American Independence day—a grand day for the world." (4)

II

As much as possible, Bright lost himself in the life of his family. He spent much time in Rochdale; he visited his daughter Helen and his grandchildren in Somerset; he stayed with his invalid daughter Mary in Brighton; he vacationed and fished in Scotland. There he met an Inspector of Lunatics and Asylums, about whom he quipped to his wife, "... perhaps some may think he might take charge of me"—a quip that showed how much his health had improved. (5)

When he was in London, he walked a great deal, especially in the area of the Serpentine. The wild fowl, the swans, the pleasure boats, the children, the dogs, the horses, the riders—all had an endless appeal for him. He also found plenty of time to read. As ever, Milton remained his favorite writer, but he read many contemporary works as well. He was shocked by the bigotry of the Mary Tudor of Tennyson's play *Queen Mary*. He responded warmly to the humanity of Whittier's poetry. He enjoyed Taine's *History of English Literature* so much that he was sorry that it was not a much longer work. He relished the broad view of the past embodied in John Richard Green's *Short History of the English People*. Furthermore, he agreed heartily with Gladstone's impassioned writings on the pretensions of the Papacy. Indeed, he took pleasure in all the theological controversies that were raging in the seventies, confident that while they would weaken the churches, they would also strengthen Christianity. (6)

In London the major event of his day was the arrival of the mail from his family. As he told his wife, "When I go to bed, I think, as a child does who is to have some new toy in the morning, that it will soon be time for another letter from thee...." If no mail came, or his wife sent one of her typically illegible letters, he protested bitterly, and he complained repeatedly when his sons were not so faithful in their correspondence as his daughters. (7)

Like other middle-class Victorian fathers, he believed in the careful supervision of children—their religion, their social life, their reading, their attendance at the theatre, which he regarded as an unhealthy influence. But he worried more about his sons than his daughters, and he endlessly advised Albert and William to take their responsibilities seriously and to give their generous Uncle Thomas no grounds for complaint. Philip, his youngest child, remained his favorite and a source of endless satisfaction. Bright was constantly delighted with his responses—his conviction, for example, that Westminster Hall would be a fine place to ride his bicycle, or his decision that he was old enough to start saving some money. Indeed, when the boy was sent off to school in Darmstadt so that he could learn German and French painlessly, Bright made it clear to his teacher that he did not want his fifteen-year-old subjected to too severe an academic regimen; and he proved himself an understanding parent when his son did poorly in mathematics. (8)

Bright continued to wonder about himself and his future. His health was better, and he was grateful to Gladstone's doctor, Sir Andrew Clark, for having prescribed helpful exercises and a special diet. But he was still oppressed by the fear of aging, and in letters to his wife he referred to himself as "thy growing-old husband." He also feared that as long as he remained in politics, stress and excitement and speeches, which made him nervous, would be unavoidable. Understandably, therefore, he again considered resigning. "To be (a Member of Parliament) or not to be—that is the question," he wondered repeatedly. Especially now that Gladstone was in semi-retirement, there was little inducement for him to remain in the House. At the same time, however, he knew that, if he gave up his seat, he would strengthen the position of the Tories and remove a voice that could help to keep them from doing some outrageous things. (9)

Tories were not the only menace. He was also disturbed by some of the reformers who were becoming increasingly vocal—the temperance people and the champions of women's political rights. In general he was suspicious of measures that would ban the liquor traffic because he was convinced that such legislation would be widely violated and in effect would encourage disrespect for the law. Certainly he favored widespread educational campaigns, especially under the auspices of religious groups, that would inform people of the dangers of drinking; he himself had often cautioned workers,

JOHN BRIGHT'S NEW REFORM BILL—
"REFORM YOURSELVES!"

☞ Mr. Bright addressed his constituents on the evils of
the Liquor traffic; urging, that it was a question—not for
Government, but for themselves.—1870.

and others, not to wreck themselves and their families through drink. But legislation was not the solution to the problem, and he said this endlessly to the temperance advocates who sought his aid. When they pointed to the legislative triumphs of American prohibitionists, he frankly confessed his lack of confidence in the wisdom or permanence of what was being done to reduce the consumption of alcohol in the United States. (10)

The women's rights advocates struck Bright as much more dangerous people. He found their arguments wrong-headed, simple-minded, and monstrous. Women were *not* a class; they did *not* suffer from the despotism of a Parliament of men; they did *not* need to arm themselves with the franchise. Politics was simply not for women, and people like John Stuart Mill, who told them otherwise, had done them a great disservice. Much as Bright admired Mill for some of his ideas, he could not condemn sufficiently what he considered the pernicious influence of *On the Subjection of Women* (1869). Out of respect for Mill, Bright himself had once voted for extending women's political rights; but even as he did so he felt that he was making a mistake, and as the years passed, he was more and more convinced of the unsoundness of Mill's position. Woman's place was in the home, and that was a very good place to be. The rearing of children was a responsibility that required endless time and energy, and the proper management of the home was essential to a happy family life. If women engaged in politics, they would neglect their domestic obligations and thus undermine the institution of the family. Women's suffrage would introduce discord into the home. It would increase the influence of priests, parsons, and ministers—a prospect that Bright feared profoundly. Moreover, it would expose women to the turbulence and turmoil of elections and political life. (11)

Bright found it reassuring that "all the best women" were against granting their sex the right to vote, but he found it distressing that the women's rights advocates were succeeding in creating such a stir—the more so because his sisters Margaret and Priscilla, his brother Jacob, and his sister-in-law were deeply committed to the cause. He went so far as to discourage his wife from becoming involved in discussions of the subject with what he considered his fanatical and misguided relatives; and, despite the pressures that his sisters tried to bring to bear on him, he voted repeatedly against bills to grant women the right to vote. (12)

III

The gradual return of his self-confidence made 1875 and 1876 notable years in Bright's life. Although he was still occasionally overwhelmed by self-doubt, more and more his feelings of inadequacy diminished and his sense of his own worth asserted itself. Already in January 1875 his growing self-confidence was reflected in two important speeches that he delivered to his constituents. In one he raised the delicate issue of the disestablishment of the Church of England, an issue that he wanted to see settled before he died. In the other he criticized the idea of working-class representatives in Parliament. While he had no objection whatever to having workers sit in the House, he insisted that they should be chosen not because they were workers but because they were able people who could serve their constituents well. (13)

Bright's growing self-confidence was also reflected in his daring to speak on a variety of subjects in the House of Commons and to do so with some of the verve of more energetic days. And it was reflected in his reversion to his old habit of writing to his wife about the compliments that were showered on him by his colleagues— compliments, it should be added, that were usually well deserved. For he supported the Burials Bill that would have ended the requirement that only Anglican services be held in parish graveyards. He defended the administration of British justice against the lawyer who insisted that his client Arthur Orton, the butcher from Wapping (who claimed to be the heir to the Tichborne estate), had been unjustly convicted. On behalf of Joseph Arch's trade union of agricultural workers, he presented a petition endorsing the household franchise for county residents. Characteristically, too, he approved of the visit of the Prince of Wales to India because he hoped that his courtesy, kindness, and respect for human dignity might encourage some of the British in India to treat the natives with courtesy, kindness, and respect. (14)

Again in 1876 Bright spoke up in the House with some of his traditional vigor. He urged the extension of the household suffrage requirement to Irish boroughs. He proclaimed the school boards created by the Education Act of 1870 a remarkable success and favored their establishment in the counties. He praised American education, recommended that the British become familiar with the educational accomplishments of a state like Massachusetts, and hoped that British education would become "wider, broader, and deeper" and embrace the whole population. He opposed the extension of the suffrage to women. He complained that the Royal Titles Bill, which enabled the Queen to become Empress of India, was not being properly discussed, though out of respect for the Queen he did not express publicly his strong misgivings about the measure. Once again he pleaded for the extension to agricultural laborers of the right to vote, deploring the social tyranny from which they suffered in the countryside. He appealed for mercy to Irish political prisoners. (15)

Bright needed his self-confidence, for toward the end of 1876 what he had feared for years seemed to be happening again. The British Government was intervening in the affairs of other countries and, in Bright's view, endangering the peace of Europe. The old type of mischief that he had associated for years with the name of Palmerston was now being practiced by the Tories, and once more the emphasis on foreign affairs was diverting attention from important domestic questions. Already in July Bright cautioned Disraeli that it was folly to attempt to maintain the integrity of the Ottoman Empire and to give moral support to the Turks in their efforts to suppress their rebellious European subjects who were seeking freedom. The right policy for Britain was neutrality, Bright insisted. Only this policy would avert the kinds of blunders that had resulted in British involvement in the Crimean War, and one Crimean War was more than enough for the nineteenth century. (16)

In the fall the Turkish Question dominated the news, and the British public could not help learning a great deal about the geography of the Balkans, for Serbia, Montenegro, and Bulgaria were places about which important decisions had to be made. To Disraeli (now Lord Beaconsfield) the proper course was plain. Britain must support Turkey, for if the dissolution of the Ottoman Empire were permitted to take place, Russia would be the chief beneficiary. To Gladstone, on the other hand, the Government's attitude was utterly immoral. Britain should not support the Turkish barbarians who had just perpetrated indescribable atrocities in Bulgaria. Indeed, in one of the most widely discussed pamphlets of the century Gladstone defended what amounted to a pro-Russian policy. Better the Russians than the Turks, he argued, and so inevitably he was attacked as a Russian agent. (17)

Bright disagreed with both Disraeli and Gladstone. Disraeli's policy would preserve the Turkish Empire even at the risk of a British war with Russia, while Gladstone's sympathy with the oppressed nationalities of the Ottoman Empire could lead to a British war with Turkey. Bright had no doubt that the subject nationalities would eventually win their freedom, but he opposed casting Britain in the role of their armed liberator. Peace was the great desideratum, and the great evil was the war spirit which Disraeli in particular was encouraging. (18)

Dealing with the Turkish question in several public letters and speeches, Bright knew that he would again be attacked as unpatriotic and un-English. Even so, he spoke out bluntly, leaving no doubt whatever about his position. The Crimean crime should not be repeated. Britain should stand aside and let Russia and Turkey settle their differences and make arrangements about the future of the Christians in the Ottoman Empire. The British Government should end its absurd partnership with the Ottoman Empire, recognizing once and for all that the Porte was "a power which curses every land that is subject to it." Furthermore, the British people should cast off their ridiculous fears of Russia. In Bright's daring words:

We can make allowances for children that are afraid in the dark, but for a great nation like this, without doubt in some respects at this moment the most powerful in the world, to be shaken by these childish and unreasoning panics, is a discredit and a humiliation which we have to bear, unfortunately, before the honest but astonished opinion of all other nations. (19)

IV

When the long-expected Russo-Turkish War began in April 1877, Bright's chief worry was that, before the Russians succeeded in defeating the Turks, Beaconsfield would involve Britain in the conflict. The one hopeful sign that Bright detected in the international situation grew out of Britain's isolated diplomatic position. No continental power would join in any British-led war to preserve Turkey and humiliate Russia, and without continental allies even Beaconsfield would see the impossibility of his pro-Turkish policy. Still, Bright was sufficiently familiar with European history to know that wars often broke out unexpectedly, and so he displayed no overconfidence that Britain would remain neutral. Peace had to be pursued actively, he emphasized repeatedly both in public and in private. Indeed, at every party he attended, he went out of his way to make his views known. Once at the Gladstones', when Tennyson dared to suggest that he admired Mohammedanism as a religion and the Turks, apart from their rulers, as a people, Bright was outraged. (20)

The bragging, bullying, and jingoism that went with Beaconsfieldism were the chief threats to peace, but the idealism that went with Gladstonism was dangerous, too, as Bright saw it. For he was convinced that the logical outcome of Gladstone's sympathy with the Christians within the Ottoman Empire would be a British war with Turkey—the more so because Gladstone feared that if these Christians were liberated by Russia they would become pro-Russian in sentiment. As far as Bright was concerned, this pro-Russianism was inevitable; Russia ought to emancipate these people because of their religious, linguistic, and cultural links with Russia. In short, Bright found Gladstone's view of the Eastern Question wrong, and he was relieved to discover that Gladstone could rally little support among Liberals. It was one thing to sympathize with Bulgarians and to admire Gladstone's noble earnestness in advocating their cause; it was quite another to go to war in their behalf. (21)

Bright followed the course of the Russo-Turkish conflict with acute anxiety, hoping that the Russians would win a speedy victory before the British Government could do any harm by its meddling. Constantly—and wisely—he counted on Britain's lack of allies as the chief fact that would prevent the war from spreading. Nevertheless, he frequently despaired because of the malicious baiting of Russia that Lord Beaconsfield seemed to relish, and he was sickened by the jingoism that pervaded some of the most widely read British newspapers and magazines. In fact, nothing gave him more of a sense of failure than to read some of the outbursts of the jingoes. It was as though he, and Cobden, had never lived. All their appeals for international peace, all their assertions of the need to stop interfering in the affairs of other countries, had obviously not made much of an impression. Sometimes Bright wondered if the British were even capable of learning; perhaps they were just a hopelessly stupid, ignorant, and brutal people. (22)

Bright's disgust with his countrymen helps to explain his response to the falling prices and profits and growing unemployment of 1877–1878. He contended that economic conditions were not being helped by the Government's militant foreign policy. On the contrary, there was a direct connection between the worsening economic picture and the Government's behavior in international relations. Indeed, Bright hoped that suffering and hardship would make his countrymen see this connection and force the Government to abandon its dangerous foreign policy. As he put it repeatedly: "With Trade sorely depressed, and the people getting into trouble, I think there will be small disposition for boasting and for war." (23)

Both during the Russo-Turkish conflict and the tense months between the armistice of January 1878 and the convening of the Congress of Berlin in June, Bright condemned Beaconsfieldism as the chief cause of trouble in Europe. Time and again he insisted that Britain had no interest whatever in preserving the Ottoman Empire and that Britain had no reason to fear Russia. It was no surprise, therefore, that he became a favorite of those who opposed the Government's bellicosity. In fact, it was hard to believe that only recently Bright himself as well as other reformers had thought that his important public work was completed. Now his mail was filled with letters praising him for his courage in exposing the folly of the Government's foreign relations. George Jacob Holyoake, the champion of the cooperative movement, could not thank Bright enough for what he had done to condemn the recklessness of the Ministry. Lewis Morris, the author of *An Epic of Hades* and other poems that Bright admired, heartily congratulated Bright for his denunciation of what the Prime Minister stood for. Anti-war groups frequently called on him to address them. (24)

Although the menace of Beaconsfieldism was Bright's main preoccupation in 1877 and the early months of 1878, he also expressed strong views on other subjects. He deplored the tendency of newspapers to print more advertisements and fewer reports of parliamentary debates. He attacked the practice of capital punishment, arguing that it undermined reverence for human life but failed to make life and property any more secure. He stressed the importance of freeing the sale of land, predicting that such a step would benefit the working classes immensely. He reasserted the wisdom of free trade, insisting that protective tariffs were the greatest enemies of industry. He praised the beneficent results that flowed from commercial treaties. He urged extending the right to vote to agricultural laborers. He appealed to workers to do all they could to support the school system and further the education of their children. He used the occasion of the unveiling in Bradford of a statue of Cobden to remind his countrymen of his friend's passionate beliefs about peace and disarmament. He denounced the unforgivable stupidity that still made possible famines in India, maintaining that an adequate system of irrigation would prevent such calamities in the future. He called for more attention to Irish affairs. Finally, he implored Liberals to organize themselves more effectively for future elections. (25)

While Bright found all these issues important, he never doubted that the overriding public question for Britain in the period of the Russo-Turkish War and its aftermath was the preservation of peace. No other matter was nearly so meaningful, and all other questions depended on it. Yet if the menace of Beaconsfieldism was critical for Britain, it was also critical for Bright, for it served to restore his health by restoring his sense of purpose—what the *Annual Register* aptly called his "old tribune-spirit." At sixty-six he was again a man with a mission. (26)

NOTES

(1) Bright to unnamed correspondent, Feb. 3, 1874, Bright MSS, FHL; Bright to Gladstone, Jan. 26, 1874; Feb. 6, 1874; Feb. 8, 1874, Gladstone MSS, BM 44,113; cf. Salisbury to Balfour, July 19, 1873, Balfour MSS, BM 49,688; *Letters,* Mar. 2, 1874; June 6, 1874; Nov. 27, 1875; Magnus, p. 228; see the sophisticated discussion in H. J. Hanham, *Elections and Party Management, Politics in the Time of Disraeli and Gladstone* (London, 1959), ch. 9 and 10.

(2) Bright to W. H. Clark, Mar. 1, 1874, Bright MSS, Friends Historical Library, Swarthmore College; Bright to Mrs. Bright, Mar. 19, 1874; Apr. 20, 1875; May 7, 1875; Jan. 22, 1878, Bright MSS, UCLL.

(3) Bright to Northy, Dec. 25, 1874; Nov. 1, 1875, Northy MSS, BM 44,877; *Letters,* Feb. 25, 1875; cf. Apr. 4, 1878; Bright to Gladstone, Jan. 17, 1875, Gladstone MSS, BM 44,113; Bright to Cyrus Field, Nov. 1, 1875, Field MSS, NYPL; Granville to Gladstone, June 13, 1874, Ramm; *Economist,* XXXIII (1875), 58.

(4) Whittier to Bright, Jan. 21, 1875, Whittier MSS, Berg Collection, NYPL; *Diaries,* June 18, 1875; June 20, 1875; Sept. 4, 1875; Apr. 27, 1876; June 1, 1876; Joseph White to Bright, Dec. 1875, Bright MSS, BM 43,391; Bright to Joseph White, Jan. 5, 1876, Bright MSS, Williams College Library; Bright to Mrs. Bright, Jan. 20, 1874; July 4, 1874; July 8, 1874, Bright MSS, UCLL; cf. Bright to J. R. Hamilton, June 21, 1876, Misc. MSS, LC.

(5) *Diaries,* p. 363; Bright to Sir David Wedderburn, Feb. 10, 1874, Bright MSS, PUL; Bright to Joseph Chamberlain, Feb. 10, 1875, Chamberlain MSS, University of Birmingham Library; Bright to Mrs. Bright, July 14, 1874, Bright MSS, UCLL.

(6) Bright to Mrs. Bright, June 6, 1874; July 7, 1874; July 12, 1874; Apr. 16, 1875; June 26, 1875; May 7, 1876, *ibid.;* Magnus, pp. 235–37; Bright to Gladstone, Jan. 17, 1875, Gladstone MSS, BM 44,113; Bright to Northy, Dec. 25, 1874, Northy MSS, BM 44,877.

(7) Bright to Mrs. Bright, Mar. 19, 1874; June 8, 1874; June 11, 1874; Apr. 22, 1875; Apr. 24, 1875; July 6, 1876, Bright MSS, UCLL.

(8) Bright to Mrs. Bright, July 8, 1874; July 12, 1874; July 16, 1874; Oct. 7, 1874; Feb. 20, 1875; July 11, 1875; Mar. 6, 1876; Mar. 9, 1876; Mar. 27, 1876; June 18, 1876; Apr. 26, 1877, *ibid.;* Bright to Gladstone, Dec. 24, 1877, Gladstone MSS, BM 44,113; Bright to Northy, Dec. 27, 1877, Northy MSS, BM 44,877; Bright to Isaac Sharp, Dec. 22, 1877; Mar. 22, 1878; Oct. 25, 1878, Sharp MSS, FHL.

(9) Bright to Gladstone, Nov. 26, 1873; Jan. 13, 1874; Jan. 17, 1875, Gladstone MSS, BM 44,113; Bright to Mrs. Bright, July 3, 1874; July 5, 1874; July 8, 1874; Apr. 26, 1875; Mar. 19, 1876, Bright MSS, UCLL; Bright to Henry Hawkes, Nov. 4, 1874, Bright MSS, PUL; Granville to Bright, Jan. 30,

1875, Bright MSS, BM 43,387; Bright to Mrs. William Rathbone, Mar. 3, 1875, Rathbone MSS, University of Liverpool Library; Bright to Northy, Dec. 26, 1875, Northy MSS, BM 44,877.

(10) Bright to Hannah Sturge, Sept. 24, 1873, Bright MSS, FHL; *Letters*, June 5, 1874; Bright to Hannah Sturge, June 6, 1874, Poetry Collection, Lockwood Memorial Library, University of Buffalo; Bright to Mrs. Bright, June 10, 1875, Bright MSS, UCLL.

(11) *Parl. Deb.*, 228 (Apr. 26, 1876), 1730, 1731–32, 1735, 1738–39; Bright to Mrs. Bright, May 10, 1873; May 11, 1873, Bright MSS, UCLL; Bright to the Mayor of Birmingham, May 5, 1877, Bright MSS, BPL.

(12) Bright to Mrs. Bright, May 10, 1873; Apr. 6, 1875; Apr. 9, 1875; Apr. 10, 1875; May 10, 1875; June 10, 1875; Apr. 29, 1876; Feb. 15, 1878, Bright MSS, UCLL; cf. Mary A. Estlin to Mrs. S. H. Gay, May 13, 1876, Gay MSS, CUL; John Morley to Cobden–Sanderson, Nov. 22, 1906, Cobden–Sanderson MSS, PML.

(13) Bright to Mrs. Bright, Apr. 29, 1875; Mar. 7, 1876; Mar. 23, 1876; June 20, 1876, Bright MSS, UCLL; *Addresses*, pp. 228–61; cf. Louis Mallet to David Wells, July 26, 1875, Wells MSS, LC; Bright to Chamberlain, May 4, 1876, Chamberlain MSS, University of Birmingham Library; Bright to Rev. Thomas Rippon, Dec. 4, 1877, Hope MSS, University of Liverpool Library; *Letters*, Feb. 13, 1875; Bright to Henry Broadhurst, Mar. 21, 1875, Broadhurst MSS, LSEL; cf. Bright to George Mitchell, Dec. 20, 1878, Bright MSS, BM 43,389.

(14) Bright to Joseph Chamberlain, Dec. 15, 1874; Feb. 10, 1875, Chamberlain MSS, University of Birmingham Library; E. Perry to Bright, Feb. 1, 1875, Bright MSS, BM 43,389; Bright to Mrs. Bright, Apr. 16, 1875; Apr. 24, 1875; Apr. 26, 1875, Bright MSS, UCLL; *Parl. Deb.*, 223 (Apr. 21, 1875), 1411ff.; 223 (Apr. 23, 1875), 1601ff.; 225 (July 7, 1875), 1061; 225 (July 15, 1875), 1517ff.; Bright to Mark Harrison, July 16, 1875, Bright MSS, National Liberal Club; *Diaries*, July 6, 1875; July 15, 1875.

(15) *Parl. Deb.*, 228 (Mar. 28, 1876), 758ff.; 228 (Apr. 5, 1876), 1289ff.; 228 (Apr. 27, 1876), 1770ff.; 229 (May 3, 1876), 1474ff.; 230 (July 24, 1876), 1830ff.; 231 (Aug. 1, 1876), 302; Bright to Mrs. Bright, Feb. 20, 1876; Mar. 19, 1876; Mar. 21, 1876, Bright MSS, UCLL; *Diaries*, Mar. 9, 1876; Mar. 16, 1876; Mar. 23, 1876; Mar. 25, 1876; Apr. 26, 1876; cf. Granville to Gladstone, Nov. 21, 1877, Ramm.

(16) Bright to Chamberlain, June 29, 1876, Chamberlain MSS, University of Birmingham Library; *Parl. Deb.*, 229 (June 16, 1876), 1975; 230 (July 3, 1876), 877.

(17) See R. T. Shannon, *Gladstone and the Bulgarian Agitation, 1876* (London, 1963); Magnus, pp. 242–49; Trevelyan, pp. 419, 422, distorts the nature of Gladstone's policy.

(18) Bright to Gladstone, Sept. 23, 1876, Gladstone MSS, BM 44,113; Bright to Chamberlain, Nov. 13, 1876; Nov. 19, 1876, Chamberlain MSS, University of Birmingham Library.

(19) *Letters*, Sept. 1, 1876; Sept. 22, 1876; Sept. 30, 1876; Nov. 25, 1876; *Parl. Deb.*, 233 (Mar. 26, 1877), 510; cf. John Williams to Rutherford B. Hayes, Oct. 3, 1876, Hayes MSS, Rutherford B. Hayes Library, Fremont, Ohio; *Diaries*, Dec. 4, 1876; Bright to Robert Leake, Dec. 11, 1876, Bright MSS, FHL; Bright to Northy, Dec. 26, 1876, Northy MSS, BM 44,877; *Addresses*, p. 309.

(20) *Diaries*, Apr. 26, 1877; Bright to Mrs. Bright, Apr. 26, 1877, Bright MSS, UCLL.

(21) *Diaries*, Apr. 27, 1877; May 1, 1877; May 7, 1877; Bright to George Baker, May 22, 1877, Bright MSS, BPL; Bright to Mrs. Bright, Apr. 26, 1877; cf. Feb. 5, 1878, Bright MSS, UCLL.

(22) Bright to Northy, Apr. 30, 1877; Dec. 27, 1877, Northy MSS, BM 44,877; Bright to Thomas Snape, Sept. 26, 1877, Misc. MSS, University of Chicago Library; Bright to Edward West, Dec. 19, 1877, Bright MSS, PUL; Bright to Gladstone, Dec. 21, 1877; Dec. 24, 1877, Gladstone MSS, BM 44,113; Bright to Charles Sturge, Jan. 1, 1878, Bright MSS; Bright to Joseph Chamberlain, Jan. 8, 1878, Chamberlain MSS, University of Birmingham Library; Bright to Mrs. Bright, Jan. 18, 1878; Jan. 20, 1878; Jan. 25, 1878; Jan. 31, 1878; Mar. 26, 1878, Bright MSS, UCLL.

(23) Bright to Northy, Apr. 30, 1877; Aug. 1, 1877; Dec. 27, 1877, Northy MSS, BM 44,877; Bright to Field, Aug. 9, 1877, Field MSS, PML; Bright to John Benjamin Smith, Sept. 7, 1877, Smith MSS, MCL; Bright to Gladstone, Dec. 24, 1877, Gladstone MSS, BM 44,113.

(24) *Parl. Deb.*, 237 (Jan. 28, 1878), 1223ff.; 237 (Jan. 31, 1878), 789, 803; 237 (Feb. 8, 1878), 1330; *Diaries*, Jan. 12, 1878; Jan. 31, 1878; Apr. 30, 1878; *Letters*, Mar. 18, 1878; May 2, 1878; Bright to James Bryce, Mar. 19, 1878, Bryce MSS, BL; Bright to Mrs. Bright, Jan. 26, 1878; Feb. 1, 1878; Feb. 2, 1878; Feb. 8, 1878; Feb. 14, 1878; Feb. 16, 1878, Bright MSS, UCLL; Bright to Joseph Sturge, Apr. 2, 1878, Sturge MSS, BM 43,723; cf. Henry Vincent to William Lloyd Garrison, June 17, 1874, Garrison MSS, Boston Public Library; George Jacob Holyoake to Bright, May 1, 1878; Lewis Morris to Bright, May 4, 1878, Bright MSS, BM 43,389; Bright to Henry Broadhurst, Feb. 16, 1878, Broadhurst MSS, LSEL; George Augustus Sala to Bright, Apr. 13, 1878, Sala MSS, YUL.

(25) *Parl. Deb.*, 233 (Apr. 20, 1877), 1585; 234 (June 12, 1877), 1698ff.; 237 (Jan. 22, 1878), 341; 237 (Feb. 15, 1878), 1814ff.; 237 (Feb. 19, 1878), 1965ff.; *Letters*, Apr. 11, 1877; Apr. 21, 1877; July 31, 1877; *Diaries*, June 12, 1877; Feb. 15, 1878; *Annual Register, 1877*, p. 67; Bright to John Benjamin Smith, Sept. 8, 1877, Smith MSS, MCL; Bright to Mrs. Bright, Jan. 20, 1878,

Bright MSS, UCLL; Bright to David Wells, Dec. 19, 1877, Wells MSS, LC; Bright to Joseph Kay, Jan. 3, 1876; Jan. 13, 1876; Bright to Mrs. Joseph Kay, Jan. 8, 1878, Kay MSS, NLI.

(26) *Annual Register, 1878*, p. 51.

CHAPTER FOURTEEN

LONELY YEARS
1878–1881

On May 13, 1878, Bright received an alarming telegram from his oldest son: Mrs. Bright had suddenly taken seriously ill. He rushed back to Rochdale, fearing the worst, and by the time he arrived home it had happened. Mrs. Bright was dead at fifty-eight, and after thirty-one years of marriage he was a widower again. Only recently he had been consoling Cobden's daughters on the death of Mrs. Cobden. And only recently he had been consoling his new parliamentary colleague from Birmingham Joseph Chamberlain on the death of his wife, wishing for him "the fortitude of a man and a Christian." Now it was his and his children's turn to be consoled. He had been entirely unprepared for the news. He had assumed that because of his own record of poor health he would die before his wife; he had not imagined the possibility of surviving her. (1)

Bright knew what an extraordinary human being he had lost. To be sure, he had scolded her repeatedly for her illegible handwriting; he had criticized her for some of her extravagances; he had teased her for grumbling about the meager returns on some of her investments; he had made fun of her for becoming upset by trifles. But he loved and admired her for a variety of qualities: kindness, warmth, compassion, patience, respect for human dignity, and profound religious feeling. He never ceased to appreciate the part she had played in caring for him during his illnesses; nor did he ever cease being grateful that, unlike other married people they knew, he and his wife had not grown tired of each other. (2)

The prospect of living without her seemed impossible. No more walking together in their garden. No more trips together. No more talks about the problems of their children—Mary's and Sophie's poor health, Philip's school life in Germany and his difficulties with mathematics, Lillie's and Mary's forthcoming marriages, Albert's and William's careers, Helen's growing family. No more visits together to Leonard's grave in Wales. No more letters, however illegible. No more attendance at Quaker meeting together. No more conversations about the affairs of their beloved Society of Friends. No more discussions of the strong and weak points of the sermons they heard or the books they read. No more free expression of his pride and vanity—that someone had compared his speeches with those of Edmund Burke, that someone had requested his autograph, that Queen Victoria had inquired about his health. No more sending along to her recipes from his hostesses. No more gossip about the people he saw at parties—about the good looks of Mill's stepdaughter Helen Taylor, the boisterousness of Sir Charles Trevelyan, the clarity of Robert Browning as a conversationalist, if not as a poet, the refreshing integrity of Thomas Hughes, and the personal charm of Henry Wadsworth Longfellow. No more unembarrassed outbursts about the human predicament, the shortness of life, the omnipresence of suffering and injustice. (3)

Bright never recovered from the loss, and for the remaining years of his life he had strong death wishes. He realized that apart from his children almost all the people he cared about were in the next world, and he was in a hurry to join them. Dispirited, dazed, and filled with self-pity, he hoped that God would bless him with a speedy death. (4)

In the meantime he knew that he had to keep busy in order to preserve his sanity. Fortunately, his children came to his rescue on a grand scale, involving him in their affairs, asking his advice, visiting him, writing to him, consoling him. He had always treasured his children as gifts of God; now that he was a widower he appreciated them all the more. Indeed, the marriages of both Lillie and Mary shortly after their mother's death affected him profoundly. It was not only that his wife was not present to see them married; it was also that he was unhappy about giving up two of his daughters at a time when he wanted and needed them for himself. He was ashamed to feel as he did, but his sense of shame did not submerge his jealousy. To his great distress even Sophie, his youngest and only "home daughter," was to marry soon. (5)

Bright's friends and acquaintances went out of their way to show their affection for him. Invitations to dinner parties arrived in staggering numbers. Lewis Morris requested—and received—his permission to dedicate his poem *Gwen* to him. Mrs. Joseph Kay asked him to write a preface to her husband's posthumously published *Free Trade in Land*. And American admirers pursued their campaign to entice him to the United States. As always, the tireless Cyrus Field led the rest, and even President Rutherford B. Hayes joined in the clamor to bring Bright among the people he had defended so long and eloquently. But Bright was much too melancholy too much of the time to expose himself to an American journey. As he wrote to President Hayes, "I have suffered much during the past year from the heaviest of all domestic bereavements, and I have lost, for a time at least, the spirit and the energy which are needful to make a visit to America useful or pleasant." (6)

II

His political friends—among them Gladstone and Joseph Chamberlain—were eager for him to resume as soon as possible his role as a stalwart critic of Beaconsfieldism. For, after the Congress of Berlin officially ended the Turkish crisis, new dangers arose—troubles in South Africa and Afghanistan. Moreover, as long as Beaconsfield remained in power and encouraged the jingoism that pervaded the Britain of the late 1870's, there was no telling what further disasters might occur. As Gladstone put it to Bright, "Dizzy has surpassed all my expectations, all my fears." But while Bright wrote some public letters in the latter part of 1878 condemning what he regarded as the Government's insane foreign policy, he was not able to assume any important responsibilities either as a Member of Parliament or as a public speaker addressing anti-Government rallies. Despite the pleas of Gladstone and others, he confessed that his private troubles had incapacitated him for public service; besides, he was weary as well as afraid of meetings and speech-making. It was time for younger men to assume leadership—younger men "not yet stricken with the sorrows which as we grow older seem destined to overtake us." (7)

Thus it was only in late February 1879 that Bright ventured to deliver a speech in Parliament—a moving speech on Britain's responsibilities to the natives of India. And it was only in April that he risked making a speech to his patient Birmingham constituents— a powerful speech in which he attacked the leaders of Beaconsfield's Government in no uncertain terms:

They have played, in my view, falsely both with Parliament and with the country. They have wasted, and are now wasting, the blood and the treasure of our people. They have tarnished the mild reign of the Queen by needless war and slaughter on two continents and by the menace of needless war in Europe; they have soiled the fair name of England by subjecting and handing over the population of a province which had been freed by Russia, through war and treaty, to the cruel and odious government of the Turk. And beyond this they have shown, in my view, during an interval of five years through which they have been in possession of office and power, that they are imbecile at home and turbulent and wicked abroad. I leave them to the judgment of the constituencies of the United Kingdom, to which they must speedily appeal, and to the heavy condemnation which impartial history will pronounce upon them. (8)

The one encouraging sign that Bright detected on the British political scene in 1879 was the glaring incapacity of the Ministry. A new election would have to take place soon, and at last the British people would be in a position to get rid of their blundering Government. For the rest, Bright viewed 1879 as one of the worst years in the whole sweep of British history. The disgraceful Afghan war, the troubles with the Zulus, the dangerous meddling in Egypt, the unfounded Russophobia that had again captured large sections of the British population, the continuing misgovernment of India, the stupid involvement in Cyprus, the neglect of vitally needed domestic reforms, the failure to extend Irish land reform by granting greater security to tenants and by further encouraging the creation of a loyal class of independent farm owners, the revival of protectionist agitation as a result of the deepening world economic crisis, the growth of protectionism in Canada, the United States, and other countries—all these made 1879 a year that Bright was anxious to see pass quickly. (9)

He was also depressed by the bold evidences of the warlike spirit of the British people. At the slightest provocation they were not only willing but eager to fight; despite dozens of unnecessary diplomatic crises, they had learned little. They had no fear of war; on the contrary, they thought of it lightly, and this Bright found alarming, for he believed that a country should think hard before it embarked on a war. In short, he was again convinced that the British needed desperately to be reeducated. Their frivolous, irresponsible, dangerous attitude towards war had to be changed; and they had to be encouraged to think of war not only as patriots but as Christians. As he wrote to the labor leader Henry Broadhurst:

What we want is that our people should regard war with abhorrence, and should deem it criminal until it is proved to be necessary—that is unavoidable. Now, war is looked upon as a reasonable thing—usual and in the common course of events—to be regretted perhaps, but not without its advantages—and the people are exhorted and expected to sanction any policy leading to or ending in war, which has received the support of the ministers for the time being. The friends of Peace are always denounced as unpatriotic, and as friends of their country's enemies. (10)

As in the past, Bright had faith in one device above all for the promotion of international peace: freer trade. Commercial treaties that reduced the tariffs between nations would serve to remove old national hostilities and create new national friendships. It is understandable, therefore, that Bright used every opportunity that presented itself to press for closer Anglo-Russian economic ties, for he saw freer trade between the two countries as the one sure basis for overcoming the hostilities that had recently dominated their relations. So, too, he took advantage of every occasion to warn Americans of the folly of their protective tariff legislation and the damage it was doing. (11)

III

Bright was overjoyed with the results of the long-awaited election of 1880. At last the Tories were thrust from power and Gladstone was back where he deserved to be—at the head of the Government. This is not to suggest, however, that Bright thought that Gladstone would have an easy time as Prime Minister. He anticipated that his friend would have great difficulty in abandoning the commitments that Beaconsfield had assumed; but at least he felt that Britain was safe now that the unscrupulous adventurer Beaconsfield with his "Jewish dispensation" and his fascination with the East had made way for the earnest Christian moralist Gladstone. (12)

Bright was pleased that Gladstone again invited him to become Chancellor of the Duchy of Lancaster. Although he knew from experience that his departmental duties would be minimal, he still hesitated to accept office. He was in his late sixties, he lacked energy, he feared the responsibilities that went with membership in the Cabinet, he suffered from severe depressions, and he expected to die soon—a prospect that had undermined both his pride and his ambition. But Gladstone insisted, and he consented. This was the least he could do to help out the colleague he had come to respect most since the death of Cobden. (13)

Bright hoped that Gladstone would quickly extricate Britain from Beaconsfield's dangerous foreign involvements and deal with vital domestic legislation in the spirit of the campaign poem of Edwin Waugh, his Lancashire friend:

> Let England remember the days of old,
>   When the Liberal leaders ruled her,
> Ere she squandered in bloodshed her hard-won gold,
>   And a Beaconsfield be-fooled her;
> When peace and plenty went hand in hand,
>   And her toilers lived in clover,
> And the aim of those who ruled the land
>   Was justice the wide world over.

But Gladstone's second Ministry had hardly begun when the House of Commons was distracted and disrupted by what for Bright was the ridiculous Bradlaugh affair. To be sure, Bright deplored Charles Bradlaugh's view of Christianity; but the fact was that the militant atheist had been duly elected Member for Northampton, and therefore, according to Bright, he should have been permitted to make the affirmation and take his seat in the House of Commons. Bright wished to avoid another John Wilkes affair that could bring only discredit on Parliament. As he put it in the House: "Hon. Members opposite will, I dare say, represent to themselves and to others that they are the defenders of religion, of orthodoxy, of decency, and of I know not what. I am here as the defender of what I believe to be the principles of our Constitution, of the freedom of constituencies to elect, and of the freedom of the elected to sit in Parliament." But many of Bright's colleagues refused to recognize these freedoms, and so for years the Bradlaugh case dragged on, taking time away from what Bright regarded as important matters. (14)

Of these the one that Bright wanted Parliament to deal with immediately was the Irish Question. The Land Act of 1870 was a splendid piece of legislation, as he saw it, but it was only a beginning. He was particularly eager to grant Irish tenant farmers greater security of tenure than they enjoyed, and he remained hopeful about the beneficial social results that would flow from further legislation to encourage Irish tenants to become independent farm owners. For the great calamity of Ireland was still the immense preponderance of tenants over proprietors. A substantial increase in the size of the proprietary class, therefore, would contribute mightily to Irish social peace. (15)

As for home rule, Bright continued to regard it as a pernicious idea. To create a House of Commons and a House of Lords in Dublin would be absurd. Home rule would be a step towards the complete independence of Ireland, and an independent Ireland was a geographical impossibility because it would threaten the military security of Britain and serve as an excuse for endless military expenditures and expeditions. How much more sensible, therefore, for the British Parliament to deal justly and generously with Ireland and demonstrate that home rule was unnecessary.

It was plain to Bright that the Liberals had to make up in a hurry for the stupidity that had marked the Tory neglect of Ireland. As early as July 1880, however, he was complaining about the slowness with which the work of the House was proceeding, and he correctly ascribed this lack of progress not only to Tories but to Charles Stewart Parnell and his Irish followers. Indeed, when Bright thought of how much the House had to do and how much the Parnellites obstructed proceedings, he could not control his rage. Having fought for Ireland almost single-handedly for decades, he resented the obstructionist tactics of the Parnellites as selfish, unscrupulous, immoral. As he told Gladstone in December, "It is evident that Parnell and Co. only want men to provoke a revolt and that their purpose is more revolution than a mere reform, however broad, of their land system." (16)

Bright had long been aware of the complexities of the Irish land problem; but he was never so aware of them—and so discouraged by them—as in the months preceding the passage of the Land Act of 1881. His own commitment was chiefly to land purchase schemes, but he kept an open mind about other proposals for land reform. He read constantly what was being published in newspapers, magazines, and books about the Irish land problem; and he kept himself informed about the recently founded Irish Land League with its slogan of "The Land for the People" and its war against rent and landlordism. He was convinced that the longer constructive legislation was delayed, the more alarming the situation in Ireland would become. Certainly he had no faith in coercion as a device for restoring social peace in Ireland—only large doses of land reform would do. Relations between Irish landlords and tenants had deteriorated not because of the Land League's agitators but because of the unwholesome social structure of Ireland. The way to defeat the League was not through repression but through alterations in Irish society. In short, Bright regarded as dangerous those of his colleagues who favored a do-nothing solution to the Irish land problem. The Government had to intervene actively, and "the received rules of political economy" had to be revised. Government-instituted land reform was the only hope for social peace in Ireland. (17)

In a confidential memorandum prepared for the members of the

Cabinet in December 1880, Bright summed up his philosophy of Irish land reform. The "Bright clauses" of the Land Act of 1870 had to be extended, since the great Irish need was for a large increase in the number of farm owners and a sharp decrease in the number of absentee proprietors. If more and more Irish tenants became landowners "bound to an industrious and peaceful life by the strongest and most natural ties," the temper of Ireland would improve markedly. Confidence, hope, and goodwill would replace the suspicion, hatred, and despair that contaminated the Irish countryside. (18)

IV

Throughout 1881—the year he reached seventy—Ireland was Bright's great preoccupation. He was sickened by the reports of atrocities that arrived from Ireland; he was hardly less sickened by the obstructionism of the Parnellites in the House. All this convinced him even more—if this was possible—of the need for a good land bill, and he was pleased that by August the months of wrangling in the Cabinet and in Parliament yielded the Irish Land Act, with its guarantees of the three F's (free sale, fixity of tenure, and fair rent) and its land purchase provisions. Despite the noisy complaints of landowners and others, major concessions were made to Irish tenants, and so Bright believed that it was now only a question of time before the crimes of the Land League would cease and the Irish countryside would became peaceful. He still assumed that economic reform would undermine Parnellism and the agitation for home rule. (19)

Bright had found the idea of home rule objectionable in the days of the gentle Isaac Butt; now in the time of Charles Stewart Parnell he found it increasingly unthinkable. For Ireland under home rule would be an Ireland ruled by the Parnellites, people whom Bright considered rebels, traitors, and agents of the Irish-American conspiracy against Britain. His hatred of them was intense; and so was his fear of them—among other reasons because of the financial backing they received from Irish Americans. In fact, when Parnell was imprisoned at Kilmainham in October for urging the intimidation of tenants who took advantage of the Land Act, Bright cautioned Gladstone about criticizing the Irish leader in public. Bright's contention was that such criticism might serve to make Parnell even more of a hero to the rowdies who worshiped him. (20)

Although Ireland was Bright's chief worry in 1881, he was troubled also by other developments in public affairs. He continued to rage at the treatment given to Bradlaugh, insisting that the Tories and Liberals who combined to prevent the Member for Northampton from taking his seat were damaging the reputation of the House. He was disturbed by the further growth of British protectionist sentiment under the guise of schemes of reciprocity and what was wrongly called "fair trade," and though he was confident that these proposals to abandon free trade would fail, he was disheartened that they should still be advanced in the country of Adam Smith more than a century after the appearance of *The Wealth of Nations*. Mainly, however, he was concerned about the slowness with which the Gladstone Ministry was extricating itself from the foreign involvements bequeathed by Lord Beaconsfield's Government. In the light of the disquieting events of 1881, Bright found the time ideal for the publication of John Morley's masterly biography of Richard Cobden. If the British people would only read and learn from the work, they could save themselves from countless blunders that were disgracing their history. (21)

It is understandable that Bright was unable to give himself wholeheartedly to the celebrations that took place in November when his seventieth birthday arrived. First of all, he missed his wife. Although it was three and a half years since her death, he continued to feel her loss intensely. Secondly, he considered himself a wretched failure as a public instructor, for the lessons he had been trying to teach the British people for so long had been poorly learned. The Irish Question, the Bradlaugh Case, protectionism, and foreign meddling, all represented triumphs of the unreason that he had devoted a lifetime, with very limited success, to combating. Certainly he was moved by some of the flattering remarks that the celebrants of his birthday made about his contributions to the Victorian era, but the truth was that the appreciation of his talents had come much too late. Years earlier he had yearned for the kind of recognition that he was at last receiving. Now he was a desolate old man, and the thrill of recognition could not mean much to him. (22)

NOTES

(1) Albert Bright to Bright, May 13, 1878, telegrams, Bright MSS, BM 43,384; *Diaries*, Apr. 23, 1877; Bright to Northy, Apr. 30, 1877, Northy MSS, BM 44,877; Bright to Chamberlain, Feb. 17, 1875, Chamberlain MSS, University of Birmingham Library; Villiers to Bright, May 24, 1878; Chamberlain to Bright, May 14, 1878; Harcourt to Bright, May 14, 1878; J. B. Smith to Bright, May 17, 1878; James E. Thorold Rogers to Bright, May 14, 1878; Kate C. Fisher to Bright, May 17, 1878; Henry Leatham to Bright, May 18, 1878; Edwin Waugh to Bright, May 18, 1878; George S. Gibson to Bright, May 24, 1878, Bright MSS, BM 43,386–43,389; *Annual Register, 1878*, p. 147; *Illustrated London News*, LXII (1878), 492–93.

(2) Bright to Mrs. Bright, Feb. 5, 1866; Jan. 20, 1874; Nov. 27, 1874; June 10, 1875; Feb. 10, 1876; July 6, 1877; Dec. 2, 1877; Jan. 18, 1878; Jan. 21, 1878; Jan. 25, 1878; Apr. 10, 1878, Bright MSS, UCLL.

(3) Bright to Field, Nov. 19, 1872, Field MSS, PML; Bright to Northy, May 21, 1874; Nov. 1, 1875; Apr. 30, 1877, Northy MSS, BM 44,877; Bright to Mrs. Bright, Dec. 1, 1863; Mar. 4, 1866; June 12, 1866; Dec. 5, 1866; Mar. 21, 1867; Sept. 12, 1867; Nov. 24, 1867; June 27, 1868; Dec. 29, 1868; Mar. 3, 1869; Mar. 15, 1874; Mar. 18, 1876; May 1, 1877; May 2, 1877; May 9, 1877; July 10, 1877; July 13, 1877; Nov. 24, 1877; Dec. 1, 1877; Jan. 20, 1878; Jan. 24, 1878; Feb. 1, 1878; Feb. 3, 1878; Feb. 6, 1878; Feb. 7, 1878; Feb. 17, 1878; Mar. 27, 1878; Apr. 14, 1878, Bright MSS, UCLL.

(4) Bright to Northy, Aug. 17, 1878, Northy MSS, BM 44,877; *Diaries*, July 19, 1879; Oct. 18, 1879; May 13, 1882; Bright to Mrs. Kay, Oct. 14, 1878, Kay MSS, NLI; Bright to Julia Goddard, Dec. 28, 1885, Bright MSS, PUL.

(5) *Diaries*, June 20, 1878; Aug. 29, 1878; Oct. 10, 1878; Nov. 9, 1878; May 2, 1879; Oct. 29, 1879; June 7, 1880; Bright to John Rylands, Sept. 5, 1878, Autograph MSS, JRL; Bright to Northy, Dec. 29, 1878; Jan. 6, 1879; Dec. 24, 1879; Dec. 28, 1880, Northy MSS, BM 44,877; Bright to Field, June 5, 1879, Field MSS, PML.

(6) *The Times*, June 6, 1878; June 8, 1878; Lewis Morris to Bright, Nov. 21, 1878; Nov. 26, 1878; C. O. Shepard to Bright, Dec. 29, 1879, Bright MSS, BM 43,389–91; Joseph Kay, *Free Trade in Land* (London, 1879), preface by Bright, dated Mar. 26, 1879; Bright to Field, Aug. 15, 1879, Field MSS, NYPL; Rutherford B. Hayes to Bright, June 15, 1879, copy; Bright to Hayes, Aug. 14, 1879; L. U. Reavis to Hayes, Jan. 18, 1880; James Beal to Hayes, Aug. 15, 1880, Hayes MSS, Rutherford B. Hayes Library, Fremont, Ohio.

(7) Bright to Chamberlain, July 13, 1878, Chamberlain MSS, University of Birmingham Library; Gladstone to Bright, Nov. 12, 1878, Bright MSS, BM 43,385; *The Times*, July 24, 1878; *Letters*, Sept. 4, 1878; Sept. 23, 1878; Nov., 1878; *Diaries*, Dec. 9, 1878; Dec. 12, 1878; Oct. 23, 1879; Bright to

Gladstone, Nov. 13, 1878; Dec. 12, 1879, Gladstone MSS, BM 44,113; Bright to Joseph Sturge, Nov. 28, 1878, Sturge MSS, BM 43,723; cf. Bright to Northy, Oct. 30, 1879, Northy MSS, BM 44,877; Bright to Bryce, Mar. 17, 1880, Bryce MSS, BL.

(8) *Parl. Deb.*, 243 (Feb. 28, 1879), 2027ff.; *Diaries*, Feb. 28, 1879; Apr. 16, 1879; *The Times*, Apr. 17, 1879; *Addresses*, pp. 506–7.

(9) *Letters*, Mar. 11, 1879; Apr. 1, 1879; Aug. 1, 1879; Aug. 16, 1879; Mar., 1880; *Addresses*, pp. 491–507; *Parl. Deb.*, 244 (Mar. 18, 1879), 1160, 1311, 1312; 245 (May 2, 1879), 1594; 247 (June 23, 1879), 430; 247 (July 4, 1879), 1499ff.; *The Times*, Mar. 18, 1879; Apr. 18, 1879; Oct. 27, 1879; Dec. 6, 1879; Jan. 21, 1880; Jan. 23, 1880; Mar. 20, 1880; Mar. 25, 1880; *Diaries*, Feb. 13, 1879; Mar. 12, 1879; Mar. 27, 1879; May 4, 1879; June 24, 1879; Bright to Field, Jan. 21, 1879, Anthony MSS, NYPL; June 5, 1879, Field MSS, PML; Bright to J. Wilson, July 8, 1879, Bright MSS, BL; Bright to Northy, July 16, 1879; Dec. 24, 1879, Northy MSS, BM 44,877; E. Perry to Bright, July 24, 1879, Bright MSS, BM 43,389.

(10) *Letters*, Aug. 18, 1879; Bright to Broadhurst, June 14, 1879, Broadhurst MSS, LSEL.

(11) *Diaries*, Feb. 15, 1879; Feb. 17, 1879; Mar. 2, 1879; Mar. 8, 1879; Dec. 18, 1879; *Addresses,* 505–6; *The Times*, Feb. 18, 1879; Dec. 19, 1879; Hartington to Bright, Oct. 18, 1879, Bright MSS, BM 43,377; Bright to unnamed correspondent, Dec. 23, 1880, Bright MSS, LC.

(12) Cf. Salisbury to Austin, Aug. 17, 1898, Alfred Austin MSS, National Liberal Club; *Diaries*, Mar. 8, 1880; Apr. 1, 1880; Apr. 7, 1880; Apr. 8, 1880; May 3, 1880; Magnus, pp. 271–3; Bright to Gladstone, Apr. 13, 1880, Gladstone MSS, BM 44,113; Bright to Chamberlain, Apr. 1, 1880; Apr. 18, 1880, Chamberlain MSS, University of Birmingham Library; Bright to J. T. Bunce, May 6, 1880, Bright MSS, BPL.

(13) Gladstone to Bright, Apr. 24, 1880, Bright MSS, BM 43,385; *Diaries*, Apr. 27, 1880; Bright to Bunce, May 6, 1880; Bright to Joseph Powell Williams, May 9, 1880, Bright MSS, BPL.

(14) Edwin Waugh, "Let England Remember," first published in Mar., 1880, in Manchester *Examiner and Times*; cf. *Parl. Deb.*, 118 (July 21, 1851), 1199; 252 (May 21, 1880), 209ff.; 253 (June 21, 1880), 496ff.; *Diaries*, June 7, 1880; June 21, 1880; June 22, 1880; Bright to Northy, July 9, 1880, Northy MSS, BM 44,877.

(15) *Diaries*, May 1, 1879; May 2, 1879; Bright to Arthur Underhill, Dec. 8, 1879, Misc. MSS, BM 49,597; *The Times*, Jan. 26, 1880; Nov. 17, 1880; Dec. 28, 1880; *Parl. Deb.*, 245 (May 2, 1879), 1647ff.; 256 (Sept. 2, 1880), 1062; despite its bias, Michael Davitt, *The Fall of Feudalism in Ireland* (London, 1904) is still invaluable.

(16) Bright to William Rathbone, Dec. 1, 1879, Rathbone MSS, University

of Liverpool Library; *Parl. Deb.*, 250 (Feb. 17, 1880), 865, 870; Bright to Northy, July 9, 1880, Northy MSS, BM 44,877; Bright to Gladstone, Dec. 7, 1880, Gladstone MSS, BM 44,113.

(17) *Diaries*, July 21, 1880; Nov. 16, 1880; Dec. 13, 1880; Jan. 2, 1881; Bright to Gladstone, Dec. 4, 1880; Dec. 7, 1880; Dec. 22, 1880; Dec. 24, 1880, Gladstone MSS, BM 44,113; Gladstone to Granville, Dec. 25, 1880, Ramm; Bright to John Stuart Blackie, Dec. 14, 1880, Blackie MSS, NLS; Bright to H. Yates Thompson, May 16, 1881, Bright MSS, NLI.

(18) *Diaries*, Dec. 17, 1880; Dec. 30, 1880; Dec. 31, 1880; Memorandum dated Dec. 17, 1880, Gladstone MSS, BM 44,625.

(19) *Parl. Deb.*, 257 (Jan. 27, 1881), 1555ff.; 260 (May 6, 1881), 1993; 261 (May 9, 1881), 94ff.; 263 (July 8, 1881), 441ff.; *The Times*, Apr. 28, 1881; Sept. 5, 1881; Bright to Northy, May 16, 1881; Dec. 26, 1881, Northy MSS, BM 44,877; Bright to Gladstone, May 27, 1881, Gladstone MSS, BM 44,113.

(20) *Diaries*, Jan. 14, 1881; Jan. 22, 1881; Mar. 10, 1881; *Parl. Deb.*, 263 (July 14, 1881), 904; 263 (July 19, 1881), 1331ff.; Gladstone to Granville, July 15, 1881, Ramm; Bright to Samuel A. Goddard, Aug. 5, 1881, Bright MSS, PUL; Bright to Edward L. Pierce, Oct. 28, 1881, Pierce MSS, HCL; Bright to Gladstone, Oct. 4, 1881, Gladstone MSS, BM 44,113.

(21) *Parl. Deb.*, 260 (Apr. 26, 1881), 1199ff.; 264 (Aug. 3, 1881), 709–10; *Letters*, Mar. 18, 1881; Mar. 29, 1881; Apr. 15, 1881; Sept. 2, 1881; Nov. 20, 1881; *The Times*, Mar. 21, 1881; Apr. 11, 1881; Sept. 10, 1881; Sept. 14, 1881; Sept. 15, 1881; Nov. 26, 1881; Dec. 3, 1881; Bright to Karl Blind, Mar. 14, 1881, Blind MSS, BM 40,125; Bright to W. G. Lord, Apr. 15, 1881, Bright MSS, National Liberal Club; Bright to Gladstone, Mar. 2, 1881; Apr. 8, 1881; Oct. 4, 1881, Gladstone MSS, BM 44,113; Bright to Pierce, Oct. 28, 1881, Pierce MSS, HCL; Bright to Nellie Cobden, Oct. 31, 1881, Cobden–Sanderson MSS, PML; Bright to Northy, Dec. 26, 1881, Northy MSS, BM 44,877.

(22) *Diaries*, May 13, 1881; *The Times*, Nov. 11, 1881; Nov. 12, 1881; Nov. 16, 1881; Nov. 17, 1881; *Letters*, Dec. 13, 1881; memorial from "the workpeople in your employ," dated Nov. 16, 1881; memorial from "your townsmen and neighbours at Rochdale," dated Nov. 16, 1881; memorial from the Butterworth Liberal Association, RGL; S. G. Osborne to Bright, Nov. 18, 1881, Bright MSS, BM 43,389; printed letter of thanks from John Bright to his friends, Nov. 18, 1881; Bright to Northy, Dec. 26, 1881, Northy MSS, BM 44,877.

CHAPTER FIFTEEN

NOUGHT AVAILETH

1882–1886

If his late sixties were difficult years for Bright, his early seventies turned out to be no easier. For in 1882, after much soul-searching, he broke with Gladstone. The estrangement had been building up for months. Already in the early stages of Gladstone's second Ministry, Bright suspected that he might have to resign from the Cabinet because of what impressed him as the unmistakably expansionist policy that the Government was pursuing in South Africa; but in 1881 the difficulties with the Transvaal Boers were settled—if belatedly, at least to his satisfaction.

The next year, however, the Government's continuing involvement in Egyptian affairs resulted in the bombardment of Alexandria. With his usual self-righteousness, Gladstone justified the action as a step toward peace and the restoration of law and order, but Bright could not follow this reasoning. For him to condone the bombardment would be to renounce the doctrine of nonintervention that he had upheld throughout his public career. Since he could discover no valid grounds for the Egyptian war—it was both unjust and unnecessary—he had no choice but to resign from the Cabinet and separate himself from his closest political friend. He bluntly told his colleagues that they had lost their heads, but no one would listen to him—not even Joseph Chamberlain, who was later to tell him that his position was sound and wise. Gladstone, for his part, expected Bright to respond as he did; he saw his resignation as a sign that the "old Adam" was still working in him. (1)

Bright's behavior caused no surprise whatever among his contemporaries. *The Times* and the *Economist* noted that he had done what he had to do, and so did many of his parliamentary colleagues as well as Liberal associations throughout the country. The only compromise that Bright made was in refusing to create a public issue of the Alexandrian episode. His reasoning was that the Gladstone Government had behaved both outrageously and inexcusably, but to overthrow it would be to bring back the Tories, who would be much worse both in foreign and domestic affairs. Better, therefore, to endure the shameful and jingoistic Egyptian policy of the Liberals than to risk a return to power of the heirs of the recently deceased Lord Beaconsfield. Yet Bright never doubted that Gladstone's Egyptian policy was in the most disgraceful tradition of Palmerston and Beaconsfield, and he was certain that if Palmerston or Beaconsfield had dared to do what Gladstone had done in Egypt, British Liberals would have been furious. (2)

Bright was also depressed by the repeated eruptions of violence in Ireland. He had taken it for granted that once the Land Act of 1881 was passed, the Irish situation would improve markedly. Yet things had not worked out that way. Like all his English—and many of his Irish—contemporaries, he was sickened in May 1882 by the brutal murder in Phoenix Park, Dublin, of two British officials. He was no less sickened by the reports of other atrocities perpetrated in Ireland on both people and farm animals. Although he had spent decades believing and preaching that force was no remedy, he now knew that Irish crimes would have to be met by British coercion. He consoled himself with the thought that the repression would last only briefly and that as soon as the effects of the Land Act made themselves felt, coercion would be unnecessary. At the same time, however, his hatred of the Irish leaders mounted. Instead of urging their countrymen to be patient and cooperative, they were inciting them to violence and playing into the hands of their traditional enemies—the Tory coercionists. (3)

Bright was angry about Irish violence and the Egyptian imbroglio (as well as the Bradlaugh mess) because they were wrong in themselves. But he was also angry because they were diverting attention from the serious questions that Parliament should have been considering: among them, the extension of the suffrage in the counties, the redistribution of seats in the House of Commons, and the revision of the British land laws. Shortly before the Gladstone–Bright rift, in fact, when Gladstone in a rare moment of discouragement had talked of resignation, Bright told him that he had to retain office until he succeeded in carrying these reforms. For Bright never had a static conception of Liberalism; he still saw a great deal of constructive work for Liberals to do. (4)

II

For many months after his resignation from the Government in July 1882, Bright found little to encourage him about the course of public events, and he feared that Gladstone's flexible conscience might permit still further follies to take place. Yet while he fretted about Britain's future, some of his admirers decided to celebrate some notable events of the past. For 1883 marked two important occasions: the fortieth anniversary of Bright's election to Parliament, and the twenty-fifth anniversary of his active connection with Birmingham. Furthermore, he was to be installed as Lord Rector of the University of Glasgow and to be granted the freedom of the city of Glasgow. (5)

The result was that in 1883 Bright was treated to many heart-warming—and accurate—testimonials to his character and his contributions to the history of his time. He was praised for his humanity, earnestness, consistency, trustworthiness, courage, independence, fidelity to principle, love of freedom and justice, and trust in the people. He was also thanked for what he had done to make Britain a better place in which to live. Indeed, he was assured that, as long as men studied the history of the Victorian age, they would dwell on his impressive achievements. "Could any veteran statesman, in the autumn of his days, desire a more noble record?" the *Illustrated London News* asked. (6)

In responding to the compliments that were heaped on him, Bright made it plain that he preferred to linger not on past accomplishments but on the gains that were still to be won. Thus he called for the broadening of the suffrage in the counties, a more equitable distribution of seats in the House of Commons, the limitation of the power of the House of Lords, the disestablishment of the Church of England, the overhauling of the land laws, the active furtherance of free trade, the extension of educational improvements, and political and economic reforms that would prepare the Indians for the independence they would inevitably attain. Bright also continued to deplore the widespread poverty that defaced late Victorian Britain, and while he granted that education and temperance would help to reduce the numbers of the poor, he insisted repeatedly that the cutting of military expenditures, and therefore of taxes, would aid the poor more than any other section of the population. In short, Liberalism, as Bright understood it, was far from having fulfilled its mission; and, properly pursued, it was the truest kind of conservatism. That Lord Salisbury's Tories did not understand this he found appalling, and more and more he was filled with hatred of them and fear of the damage they would do to Britain. It depressed him that people—especially Tories—rarely learned anything from history. (7)

As so often in the past, he was overwhelmed by the power of ignorance and irrationality in both British and world affairs. If not for ignorance and irrationality, would Americans still be resisting free trade? Would the British treat the Indians as they did? Would the Irish follow leaders like the Parnellites? Would Liberals permit the Gladstone Government to pursue its Egyptian policy? Would Tories fight the extension of the right to vote to agricultural workers? Would all kinds of people oppose the construction of a tunnel under the English Channel? (8)

III

As the parliamentary session of 1884 approached, Bright expected trouble. He was certain that the Tories would do all they could to prevent any constructive work from being accomplished, and that the Parnellites would cause as much mischief as they could. In part Bright was proven right in his anticipations. The Bradlaugh controversy continued to distract the attention of the House of Commons from important matters; and the House of Lords ostentatiously opposed Gladstone's scheme of suffrage reform.

To Bright's surprise and pleasure, however, the Reform Bill of 1884 was enacted toward the end of the year, and large numbers of agricultural laborers were belatedly granted the suffrage. (9)

This measure, which Bright had advocated for many years, was at last the law of the land, and if he took pride in having prepared the way for its enactment, his pride was justified. Certainly he saw the enfranchisement of farm workers as right in itself—these people had every reason to be first-class citizens. But Bright also saw the legislation as a further stage in the weakening of the position of the great landowners, for it would serve as a prelude to land law reform. Above all, he saw it as a step towards peace and the cutting of military expenditures, since he assumed that Members of Parliament who wished the support of agricultural laborers would inevitably favor the reduction of the heavy tax burden borne by the poor in relation to their income. (10)

If 1884 was a good year for Bright because of the Reform Act, it was also a good year for him because of the recognition that continued to come to him. There was no longer any doubt that he was widely accepted as a statesman. Indians overwhelmed him with praise and expressions of gratitude. A Latin-American merchant told him that his young son could quote from memory large sections from his speeches. Americans continued to write to him, call on him, and beg him to visit the United States. Although he continued to decline their invitations, he assured them that he regarded the British and the Americans as one people even if they were two nations, and that "on them the growth of all that is good in the world greatly depends." At the same time he seized every opportunity to urge Americans to agitate against the protective tariff policy that was endangering their country's economy. (11)

His own countrymen gave him many signs of affection and respect. Some dedicated books to him. Some cited him in sermons. Some tried to enlist his support for all kinds of causes. But while he often sympathized with their aims, he used his age as a reason for not joining actively in any new agitation. He was particularly pleased that Gladstone turned repeatedly to him for advice and even confessed that he "would give much" to have him back in the Cabinet. He was also pleased that, when for a few weeks he developed a lung ailment, his health became an important news item, and he was deluged with good wishes for a speedy recovery and with pleas that he take better care of himself. (12)

He would not have been John Bright, however, if he had not continued to be alarmed by much that happened in the Britain of 1884. A series of brutal hangings made acute his shame over the barbarous state of British criminal justice. The campaign to keep Bradlaugh from joining the House of Commons stirred up his horror of the bigotry that opportunistic Tory leaders were exploiting. The insolence of the House of Lords convinced him that the House of Commons must do something about its humiliating position. The activities of Fair Traders demonstrated painfully that free trade had not won a permanent victory even in Britain, and that if the foreign competition and the falling prices and profits of recent years continued, it might be necessary to launch a new crusade against the delusion of protectionism. Further outbreaks of Irish violence intensified his hatred of the Parnellites and his fear that the beneficent measures enacted by Parliament might not have a chance to prove their worth. Moreover, the continued embroilment of the Gladstone Government in Egyptian affairs revealed that Palmerstonianism and Beaconsfieldism were chronic dangers in British life—especially because of the vicious jingoism of the newspaper press. (13)

Bright did not deceive himself—Britain had a long way to go before it could justly be called a good society—and he knew that he would not live to see that society. He was seventy-three, he marveled that he had lived so long, he was constantly aware of death. It seemed as if he were always going to a funeral or coming from one, and almost every day marked the anniversary of the death of someone dear to him. He was certain that his own life was soon to end and that in any case his political career was about finished. The parliamentary session of 1884, he told Gladstone, was probably the last he would attend. (14)

Even so, the achievement of suffrage reform at the end of the year encouraged him to hope that it might now be possible to carry a satisfactory redistribution bill. As an old hand at parliamentary reform schemes, he had consistently urged Gladstone to keep suffrage reform and the reallotment of seats in the House of Commons distinct measures. But now that the household franchise had been won for the counties, the important thing was to rearrange seats in the House in keeping with the distribution of population in the country. Beyond that, it was a question of reforming the land laws. And he was quick to inform Gladstone of his views and preferences. (15)

IV

As Bright had hoped, a satisfactory redistribution of parliamentary seats was accomplished in 1885; but otherwise the new year was filled with alarming news. First came the death of the misguided and reckless General Gordon in the Sudan, an event seen by Bright as yet another consequence of the folly of Gladstone's involvement in Egyptian affairs. Then a serious threat of war arose between Britain and Russia over the Afghan frontiers. In his long public career Bright had rarely been so depressed by the course of public events. More than ever it struck him that the British had learned nothing from the past; if they had, they would not have talked so readily about bigger and better wars. What enraged him chiefly was that with a modicum of goodwill both the Egyptian and the Afghan difficulties could have been settled; if ever disputes called for arbitration, it was these. Yet the London press and a host of superpatriots were clamoring for bold displays of force, and the Gladstone Government was being attacked for having done too little when, as far as Bright was concerned, it had done far too much. At times Bright thought that the Ministry was "afflicted with madness." But he never doubted that if Gladstone had been strong and wise enough to take the advice he had given him, he would not have been in his present difficulties. (16)

Bright was sickened by the uproar created both by those who wished to avenge the death of General Gordon and by those who sought to teach the Russians a lesson. And no wonder. It was as if he had never lived, and preached, and tried to teach. How he envied the lucky Americans—and other people—who had no colonies. But the wretched British were saddled with an empire, and at almost any moment they could become involved in war in almost any part of the world. Partly, Bright realized, the danger was the result of the immense power British officials exercised in these far-off places; with little to restrain them, they were frequently in a position to force Britain into a war. "You know better than I do how often our Government is misled by its agents abroad," Bright bluntly reminded Gladstone, referring to Lord Stratford and the Crimean War, Sir John Bowring and the China War, Sir Bartle Frere and the Zulu War, and Sir Beauchamp Seymour and the bombardment of Alexandria. (17)

Bright was so appalled by the course of events that he felt no great regret that the Gladstone Ministry ended in June after a defeat on a relatively unimportant matter. To Bright's mind what had really brought about the Government's downfall was the Egyptian war; and it was no consolation to him that he had predicted that the bombardment of Alexandria would yield this result. Nor was it any consolation that his admirers congratulated him on his prescience, assuring him that his resignation over the Alexandrian affair stood out as one of the noblest acts of his career. The truth was that he despised his countrymen for their ignorance, irrationality, and pride. He saw them as irrepressible Palmerstonians and incorrigible Beaconsfieldians. Although they should have been occupying themselves with their own difficult domestic problems, they were stupidly consuming their energies in parts of the world where they should not have been in the first place. As one who believed in the application of intelligence and Christian ethics to human affairs, Bright was horrified by the abiding power of unreason and immorality in British life. Indeed, in the hope of doing something to spread the notion that morality applied to international relations as well as to private affairs, he even helped to subsidize the publication of a new edition of Jonathan Dymond's *Essays on the Principles of Morality* (1829). More than ever it was plain to Bright that a profound change in the British idea of foreign policy was needed. "When it will come I know not—perhaps some great catastrophe is approaching. I sometimes suspect it. Earthquakes come without noise. . . . Europe is nearly ready for one, and its nations, we amongst them, may need a lesson," he wrote revealingly to an American admirer. (18)

Lord Salisbury's short Ministry of 1885–1886 confirmed Bright's belief in the soundness of his thinking at the time of his resignation. He had reasoned that there was no sense in embarrassing the Government unduly, an attitude that Gladstone, of course, appreciated, for if it fell it would be succeeded by a Tory Administration that would be infinitely worse. After all, except for its Egyptian policy, Bright considered the Gladstone Ministry the best the British had had in the nineteenth century. He thought so even more when the Salisbury Government came into being, for the Tories quickly proceeded to annex Burma. Years of instructing the British about the disadvantages of colonies—that they were costly, that they increased military expenditures and the dangers of war, that they were temporary in any case—were wasted. (19)

The behavior of the Tories during Salisbury's first Ministry was sufficient to convince Bright that the Liberals simply had to return to office. He was disappointed by their failure to win more seats than they did in the election in November 1885, but he hopefully interpreted the returns as evidence of voters' disapproval of Gladstone's Egyptian adventure. Tory leaders saw things differently, to be sure. Lord Salisbury and Arthur Balfour were certain that Whigs were deserting Gladstone's party chiefly because they feared the social radicalism of Joseph Chamberlain, a view with which Chamberlain himself agreed. At any rate, Gladstone controlled enough seats to form a Government. From the outset, however, it was clear that a coalition of Tories and Parnellites could force him out at any time. (20)

V

Gladstone had hoped that Lord Salisbury would make an arrangement with the Parnellites for the settlement of the Irish Question—an arrangement to which the Liberals would then lend their support. But this hope proved to be another of the fantasies to which Gladstone was sometimes prone. He saw no other way out, therefore: he himself had to take the initiative, and with the support of the Liberals and the Parnellites he thought he might succeed. As he had pointedly told Bright some years before: "It is I think one of the advantages of the last stage of public life that one may use it to say things which, though true and needful in themselves, could not properly be said by any man with twenty or even ten years of his career before him." Thus, Gladstone's decision to end the Irish Question by granting home rule became the hotly debated issue of his brief third Ministry (February–July, 1886). Joseph Chamberlain did not exaggerate when he noted, "The strain of the political situation is very great and the best and strongest of us may well find it difficult to keep an even mind." (21)

Gladstone made every effort to win Bright's support. He praised him, he flattered him, and he convinced himself that his old friend and ally would back him. Other home rulers did the same. They told Bright how influential and powerful he was. They reminded him of what a glorious record of service he had. He had helped to give the people cheap bread, an inexpensive newspaper press, the right to vote; he was chiefly responsible for the disestablishment of the Church of Ireland. Now he could crown his career by defending home rule. (22)

But Bright was also subjected to other pressures. Anti-home rulers from Ireland wrote and spoke to him about their fears; and so did British anti-home rulers. Above all, Lord Hartington and Joseph Chamberlain urged him to play a prominent part in the struggle to block home rule. He refused, partly because of loyalty to Gladstone, but chiefly because he knew that the fate of the Liberal Party depended on the fate of Gladstone's home rule bill. If the measure were defeated as a result of the cooperation of Tories and those Liberals who wished to preserve the Act of Union with Ireland (the Liberal Unionists), the future of the Liberal Party would be bleak indeed; and there would be years and years of Tory rule ahead. If only Gladstone would think of the consequences of his behavior! If only he would abandon his scheme before he did irreparable damage to his party and his country! (23)

Bright's position was not so clear as he later came to think it was. At times he thought that it would be splendid to rid Westminster of the Parnellites so that Parliament could get some important work done. More and more, however, he was obsessed with the implications of a Parliament in Dublin. Such a Parliament would be dominated by the very Parnellites who for years had been bringing British parliamentary government into disrepute, who for years had demonstrated their disloyalty to Britain, who for years had accepted money from Irish Americans in order to subvert British institutions. More and more, therefore, Bright saw Gladstone's home rule proposals as a capitulation to scoundrels, ruffians, rebels, and traitors. To give such people a Parliament in Dublin would be no answer to the Irish Question; on the contrary, home rule would raise new difficulties. Bright, in other words, could not divorce the idea of home rule from the character of Parnell and his cohorts. He was honest enough to recognize that he could have conceded much if he had been able to trust the Parnellites; but he would never be able to trust them. And to give to them control over the lives of those Irish—both Catholic and Protestant—who were loyal to Britain would be, he felt, an act of unwisdom and injustice with few parallels in the sweep of British history. The home rule bill, he told Gladstone, "will only place more power in their hands to war with greater effect against the unity of the three kingdoms with no increase of good to the Irish people." (24)

At the same time, however, he made it clear that although he did not agree with Gladstone neither did he agree with the scheme of federation for which Joseph Chamberlain was pressing. He felt alarmingly alone, "outside all the contending sections of the Liberal Party," as he put it. Bright, in short, knew something that historians since his time have often forgotten: that the struggle over home rule was enormously complex, that it was not simply a struggle between Gladstonians and anti-Gladstonians but between Gladstonians of different degrees of intensity and a variety of anti-Gladstonians, who disagreed with one another. (25)

It was plain to contemporaries that, even if Gladstone's bill had passed the House of Commons in June, it would in any case have been thrown out by the Lords. Nevertheless, what Bright feared was the aftermath of the defeat. It was one thing for a Sir Robert Peel to split his party over an important moral issue; it was quite another thing to do what Gladstone had done. For Bright this latest action was the most disastrous in a long line of blunders that betrayed a fundamental character defect in Gladstone. And in his fury with him for having wrecked the Liberal Party, Bright recalled that, among other things, Gladstone had supported the Crimean War, he had favored the South in the Civil War, and he had rivaled the Tories in his imperialistic ventures in Egypt. Now he had been willing to destroy his party in order to give power to the unscrupulous Parnellites. As the year ended and Bright reached his seventy-fifth birthday, he knew that the kind of Liberal Britain he favored was doomed. (26)

NOTES

(1) *Diaries,* Mar. 1, 1881; Mar. 3, 1881; Mar. 5, 1881; Mar. 12, 1881; Feb. 1, 1882; May 13, 1882; May 31, 1882; June 20, 1882; July 2, 1882; July 8, 1882; July 10, 1882; July 11, 1882; July 12, 1882; July 13, 1882; July 14, 1882; *Letters,* Feb., 1881; Mar. 14, 1881; Mar. 23, 1881; Bright to Gladstone, July 12, 1882; July 13, 1882; July 15, 1882; July 22, 1882, Gladstone MSS, BM 44,113; Gladstone to Bright, July 12, 1882; July 13, 1882; July 14, 1882, Bright MSS, RGL; Chamberlain to Bright, Dec. 31, 1882; Jan. 14, 1884, Bright MSS, BM 43,387; Bright to Chamberlain, Jan. 18, 1884, Chamberlain MSS, University of Birmingham Library; Magnus, p. 290; Gladstone to Granville, July 12, 1882; July 14, 1882; Oct. 3, 1882; Oct. 12, 1882, Ramm.

(2) *Parl. Deb.,* 272 (July 17, 1882), 722ff.; *The Times,* July 17, 1882; July 22, 1882; Sept. 30, 1882; *Economist,* XL (1882), 902–3; *Punch,* LXXXIII (1882), 39; *Letters,* Sept. 25, 1882; Granville to Bright, July 13, 1882; Chamberlain to Bright, July 15, 1882; Harcourt to Bright, July 18, 1882; Ripon to Bright, Dec. 30, 1882, Bright MSS, BM 43,387–43,389; Bright to D. Williams, Aug. 18, 1882, Bright MSS, NLW; Bright to Chamberlain, Jan. 4, 1883, Chamberlain MSS, University of Birmingham Library; Bright to Pierce, Jan. 10, 1883, Bright MSS, HCL; Bright to Moncure Conway, Apr. 9, 1885, Conway MSS, CUL; Robert Rhodes James, *Rosebery* (London, 1963), p. 131.

(3) *Diaries,* Jan. 10, 1882; Mar. 30, 1882; May 7, 1882; May 11, 1882; June 8, 1882; June 23, 1882; Nov. 27, 1882; *The Times,* Jan. 4, 1882; Jan. 28, 1882; *Parl. Deb.,* 268 (Mar. 30, 1882), 325; 269 (May 11, 1882), 480ff.; 271

(July 6, 1882), 1637ff.; 272 (June 23, 1882), 275; Bright to Karl Blind, Jan. 28, 1882, Blind MSS, BM 40,125.

(4) *The Times,* Jan. 5, 1882; Jan. 6, 1882; Oct. 24, 1882; *Parl. Deb.,* 268 (May 1, 1882), 1892ff.; 274 (Nov. 16, 1882), 1612; *Diaries,* Feb. 5, 1882; Feb. 7, 1882.

(5) Bright to Northy, Jan. 4, 1883, Northy MSS, BM 44,877; Bright to Pierce, Jan. 10, 1883, Bright MSS, HCL; Bright to Mrs. Joseph Kay, Feb. 11, 1883, Kay MSS, NLI.

(6) Memorials from the executive of the Glasgow Liberal Association, Mar. 22, 1883; the executive council of the Liberal Association of the Borough of Gateshead, June 12, 1883; the Rochdale Reform Association, June 13, 1883; the Liberals of Leeds, June 13, 1883; the Greenock Liberal Association, June 13, 1883; East Worcestershire Liberal Association, June 13, 1883; West-Bromwich Liberal Association, June 13, 1883; North Staffordshire Liberal Association, June 13, 1883; Nottingham Liberal Union, June 13, 1883; Coventry Liberal Association; Salford Liberal Association, RGL; *Annual Register, 1883,* pp. 70ff.; *Economist,* XLI (1883), 690–91; *Pall Mall Gazette,* June 18, 1883; *Illustrated London News,* LXXXII (1883), 594.

(7) *Annual Register, 1883,* pp. 139ff.; *The Times,* Mar. 23, 1883; Mar. 24, 1883; July 3, 1883; July 5, 1883; Dec. 13, 1883; Dec. 15, 1883; *Diaries,* May 2, 1883; June 28, 1883; Aug. 1, 1883; *Letters,* Sept. 3, 1883; Bright to Lady Dorothy Neville, Aug. 15, 1883, Bright MSS, MCL; Bright to Northy, Dec. 26, 1883, Northy MSS, BM 44,877.

(8) *Letters,* Apr. 6, 1883; Aug. 25, 1883; Nov. 30, 1883; cf. David S. Muzzey, *James G. Blaine* (New York, 1934), p. 268; *Parl. Deb.,* 280 (June 18, 1883), 805ff.; *The Times,* Aug. 2, 1883; Oct. 17, 1883; Oct. 19, 1883; Oct. 31, 1883; cf. Bright to J. Fox Turner, Aug. 4, 1882, Bright MSS, Local History Department, MCL; Bright to Pierce, Jan. 10, 1883, Bright MSS, HCL; Ripon to Bright, Aug. 27, 1883, Bright MSS, BM 43,389; Bright to R. Barry O'Brien, Oct. 4, 1883, facsimile, Bright MSS, FHL; Bright to Northy, Dec. 26, 1883, Northy MSS, BM 44,877.

(9) *Ibid.;* Bright to W. T. Stead, July 23, 1884, Bright MSS, Friends Historical Library, Swarthmore College; *Parl. Deb.,* 286 (Mar. 24, 1884), 634, 690; *Diaries,* July 10, 1884; *Punch,* LXXXVII (1884), 67.

(10) *Letters,* Feb. 13, 1884; Feb. 27, 1884.

(11) *Diaries,* Jan. 26, 1884; Mar. 9, 1884; Mar. 18, 1884; Mar. 25, 1884; Nov. 29, 1884; Bright to Edward Atkinson, Aug. 17, 1882, Atkinson MSS, MHS; William Evarts to Bright, Dec. 12, 1882; Edward L. Pierce·to Bright, Jan. 25, 1884; Nov. 19, 1884, Bright MSS, BM 43,390–43,391; Bright to J. B. Andrews, June 16, 1884, Field MSS, PML; *Letters,* Mar. 10, 1884; Nov., 1884.

(12) *The Times,* Jan. 23, 1884; *Diaries,* Feb. 18, 1884; Apr. 9, 1884; Apr. 16, 1884; Oct. 25, 1884; Bright to Edmund Sturge, July 11, 1884, Anti-

Slavery MSS, Rhodes House Library, Oxford; George Jacob Holyoake to Bright, July 16, 1884, Holyoake MSS, Co-operative Union Ltd. Library; Bright to John Stuart Blackie, July 16, 1884; July 18, 1884, Blackie MSS, NLS; Bright to Blackie, Apr. 13, 1885, Autograph MSS, ULL; Bright to Stanley Withers, Sept. 4, 1884, Withers MSS, MCL; *Letters,* Oct. 23, 1884; Bright to William Jack, Dec. 22, 1884, Jack MSS, NLS; Gladstone to Bright, May 28, 1884, Bright MSS, BM 43,385.

(13) Bright to Mrs. Kay, Oct. 21, 1884, Kay MSS, NLI; *Diaries,* Feb. 5, 1884; Feb. 11, 1884; Feb. 21, 1884; Feb. 26, 1884; Bright to William Tallack, Jan. 6, 1884; Jan. 11, 1884, Tallack MSS, BM 38,835; cf. Bright to Rev. John B. Wright, Dec. 13, 1885, Bright MSS, Fitzwilliam Museum, Cambridge; *The Times,* Jan. 30, 1884; *Parl. Deb.,* 284 (Feb. 11, 1884), 481; *Letters,* Apr. 1, 1884; June 19, 1884; July 18, 1884; Nov. 17, 1884; Dec. 19, 1884; Dec. 23, 1884; Bright to H. McDermott, Nov. 23, 1884, Anthony MSS, NYPL; Granville to Bright, Nov. 7, 1884, Bright MSS, BM 43,387; Bright to Gladstone, June 5, 1884, Gladstone MSS, BM 44,113; Bright to Northy, Dec. 26, 1884, Northy MSS, BM 44,877.

(14) *Diaries,* Mar. 13, 1884; Sept. 18, 1884; Sept. 26, 1884; Sept. 29, 1884; Nov. 8, 1884; Nov. 16, 1884; Dec. 31, 1884; Bright to Northy, Feb. 28, 1884, Northy MSS, BM 44,877; Bright to Gladstone, June 5, 1884, Gladstone MSS, BM 44,113; cf. Chamberlain to Bright, Jan. 3, 1885, Bright MSS, BM 43,387.

(15) Bright to A. J. Mundella, July 24, 1884, Mundella MSS, University of Sheffield Library; *Letters,* Oct. 9, 1884; Dec. 29, 1884; July 9, 1885; *Diaries,* Nov. 18, 1884; Nov. 27, 1884; William Lord, *Mr. Bright on Redistribution* (Manchester, 1884); Bright to Gladstone, Nov. 26, 1884, Gladstone MSS, BM 44,113; Bright to Mrs. Kay, Jan. 3, 1885, Kay MSS, NLI; Bright to Albert B. Shaw, Jan. 22, 1885, Charles Roberts Autograph MSS, Haverford College Library; Bright to Thomas Gee, July 15, 1885, Bright MSS, NLW.

(16) *Diaries,* Feb. 5, 1885; Mar. 2, 1885; Mar. 21, 1885; Apr. 23, 1885; Apr. 24, 1885; Whittier to Bright, Mar. 31, 1885, Whittier MSS, Berg Collection, NYPL; Lord Elton, *Gordon of Khartoum* (New York, 1955); cf. Magnus, p. 326; Bright to Gladstone, Apr. 23, 1885, Gladstone MSS, BM 44,113.

(17) Bright to Pierce, Jan. 5, 1885, Bright MSS, HCL; Bright to Gladstone, May 1, 1885, Gladstone MSS, BM 44,113; *Diaries,* May 1, 1885.

(18) Trevelyan, p. 443; *Diaries,* June 8, 1885; July 23, 1885; Whittier to Bright, Mar. 31, 1885, Whittier MSS, Berg Collection, NYPL; Pierce to Bright, Nov. 16, 1885, Bright MSS, BM 43,390; Bright to Chamberlain, Apr. 7, 1885, Chamberlain MSS, University of Birmingham Library; Bright to Mrs. Kay, May 16, 1885, Kay MSS, NLI; *Letters,* May 17, 1885; Bright to Northy, Aug. 14, 1885, Northy MSS, BM 44,877; Bright to Moncure Conway, Apr. 9, 1885, Conway MSS, CUL.

(19) Bright to Thomas Bentley, Feb. 2, 1885, Bright MSS, FHL; Bright

to Conway, Apr. 9, 1885, Conway MSS, CUL; Gladstone to Granville, Apr. 24, 1885, Ramm; Gladstone to Bright, June 1, 1885; Granville to Bright, June 2, 1885; Ripon to Bright, Oct. 24, 1885, Bright MSS, BM 43,385, 43,387, 43,389.

(20) *Diaries* Nov. 25, 1885; Balfour MS memorandum, Dec. 10, 1885, Balfour MSS, BM 49,838; Salisbury to Alfred Austin, Sept. 12, 1885; Chamberlain to Austin, Feb. 16, 1891, Austin MSS, National Liberal Club.

(21) The best treatment is still J. L. Hammond, *Gladstone and the Irish Nation* (London, 1938); Magnus, pp. 330–35; Balfour to Salisbury, Dec. 23, 1885, Balfour MSS, BM 49,688; Gladstone to Bright, Sept. 29, 1881, copy, Gladstone MSS, BM 44,113; Chamberlain to Dilke, May 6, 1886, Dilke MSS, BM 43,888.

(22) Gladstone to Bright, Jan. 7, 1886, Bright MSS, BM 43,385; cf. Granville to Gladstone, Mar. 17, 1886; Mar. 20, 1886; Gladstone to Granville, Mar. 20, 1886, Ramm; Northy to Bright, June 15, 1886, Northy MSS, BM 44,877.

(23) *Diaries,* Jan. 4, 1886; Mar. 10, 1886; Mar. 17, 1886; Mar. 27, 1886; Mar. 29, 1886; Apr. 3, 1886; May 14, 1886; *The Times,* Feb. 2, 1886; Chamberlain to Bright, Jan. 28, 1886; Feb. 5, 1886; May 30, 1886; June 2, 1886; Hartington to Bright, Mar. 8, 1886; Mar. 26, 1886; Apr. 11, 1886, Bright MSS, BM 43,387; Bright to G. Barnett Smith, Mar. 4, 1886, Bright MSS, PML; Bright to Chamberlain, May 31, 1886; June 1, 1886; June 9, 1886, Chamberlain MSS, University of Birmingham Library; Bright to Gladstone, May 13, 1886, Gladstone MSS, BM 44,113.

(24) Cf. *The Times,* Apr. 15, 1889; Bright to Chamberlain, Dec. 15, 1885; Feb. 4, 1886, Chamberlain MSS, University of Birmingham Library; Bright to Northy, Dec. 28, 1885, Northy MSS, BM 44,877; Bright to Pierce, Jan. 17, 1886, Bright MSS, HCL; *Diaries,* Mar. 12, 1886; Mar. 20, 1886; cf. *Parl. Deb.,* 300 (July 28, 1885), 265; Electoral Address to the electors of the Central Division of Birmingham, June 24, 1886, Bagshawe MSS, JRL; Bright to Gladstone, May 13, 1886, Gladstone MSS, BM 44,113.

(25) *Ibid.;* C. H. D. Howard, ed., *A Political Memoir, 1880–92, by Joseph Chamberlain* (London, 1953); Chamberlain to Bright, May 15, 1886, Bright MSS, BM 43,387; Bright to Chamberlain, June 9, 1886, Chamberlain MSS, University of Birmingham Library.

(26) *Diaries,* June 7, 1886; Dec. 7, 1886; Bright to Chamberlain, Aug. 28, 1886, Chamberlain MSS, University of Birmingham Library; Bright to Northy, July 27, 1886; Dec. 27, 1886, Northy MSS, BM 44,877.

CHAPTER SIXTEEN

STAND AND WAIT
1886-1889

During the course of the home rule battle nothing pained Gladstone more than Bright's hostility; but nothing pained Bright more than what he saw as Gladstone's irresponsibility. Now the prospect was of years of government by the Tories—the party of the jingoes, imperialists, bigots, and protectionists. For this Bright held Gladstone solely responsible. The three-time Prime Minister had demonstrated that one man could smash a great party, for, if he had not insisted on home rule, few of his followers would have favored it. At the same time, Bright never ceased, even on his deathbed, to acknowledge that Gladstone had done some great things in the past, and he steadfastly criticized those who attributed Gladstone's conversion to home rule to a Jesuit conspiracy or a secret yearning for Rome. (1)

Bright's feelings about Gladstone did not soften as the months went by. When intermediaries urged a reconciliation, Gladstone suggested characteristically that Bright and he were not far apart and that if reason were permitted to operate they could be friends and allies again. But Bright would hear nothing of a reconciliation—it was out of the question. Gladstone's behavior had been reprehensible, and the wreckage of the Liberal Party was his monument. Indeed, when Bright was chided for criticizing Gladstone, he could only be struck, in view of his passionate convictions, by his relative restraint and discretion; but *Punch* was not excessive when it ran the lines:

> Mr. BRIGHT—*et tu Brighte!*—at Birmingham said
> His old friend, Mr. GLADSTONE, had quite lost his head. (2)

THE OLD LION AROUSED!

In one respect Bright could not help feeling self-righteous. For much more than a generation he had been preaching justice for Ireland. Long before Gladstone discovered the Irish Question and long before Parnell and his followers began clamoring about Irish grievances, he had been telling both the public and his colleagues in the House that they ought to improve Anglo-Irish relations. He did not exaggerate when he noted, somewhat priggishly, "I was before

them all in pointing out the evil and the remedy." Nor could he
help thinking that, if the British Parliament had listened to him and
acted earlier, the present situation would not have come about. But
as in the beginning of his career, so now at what he knew was the
end, he was impressed with the rarity of statesmanship. Politicians
simply did not think in long-range terms or try to anticipate the
future. They were immersed almost exclusively in trivialities. And
a result of their lack of foresight was the deplorable state of Anglo-
Irish relations. (3)

In the light of his depression about the condition of public affairs,
it was natural that Bright tried to lose himself in his private life.
He spent as many hours as possible with his children and grandchildren, he vacationed and fished in Scotland as often as he could,
and he spent a great deal of time in Rochdale. But he could not keep
his mind off the recent past; nor would the people he saw or those
with whom he corresponded permit him to do so. On the one hand,
he was overwhelmed with praise—even from the Queen—for op-
posing Gladstone. On the other hand, he was denounced as a lost
leader, deserter, and traitor. Absurd stories were circulated about
him, including one that his factories in Rochdale carried signs saying
that no Irish need apply. (4)

Even his own children were strongly divided in opinion, some
of them insisting that he should have supported Gladstone. (Helen
went so far as to write secretly to Gladstone about her views.) But
while Bright was pleased that his children expressed their opinions
to him, he ran no risk whatever of being converted by them. He
never questioned the soundness of his estimate of Parnell: He was
a wicked man, and the kind of freedom the Parnellites were seeking
would mean tyranny for Ireland and danger for Britain. "Parnell
and Co." were, after all, utterly dependent on the funds that came
from Irish Americans, and these were people who would have liked
nothing more than a war between Britain and the United States.
In short, Bright insisted that he was never more the friend of the
Irish than now that he had refused to subject them to the rule of
the Parnellites. (5)

In 1887 Bright noted in his diary that he had heard that home rule for Ireland had become Gladstone's *idée fixe*; he could have noted just as accurately that opposition to home rule had become his own *idée fixe*. Endlessly he rehearsed his arguments, and invariably he concluded that he had acted properly. To be sure, he despised the Tories with whom he and the other Liberal advocates of Union with Ireland were forced to cooperate. But as long as he lived he would do everything he could to prevent the return to office of Gladstone—unless, of course, Gladstone renounced his outrageous views on Ireland. In Bright's blunt words: "I prefer to join hands with Lord Salisbury and his colleagues than with Parnell and his friends—the leaders of the Irish rebellion." The result of this preference was the curious sight and sound of Tories cheering Bright as he walked up the floor of the House. (6)

It is revealing, nevertheless, that for all his self-assurance, Bright was constantly pleased to hear people tell him that he was right. When he headed a delegation of the Society of Friends to congratulate the Queen at the time of her Jubilee of 1887, he was delighted that she made a point of again telling him how much she approved of his stand. When he attended parties at which the Irish Question was discussed, he was happy to discover how many people shared his hostility to a parliament in Dublin. Moreover, when he read his mail, he rejoiced to learn how repugnant so many of his correspondents found home rule. (7)

He recognized the simplemindedness of those who hoped that the Irish Question would miraculously vanish, but he doubted his own ability to hit upon a satisfactory settlement. And for a political leader who had always prided himself on finding answers to questions, this was unnerving. At times he thought the constitution would have to be suspended in Ireland. At other times he suspected that only some altogether unanticipated event would make possible a solution to the Irish political difficulty—in much the way that the unforeseen Great Famine had brought about the repeal of the corn laws. He had some faith in the establishment of an Irish parliamentary committee that would make recommendations to Parliament about specifically Irish needs; but a Parliament in Dublin was out of the question, and so, too, was Chamberlain's federal plan. For fear of associating himself with such a plan he refused, in fact, to write an introduction to a collection of Chamberlain's Irish speeches even though his refusal might be misunderstood by his colleague. *Punch*, to be sure, called them "Johnny and Joey," but the label did not really fit. (8)

Bright's hatred of Parnell bordered on the pathological. He relished every bit of information that cast discredit on the Irish leader, and he rejoiced at each new defeat Parnell suffered at the hands of the Tory Government. Always he saw him as a scoundrel who never gave the English a chance to show their goodwill, and always he viewed him as a traitor who would do anything to ingratiate himself with his Irish-American masters and financiers. To be sure, Bright thoroughly enjoyed the exposures that *The Times* published in the series of articles on "Parnellism and Crime"—the more so because the evidence was drawn from the words of "the rebel conspirators" themselves. That the articles were based on forged documents Bright did not live long enough to find out. (9)

Although the public issue that concerned him most in his last years was the Irish Question, he also worried about other topics in the news. He was upset by the renewed clamor of protectionists, militarists, xenophobes, and imperialists, not only in Britain but in other countries. And he was disturbed by the changes that British Radicals and Socialists were proposing. He granted, for example, that many of Joseph Chamberlain's suggestions concerning educational, land, and social reform deserved serious public discussion, but he could not help wondering about the motivation of his colleague from Birmingham. Although they had got along well since the beginning of their close association in the seventies—Chamberlain was, in fact, most flattering and deferential to him—Bright suspected that personal ambition rather than patriotism or humanitarianism provided the clue to an understanding of his colleague. (10)

Bright, for his part, had never been a doctrinaire advocate of laissez-faire; like Cobden, he saw state intervention as a necessity in important phases of social and economic life. But he had worried for a long time about the tendency of some reformers to call for parliamentary interference in spheres where self-help and an en-

lightened public opinion were more appropriate—the restriction of
what people should drink, the control of corporal punishment in
schools, the regulation of the relations of parents and children, and
the further limitation by law of adult working hours. (11)

II

For years Bright had marveled that he had lived so long, but the
time for marveling was drawing to a close. He could not help notic-
ing that he was losing his old skill with numbers, that he could
write only with great difficulty, and that his script was becoming
shaky. In the spring of 1888 his lung ailment returned, but he man-
aged to recover—if slowly and fitfully. As *Punch* put it:

> We are glad you're on the mend,
> For you're everybody's friend,
>   And the troops of your admirers still increase, JOHN BRIGHT!
>
> You've a fashion of your own,
> Which the English race has grown
>   To bear with even when it does not please, JOHN BRIGHT!
>
> So when you're well once more,
> A congratulatory roar
>   Will sound from every section of the State, JOHN BRIGHT!
>
> And each will brim his glass
> To a patriot first-class
>   Who's as sturdy in his love as in his hate, JOHN BRIGHT! (12)

In the autumn, however, he suffered a relapse, and it seemed
unlikely that he would live much past his seventy-seventh birthday
in November. His children were summoned to Rochdale, and the
public—including the Queen and Gladstone—was alerted. Again he
made an unexpected recovery, but even when his doctors considered
him out of immediate danger, his feeling of weakness was overwhelming.

On March 27, 1889, he died, and on the thirtieth he was buried
with great simplicity, for he deplored elaborate and expensive fu-
nerals, in the small graveyard attached to the Friends' Meeting
House in Rochdale. Home rulers, imperialists, feminists, xenophobes,
jingoes, and protectionists had lost a fierce enemy. Democrats,

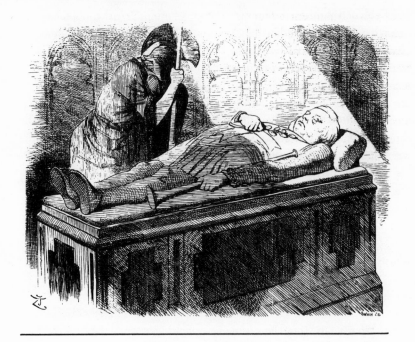

JOHN BRIGHT
Born, Nov. 16, 1811   Died, March 27, 1889
"The Trumpet's Silver Sound Is Still!"

humanitarians, advocates of the arbitration of international disputes, free traders, Indians, Americans, and the Irish people had lost a strong friend. (13)

Bright had often thought of himself as a prophet without honor, but during his last years he was accorded recognition of a sort that he had not believed possible. He was now a veteran statesman. His colleagues deferred to him; the newspapers, even when they disagreed with him, treated his opinions with respect; and his advice on a multitude of subjects was sought by many people. Oxford awarded him an honorary degree. Humphry Ward asked permission to write his biography. The compiler of his *Public Letters* wished to bring out another edition of the work. His son William was

elected to Parliament as Member for Stoke-upon-Trent. Indian patriots thanked him endlessly for his efforts in their behalf. And
Americans were, as always, kind and generous. Some wished that he
were eligible to serve as President of the United States; some begged
him to attend the celebrations of the centennial of the framing of
the American Constitution—an event that he considered "one of the
most important in the annals of men"; some who lived in Massachusetts went out of their way to assure him that their experience
with the Irish Americans—disorderly, violent, easily misled—justified
his resistance to home rule; and others named a new but ill-fated
university for him in Wichita, Kansas. To his own surprise, in short,
he lived long enough to find himself ranked as a giant among his
contemporaries. (14)

His death quickly submerged the hostilities that he had been so
adept in arousing during decades of agitation. Gladstone led the
rest in his words of praise, but Tories vied with Parnellites in their
eulogies and the citizens of Manchester with those of Birmingham.
Bright would certainly have been amused, for he had never been able
to separate a man from the causes he upheld. But many of his erstwhile opponents had this ability, and so even his enemies could insist
that his moral stature was more important than his politics—that he
was more important than his opinions. At the same time, however,
his sister Priscilla could note with a bitterness unusual for her:
"Great has been the tribute of praise given to my Brother—but alas!
how little do those who joined it follow his example. Where is the
moral courage and fidelity to principle which was so much lauded?
Where do we see them? Not in that House of Commons...." (15)

Of the countless tributes that Bright received two would have
pleased him particularly. One came from the Lancashire and Chesh-
ire Quarterly Meeting of the Society of Friends: "We feel it our
duty to bear testimony to the power of that Divine Grace, which we
believe enabled our friend John Bright to be a true minister of Jesus
Christ in the remarkable line of service to which he was called." The
other appeared in a provincial newspaper. It was not the product
of a Victorian Milton, but the kind of popular poetry that Bright
enjoyed along with *Paradise Lost*.

> Where shall we look for one to fill his place
>   In coming Ages?
> His work is done. But he shall leave his trace
> As grand exemplar of the Saxon race
>   On history's pages.
> His epitaph—"A noble path he trod,
> He served his country; and he served his God." (16)

Several other tributes, delivered long after his death, would also have meant a great deal to him. One was written during the Boer War to Bright's daughter Helen by the Liberal anti-imperialist Leonard Courtney: "The image and example of your father have often been in my mind...." Another was written in 1906 by the young Winston Churchill after the electoral defeat of the Chamberlain protectionists and the victory of the free traders: "Could anything be a plainer tribute to the wisdom of an instructed democracy than this emphatic asseveration of the economic doctrines of Mr. Bright and Mr. Cobden, after the successful practice and matured consideration of [sixty] years?" (17)

By his own standards, however, Bright was a failure, and he was acutely aware of it. For almost a half-century, from the early forties to the late eighties, he had tried to teach the British that they must abandon eighteenth- and early nineteenth-century methods, and although he had been successful in certain respects, he knew that he had failed in the sphere that mattered most to him. For everything else he stood for depended on the maintenance of international peace, and Bright accepted the painful fact that the British were not a peace-loving people, that they had made no progress towards banishing war as an instrument of policy. Indeed, at the slightest provocation their anti-French, anti-American, and anti-Russian feelings would burst forth, and they would clamor for a fight.

Bright never forgot the treatment he had received during the Crimean conflict. Nor did he forget—as have many historians—the war scares in which the Victorian age luxuriated. That they continued to occur depressed and alarmed him; and as long as they could occur, he questioned his effectiveness as a leader. He was, to be sure, no pacifist, as his stand during the American Civil War showed, but his study of history had convinced him that most wars—certainly since the Glorious Revolution—could have been avoided. That his countrymen did not understand this central truth was their greatest failing. And that he could not make them grasp this truth was his own great failing.

He was proud of what he had done to bring about freer trade, the repeal of the taxes on knowledge, an inexpensive press, the secret ballot, the extension of the suffrage, the redistribution of parliamentary seats, the weakening of the power of the great landowners, educational reform, the disestablishment of the Church of Ireland, and the Irish land acts. But he considered love of peace and the conciliatory spirit far more important than any and all of these. Yet despite his prodigious efforts as a public instructor, he discovered repeatedly that the nineteenth-century British remained slow and reluctant learners. Dangerously subject to the jingo spirit, they were setting a woeful example in an age and world of strident nationalism. They had yet to learn to apply Christianity to their affairs. (18)

NOTES

(1) *Letters,* Feb. 9, 1887; Bright to Howard Morley, Dec. 6, 1887, Bright MSS, BPL; cf. Granville to Bright, May 6, 1877, Bright MSS, BM 43,387; Albert Bright to Gladstone, Nov. 27, 1888; Helen Clark to Mrs. Gladstone, Apr. 23, 1889, Gladstone MSS, BM 44,505–44,506; Bright to Mrs. Leatherbrow, Aug. 9, 1886, Bright MSS, RGL; cf. Cobden to Bright, Dec. 7, 1850, Cobden MSS, BM 43,649.

(2) Bright to Chamberlain, Aug. 28, 1886, Chamberlain MSS, University of Birmingham Library; Gladstone to Northy, Dec. 11, 1886; Bright to Northy, Dec. 27, 1886; June 22, 1887, Northy MSS, BM 44,877; Gladstone to Bright, July 2, 1886; June 11, 1887; June 16, 1887, Bright MSS, BM 43,385; Gladstone to Granville, July 9, 1886, Ramm; Gladstone to Bright, June 26, 1886, copy; July 2, 1886, copy; June 16, 1887, copy; Bright to Gladstone, June 14, 1887, Gladstone MSS, BM 44,113; *Diaries,* Feb. 24, 1887; Bright to Lord Grey, Feb. 21, 1888, Grey of Howick MSS, The Prior's Kitchen, The College, Durham; *Punch,* XCI (1886), 22.

(3) *The Times,* June 25, 1886; July 2, 1886; *Letters,* Nov. 11, 1887; Bright to Francis J. Garrison, Feb. 17, 1886, Autograph MSS, University of Rochester Library.

(4) Bright to Sir John Millais, Aug. 28, 1886; Oct. 4, 1886, Millais MSS,

PML; Bright to James A. Manson, July 14, 1886, Bright MSS, Brotherton Library, University of Leeds; Bright to Emma Todd, Nov. 19, 1886, Bright MSS, RGL; *Diaries,* June 28, 1886; Chamberlain to Bright, May 15, 1886, Bright MSS, BM 43,387; John Morley to George Jacob Holyoake, Feb. 28, 1887, Holyoake MSS, Co-operative Union Ltd. Library; cf. *The Times,* May 28, 1885.

(5) *Diaries,* July 4, 1886; Bright to Helen Clark, Sept. 29, 1886; Mar. 17, 1887, Bright MSS, S; Helen Clark to Gladstone, Oct. 15, 1887, Gladstone MSS, BM 44,502; *The Times,* July 29, 1886; *Letters,* Mar. 15, 1887; May 30, 1887; Oct. 1, 1887.

(6) *Diaries,* July 26, 1887; *Letters,* Nov. 21, 1887; cf. *The Times,* June 28, 1886.

(7) *Diaries,* Apr. 1, 1887; Apr. 30, 1887; May 16, 1887; Bright to William Knight, May 24, 1888, Knight MSS, PML.

(8) Bright to Charles Rubins, Nov. 28, 1887, Bright MSS, NLI; Bright to Lord Grey, Feb. 21, 1888; Feb. 24, 1888, Grey of Howick MSS, The Prior's Kitchen, The College, Durham; Priscilla B. McLaren to Mina and Edith (daughters of J. B. Smith), Apr. 8, 1889, Smith MSS, MCL; Bright to Arthur Chamberlain, Feb. 11, 1887; Feb. 15, 1887, Chamberlain MSS, University of Birmingham Library; *Punch,* C (1886), 279.

(9) *The Times,* May 10, 1887; May 13, 1887; *Letters,* June 15, 1887; *Diaries,* June 17, 1887; see L. P. Curtis, Jr., *Coercion and Conciliation in Ireland, 1880–1892* (Princeton, 1963).

(10) Bright to Pierce, Jan. 5, 1885; Jan. 17, 1886, Pierce MSS, HCL; Bright to J. A. Morris, Sept. 6, 1885, Bright MSS, NLW; Bright to Richard Tangye, Nov. 17, 1886, Northy MSS, BM 44,877; Bright to Charles Thompson, Dec. 23, 1886, Bright MSS, Friends Historical Library, Swarthmore College; *Diaries,* Feb. 22, 1887; Bright to James H. Rawlins, Aug. 10, 1887, Bright MSS, PUL; Robert Rhodes James, *Rosebery* (London, 1963), p. 158; *Letters,* Jan. 12, 1887; Apr. 21, 1887; Nov. 25, 1887; cf. Gladstone to T. Fisher Unwin, June 23, 1896, Gladstone MSS, D; Bright to Gladstone, Apr. 16, 1873; Oct. 23, 1885, Gladstone MSS, BM 44,113; Bright to Chamberlain, Nov. 7, 1876, Chamberlain MSS, University of Birmingham Library; Gladstone to Granville, Oct. 24, 1885, Ramm; Chamberlain to Bright, June 9, 1886, Bright MSS BM 43,387; cf. Chamberlain to Alfred Austin, Feb. 18, 1891, Austin MSS, National Liberal Club.

(11) Cobden to Bright, Nov. 5, 1855, Cobden MSS, BM 43,650; Bright to John Reed, Feb. 16, 1858; Feb. 28, 1860, Northy MSS, BM 44,877; Bright to John H. Ingram, Nov. 29, 1883, Bright MSS, PML; *Letters,* Jan. 1, 1884; *The Times,* May 11, 1887; cf. John Spargo, "Reminiscences," p. 105, Oral History, CUL.

(12) *Diaries,* June 8, 1887; Bright to Percy W. Bunting, Apr. 5, 1888,

Bunting MSS, University of Chicago Library; Bright to Chamberlain, May 10, 1888; May 25, 1888, Chamberlain MSS, University of Birmingham Library; Helen Clark to Gladstone, June 15, 1888, Gladstone MSS, BM 44,504; Helen Clark to Northy, June 1, 1888; June 15, 1888; Mary Curry to Richard Tangye, July 31, 1888; Mary Curry to Northy, Sept. 10, 1888, Northy MSS, BM 44,877; *Punch,* XCIV (1888), 279.

(13) Albert Bright to Gladstone, Nov. 27, 1888; Nov. 28, 1888, Gladstone MSS, BM 44,505; Albert Bright to Bailey, Mar. 27, 1889, telegram, Bright MSS, BPL; *The Times,* Feb. 6, 1885; Mar. 28, 1889; *Illustrated London News,* XCIV (1889), 432–33; *Punch,* XCVI (1889), 162–63; *Annual Register, 1889,* p. 15.

(14) *Economist,* XLV (1887), 1458–1459; *Diaries,* June 30, 1886; July 9, 1887; July 26, 1887; Bright to Charles W. Wilson, Oct. 10, 1887, Bright MSS, Trinity College, Dublin; Bright to H. J. Leech, Jan. 17, 1887, Leech MSS, FHL; Bright to J. E. Thorold Rogers, Mar. 15, 1888, Bright MSS, National Liberal Club; *The Times,* July 1, 1886; Sept. 12, 1887; *Letters,* Sept. 9, 1887; A. Coles to Bright, May 24, 1885; Ellis Yarnall to Bright, Oct. 14, 1887; Pierce to Bright, Dec. 20, 1885; Nov. 20, 1887, Bright MSS, BM 43,390–43,391; Richard Tangye to Mary Curry, July 20, 1888, Northy MSS, BM 44,877; John Bright University progressed no further than the laying of its foundation in 1888; Amy F. Cobb to the author, Aug. 28, 1963.

(15) Gladstone to Albert Bright, Nov. 27, 1888, Bright MSS, RGL; *Parl. Deb.,* 334 (Mar. 29, 1889), 1169ff.; Trevelyan, p. 463; Manchester Chamber of Commerce MSS, Mar. 27, 1889; Apr. 4, 1889; June 6, 1889; June 26, 1889; July 29, 1889; Sept. 25, 1889; Oct. 28, 1889, MCL; printed document entitled "National Memorial to the Rt. Hon. John Bright," July 1889, Gladstone MSS, BM 44,113; *The Times,* May 28, 1889; May 31, 1889; June 17, 1889; June 19, 1889; June 26, 1889; Priscilla B. McLaren to Mina and Edith (daughters of J. B. Smith), Apr. 8, 1889, Smith MSS, MCL.

(16) *A Testimony of Marsden Monthly Meeting . . . ,* Local History Department, MCL; Staffordshire *Advertiser,* Apr. 6, 1889, clipping, Gladstone MSS, BM 44,113.

(17) Leonard Courtney to Helen Clark, Oct. 18, 1899, Courtney MSS, LSEL; Churchill to Bourke Cockran, June 5, 1906, Cockran MSS, NYPL.

(18) Bright to R. H. Horne, Oct. 9, 1882, Bright MSS, Ashley Library, BM; *Letters,* Aug. 30, 1887; Helen Clark to Leonard Courtney, Oct. 17, 1899, Courtney MSS, LSEL; Jonathan Dymond, *War: An Essay* (New York, 1889), introduction by Bright.

INDEX